# Integrating Geek Culture into Therapeutic Practice: The Clinician's Guide to Geek Therapy

*Integrating Geek Culture into Therapeutic Practice: The Clinician's Guide to Geek Therapy* is a comprehensive compendium of how Geek Therapy clinicians and scholars currently use a variety of games, media artifacts, and other geek culture items in therapeutic context and intervention. Even more important, the authors within this book are currently at the forefront of their research worlds and are accordingly considered experts within the growing field of Geek Therapy clinical practice. Throughout, leading researchers within the fields of Psychology, Communication Studies, and more have been able to provide clinical examples, research-based approaches, and specifics about how to utilize these items therapeutically - further enhancing the material and providing solid supportive guidance for clinicians. Clinicians reading this can develop further competence and understanding of the concepts found within their practices which will be helpful for their personal success and cultural competence to best serve their clientele.

**Anthony M. Bean, PhD,** is a Licensed Psychologist, video game researcher, and executive director at The Telos Project, a nonprofit mental health clinic in Fort Worth, Texas. He specializes in the therapeutic implications of video games and gaming, working with children and adolescents, and the use of video game character identification as a therapeutic technique. He trains professionals in Geek Therapy at geektherapytraining.com. He has authored multiple academic articles, book chapters, and the books *Working with Video Gamers and Games in Therapy: A Clinician's Guide, The Psychology of Final Fantasy* and *The Psychology of The Legend of Zelda.*

**Emory S. Daniel Jr., PhD,** is an Assistant Professor in the Department of Communication at Appalachian State University. His research specializes in parasocial relationships/interactions, gaming, interactive media, strategic communication, and advertising pedagogy. His research has been published in outlets such as *Journal of Interactive Advertising, Communication Research Reports, Journalism Studies, Internet and Higher Education Journal, and Journal of Advertising Education.*

**Sarah A. Hays, PsyD,** is a Licensed Mental Health Counselor and associate clinician at Sound Psychopathology and Assessment in Seattle, Washington. She specializes in integration of geek culture in the therapeutic setting, working with adults and youth, and the application of favored fictional anthologies as a therapeutic technique via role-modeling and analogous experience discussion. She has authored a clinical article for *iThrive Organization* and spoken on multiple academic panels.

# Integrating Geek Culture into Therapeutic Practice: The Clinician's Guide to Geek Therapy

Edited by Anthony M. Bean, PhD,
Emory S. Daniel Jr., PhD,
and Sarah A. Hays, PsyD

First Published in 2020
By Leyline Publishing
1650 West Rosedale Street, Suite 305, Fort Worth, TX 76104

Leyline Publishing, Inc.
1650 West Rosedale Street, Suite 305
Fort Worth, Texas 76104

www.leylinepublishing.com | www.geektherapytraining.com

Trademark notice: Product or corporate names may be trademarks or registered trademarks, and are used only for identification and explanation without intent to infringe.

Printed in the United States of America
10 9 8 7 6 5 4 3 2 1

Library of Congress Cataloging-in-Publication Data is available upon request.
9781734866032 (hardcover book)
9781734866025 (trade paper)
9781734866049 (e-book)

Editing and Proofreading by Anthony M. Bean
Copyediting by Madeline Jones
Text Design and composition by Asya Blue
Cover Design and Illustration by Tara Packey
Printed by Versa Press

# Dedication

*"Another definition of a hero is someone who is concerned about other people's well-being, and will go out of his or her way to help them — even if there is no chance of a reward. That person who helps others simply because it should or must be done, and because it is the right thing to do, is indeed without a doubt, a real superhero."*
— Stan Lee

To all of the Geeks, children who dream, loners, and people who feel misunderstood out there — know that you are not alone.

Anthony Bean dedicates this book to his wife and children. Without them, it would not have come to fruition.

Emory Daniel Jr. dedicates this book to his wife. She is always his favorite geek of all.

Sarah Hays dedicates this books to her brother, Ben. He has been her Player 1 and perpetual inspiration.

# Contributors

**Chrisha Anderson, PhD**, Private Practice, Cincinnati, Ohio.

**Joseph F. Atanasio, PsyD**, Owner of Mindful Path Psychology PC, New York, New York.

**Anthony M. Bean, PhD**, Executive Director of The Telos Project, Fort Worth, Texas.

**Jason M. Bird, PhD**, Psychologist at Southeast Psych, Charlotte, North Carolina.

**Megan Connell, PhD**, Psychologist at Southeast Psych and Cofounder of Geeks Like Us Media Company, Charlotte, North Carolina.

**Aaron C. Cross, PhD**, Researcher and Author, Fargo, North Dakota.

**Emory S. Daniel Jr. PhD**, Assistant Professor at Appalachian State University, Boone, North Carolina

**Adam Davis, MA Ed**, Executive Director of Game to Grow, Kirkland, Washington.

**Kelli Dunlap, PsyD**, Private Practice, Gaithersburg, Maryland.

**Matthew J. Fellows, MA**, Clinical Therapist with the Department of Human Services, Duluth, Minnesota

**Sarah A. Hays, PsyD**, Associate at Sound Psychotherapy & Assessment, Seattle, Washington.

**Adam Johns, MA**, Executive Director of Game to Grow, Kirkland, Washington.

**Ryan M. Kelly, PhD**, Psychologist at Southeast Psych and Cofounder of Geeks Like Us Media Company, Charlotte, North Carolina.

**Elizabeth D. Kilmer, PhD**, Game to Grow, Tacoma, Washington

**Jared N. Kilmer, PhD**, Game to Grow, Tacoma, Washington

**Rachel Kowert, PhD**, Research Director of Take This, Seattle, Washington.

**Joseph Lasley, PhD**, Founder of Gamenamic Leadership, Assistant Professor of Leadership and Organizational Studies at the University of Southern Maine, Portland, Maine.

**Stephanie Orme, PhD**, Emmanuel College, Boston, Massachusetts.

**Jessica Stone, PhD, RPT-S**, Private Practice and Co-Founder of the Virtual Sandtray, LLC, Fruita, Colorado.

**Shane Tilton, PhD**, Associate Professor of Multimedia Journalism, Ohio Northern University, Ada, Ohio.

# Contents

# Introduction

Being a geek can be seen as difficult for many; the social awkwardness, ineptitude, and judgment from others leads individuals to feel isolated in a world of their own. Geeks, by traditional definition, are passionate about anthologies and characters from a variety of fictional, fantasy, and virtual formats that are sometimes niche or unpopular, creating feelings of relatedness towards avatar experiences in an often lonely life. Yet there are even more morphings of the term Geek when viewed from a historical perspective, dating back to 1997 - most being identified with a negative connotation. However, with the rise of popular media over the past several years, (e.g. Big Bang Theory, Buffy The Vampire Slayer, Marvel's Avengers, Anime, etc.) self-identification as a "geek" or "nerd" has become more mainstream. Yet, even with the rise of cultural normalization and shows discussing "geek" items, there is still significant mystery surrounding geek culture that perplexes individuals who are not intimately familiar with them. This is why this book exists, to help inform professionals about the phenomenal power of Geek Therapy.

Geek Therapy encompasses many different paradigms of thought, intellectual curiosities, and specialized interests outside of "normal" social conformity. This can range from the more well-known areas of video games, comic cons, and TV shows to the less well-known topics of board games and verbose fantasy novels. Yet there are clinicians who use these geek cultural artifacts to promote social normalcy and community, reduce anxiety and depression, and help clients understand who they are through their interests.

It is important not to condemn the concept of being a geek or the activity being enjoyed based on rating, time spent, or games played (as seen in the past definitions of geek), but to see through the play itself into what the player is experiencing, what drives them to a certain character or avatar, or the individual's experience of the virtualized and fantasy worlds. This may require an observer to participate in the different worlds in order to fully comprehend the player's abilities, draws, and engagement. Indeed, the authors would all agree that in order to understand Geek Culture, one has to immerse oneself in it. This is the same for these different areas of Geek Therapy. Each area has its own draws, revelations, and clinical applicability if one is willing to step forth into it. Playing within these domains is not inherently negative or bad, as some individuals suggest, but it allows the creativity of the individual to shine through with utilization of imagination. This is just one of the possibilities and examples of "seeing through" the behavioral actions psychology sometimes gets caught up with. By conducting ourselves in this manner, it allows a deeper and more meaningful understanding to unfold about the game played, the character or avatar chosen, and the person playing in front of us.

This book is a comprehensive compendium of how Geek Therapy clinicians and scholars currently use a variety of games, media artifacts, and other geek culture items in therapeutic context and intervention. Even more important, the authors within this book are currently at the forefront of their research fields and are accordingly considered the experts within the growing field of Geek Therapy clinical practice. Throughout, leading researchers within the fields of Psychology, Communication Studies, and more have been able to provide clinical examples, research-based approaches, and specifics about how to utilize these items therapeutically - further enhancing the material and providing solid supportive guidance for clinicians. Clinicians reading this can develop further competence and understanding of the concepts found within their practices that will be helpful for their personal success and cultural competence to best serve their clientele.

By collecting texts from the leading experts and leaders in the field, this book provides to clinicians and mental health experts the knowledge that has been developed by experts who consistently work with their clients using Geek Therapy. These modalities have resulted in clients having less anxiety (e.g., social), less depressive symptoms (e.g., after playing video games), improved self-esteem, richer interpersonal interactions, greater social and school engagement, and greater development of social skills and problem solving. They are being used to improve overall psychological well-being across all ages, as well as focusing on the specific needs of targeted populations, such as those with ADHD, ASD, PTSD, and mood and anxiety disorders. This endeavor is one of love and passion. Creating a book of this caliber takes extraordinary time, effort, and resources and would not be possible without each of the authors in this book.

The book itself is divided into several different critical topics that clinicians commonly see in their everyday practice. These topics consist of five more well-known geek subcultures in total: Video Games and Gamers, Dungeons & Dragons, Comic Cons and Fandoms, Comics, Superheroes, Anime, and Supplementary Topics. These topics were chosen due to the higher chance that clinicians will experience a client with the knowledge of the topic. With adequate knowledge of what the topics encompass, what they mean to the clients, and how they can be used in a therapeutic context, the sky becomes the limit for a clinician who is well-rounded in these areas of focus.

If after reading this book you continue to want more clinical and applicable knowledge in the area of Geek Therapy it is suggested that you, the reader, check out Leyline's Geek Therapy Training at www.geek-therapytraining.com and the resources page at the end of the book. These resources and trainings are aimed specifically at enhancing the learning content in this book, but additionally have more hands-on and in-depth training from superb practitioners.

We hope you enjoy getting Geeky with us!

Anthony M. Bean, PhD
CEO of Leyline Education and Geek Therapy Training
Executive Director of The Telos Project

# Video Games and Gamers

# Video Games: An Introduction

**1**

Rachel Kowert, PhD

Video games are a cultural phenomenon. From the commercial success of *Pong* in 1972 (Atari) to the unprecedented popularization of *Fortnite* in 2019 (Epic Games), video games are a multi-billion dollar business. What was once considered a niche activity is now a global movement. From a reported $200 million dollar industry in 1978 (Aoyama & Izushi, 2003) to $137 billion dollar industry in 2018 (NewZoo, 2018), the video game market has experienced considerable growth, particularly in comparison to other media markets (Zimmerman, 2002). Today, video games continue to grow in popularity as an activity for children and adults across sectors: leisure, education, occupational skills training, and more.

## What is a Video Game?

At the most basic level, video games are playful, interactive spaces that require a user to actively participate in order to progress through the content (Bogost, 2011; Kowert, 2015; Wolf, 2002). Video games are commonly played on personal computers, dedicated gaming consoles (e.g., Nintendo Switch, Sony Playstation, Microsoft Xbox) and handheld gaming platforms (e.g., Nintendo DS, Sony Vita). It is also now commonplace for video games to be played on non-traditional gaming machines, such as smartphones and smart watches.

There are many differences across video game titles in terms of their in-game content, setting, and game play features. These differences are often discussed in terms of genres.

*Video Game Genres*

Classifying media into different genres based on their characteristics is common across media systems, such as literature and movies (Wolf, 2001). In this sense, video games are no different, as several genre classification systems have been developed for this particular media. However, unlike genre classification systems for other kinds of media, video games tend to be classified based on their gameplay rather than aesthetic features (Apperley, 2006). For example, a game where an individual shoots at or destroys a series of opponents is often classified under the shooter genre, regardless of whether the setting is a battlefield, such as in *Call of Duty* (Activision), or a dystopian fantasy environment, such as in *BioShock* (2K Games).

Video games range from so called "casual" game genres that do not require substantial amount of time or skill to play, such as a game in the puzzle genre like *Angry Birds* (Rovio Entertainment), to more complex games and "hardcore" genres, such as role-playing games that take hundreds of hours to complete, like games from the *Final Fantasy* series (Square Enix). While many different classification systems for genres have been developed (with various levels of sub-classifications), several of the more popular video game genres are outlined in Table 1.1.

| Genre | Description | Examples |
|---|---|---|
| Battle Royale/ Survival | Also called "survival" games, these games rely on exploration and scavenging and "last man standing" gameplay. | *Fortnite, PUBG* |
| Racing | Games that involves the player partaking in a racing competition with any type of land, water, air, or space vehicle. | *Need for Speed, Gran Turismo Sport* |
| Role playing | Games that involve taking on the "role" of a player and progressing through a narrative | *Final Fantasy Series, World of Warcraft* |
| Shooter | Games that involve shooting at, or destroying, a series of opponents or objects | *Call of Duty, Unreal Tournament* |
| Simulation | Games that simulate real-world activities | *SimCity, The Sims* |
| Strategy | Games that emphasize the use of strategy | *Starcraft, Civilization* |
| Sports | Games that are adaptations of existing sports or variations of them | *FIFA, Madden NFL titles* |
| Party | Games that are typically played as forms of entertainment at social gatherings | *Mario Party, Jackbox* |
| Puzzle | Games that emphasize puzzle solving | *Tetris, Portal* |

Table 1.1 Video Game Genres and Descriptions

Play motivations, uses, and effects vary widely across game genres. For example, players of shooter games have been found to be highly motivated to achieve (Ghuman & Griffiths, 2012) and be challenged (Jansz & Tanis, 2007), with the motivation to compete being the strongest predictor of the frequency of game play among players of shooter games—stronger than in any other genre (Vorderer et al., 2003). Conversely, players of role-playing games are often motivated to engage to immerse themselves in a virtual world by assuming the role of another and progressing through a narrative (Bean, 2018; Kowert, 2015; Shen & Williams, 2010).

## Who Plays Video Games Today?

Video game play is no longer a niche activity taking place in remote arcade parlors or darkened basements. As of 2018, 64% of households in the US have a device to play video games within their home, with 70% of the video game-playing population being over the age of 18. In this same survey, 60% of Americans reported playing video games daily (Entertainment Software Association, 2018).

Globally, there are more than 2.3 billion active video game players, supporting a market worth of more than 137 billion dollars (NewZoo, 2018). According to the 2018 Global Games Market Report by Newzoo, games played on mobile devices (such as a smartphone) constitute the largest proportion of this market (70.3 billion). This is followed by console (34.6 billion) and PC (32.9 billion) games. China is the country with the highest video game revenue, topping 37.9 billion, followed by the United States (30.4 billion) and Japan (19.2 billion).

While video game play has historically been stereotyped as a male-dominated leisure activity (Kowert et al., 2013; Kowert, 2012; Lucas & Sherry, 2004), the proportion of male to female game players has become more evenly distributed over time. While male players constituted 62% of the U.S. game playing community in 2006, this number has reduced to 55% in 2018 (Statista, 2018). Even though game playing has grown to mainstream status, the identification with the community of "gamers" remains a bit more exclusive.

*What is a Gamer?*

While a video game player refers to anyone who plays a video game, the term gamer refers to someone whose self-identifies as a member of the gaming community. This is an important distinction, as how one chooses to identify with a particular social group, such as gamers, is a vastly different determination of the role video games play in their lives than the objective distinction of whether they play video games or not.

One's social identification is the self-definition of the individual, rather than a categorization based on static definitions of identity applied from the outside. As discussed by Tajfel and Turner (1979), social identity is "that part of the individual's self-concept which derives from their knowledge of their membership of a social group (or groups) together with the value and emotional significance of that membership" (p. 255).

This concept originates from Social Identity Theory, which is a theoretical framework that was developed to explain the tendency for individuals to categorize the social world into groups and, consequently, generate in-group and out-group biases in their thoughts and behaviors (Tajfel, 1970, 1974; Tajfel & Turner, 1979; Turner, 1984). Individuals are continuously cataloguing themselves and others into various social groups, such as those based on organizational membership, religious affiliation, gender, and age (Tajfel & Turner, 1985). These categorizations bring order to the social environment and enable individuals to identify themselves within the social landscape. An individual can belong to multiple categories simultaneously (e.g., "female" and "gamer"), however, the extent to which an individual identifies with and values each category exists along a continuum. These social identities are also comparative and relational in nature. Individuals who seek and find positive differences between themselves and other social groups achieve and retain a positive social identity (Tajfel, 1978). This is important, as a positive social identity fosters feelings of belongingness and self-worth (Branscombe & Wann, 1991), and can enhance self-esteem (Barreto & Ellemers, 2000; Branscombe, 1998).

Thus, identifying as a gamer refers to more than the act of playing, it refers to an identification with the larger social group of gamers and all that can potentially come with that: knowledge of video game related news, attendance to game-related conferences and conventions, membership in video game clubs and societies, and video game-themed attire and fashion accessories, among others. Notably, research has found identifying as a gamer to be associated with a range of positive psychological benefits, such as self-esteem and social competence and negatively related to loneliness (Kaye et al., 2017), as well as a stronger predictor of video game play frequency (Ghuman & Griffiths, 2012).

## Transformation of the Video Game Industry

Video games have experienced vast transformations since their inception in the late 1970s. Perhaps the most obvious change has been the transition from the black and white screen of *Pong* (Atari) to the visual masterpieces we see today. However, video games have also undergone significant changes in the way they are played. No longer confined to large, clunky boxes in arcade parlors, video games have transformed into seemingly invisible strings of information floating in the clouds. The growth of the downloadable content market (that is, content that is downloaded to one's console, computer, or other device than purchased as a physical item in a store) has jumped from 20% of the market share in 2011 to 54% of the market share in 2017 (Capcom, 2017).

Alongside the transition of game content from physical to virtual, has come the transition from offline to online gaming cultures. Today, video game experiences are (for the most part) perpetually online. Even when individuals choose to play alone, in a single-player game, for example, they are still often connected to a vast network of other players.

## The Social Nature of Online Games

The proliferation of the Internet has broadened video games' scope and expanded their multi-player functionality by allowing players to connect with others in a shared gaming space beyond the boundaries of their geographical location (Kowert, 2015). The addition of a multi-player dimension has changed video game play from "a solitary or small group activity into a large, thriving social network" (Smyth, 2007, p. 178). Online gaming has seen incredible growth over the last decade. A report from Statista (2019) reports that the value of the worldwide online gaming will grow from a 21.1 billion in 2011 to a predicted 44.2 billion in 2020.

Like traditional video games, online video games are playful activities that one engages in for the primary purpose of entertainment. However, unlike traditional video games, online games are designed to encourage and facilitate social interaction among co-players, as in-game challenges often require a complementary group to accomplish (Chen, 2009; Ducheneaut & Moore, 2005; Jakobsson & Taylor, 2003; Moore et al., 2007). In this sense, online games have provided a social space that can grant access to new friendships as well as supplement pre-existing ones (Griffiths et al., 2003; Hussain & Griffiths, 2009; Steinkuehler & Williams, 2006). This social component of play is an important distinction between offline and online games.

For example, for individuals with a history of poor interpersonal relationships, online games provide a space with easily accessible and less risky friendships (Cole & Griffiths, 2007; Jakobsson & Taylor, 2003; Suler, 2004). This is particularly the case for those with low social resources, such as less perceived social support, lower interpersonal activity, or fewer group memberships (Kowert, 2015). Researchers have found that lonely (Caplan et al., 2009; Lemmens et al., 2011), depressed (Bessiere et al., 2012), socially anxious (Kim et al., 2008; Kowert & Oldmeadow, 2014; Lo et al., 2005; Peters & Malesky, 2008), and socially shy (Kowert et al., 2014) individuals are particularly apt to use online games to reduce negative moods and expand their social networks. Longitudinal studies in the area have also noted the compensatory nature of online games in relation to social difficulties (Kowert et al., 2015; Lemmens et al., 2011).

This is, at least partially, because the lack of non-verbal cues in online games provide the unique combination of dissociative anonymity (i.e., "You do not know me") and invisibility (i.e., "You cannot see me"), often referred to as the Online Disinhibition Effect (Suler, 2004). This stimulates open and intimate conversations because the fear of any "real-world" social repercussions are largely removed. For example, individuals have been found to disclose personal information at a quicker rate than is found in non-visually anonymous relationships (Joinson, 2001; McKenna & Bargh, 2000; Suler, 2004) and be more honest and open (Whitty & Gavin, 2001).

Online games have also been found to augment pre-existing friendships by playing online together. As a shared social activity, where the ability to participate is not limited to one's current geographical location, players are able to engage with their friends from down the street, friends from their hometown, and friends from a continent away, all from the comfort of their own homes. Individuals who play online games with their pre-existing friendship networks report less loneliness and greater social engagement of a higher quality with their friends whom they played with than those who played with strangers (Shen & Williams, 2010). While individuals are also able to play video games offline with each other (often referred to as co-located gaming), the ability to connect regardless of location has greatly eased the accessibility of social play.

The unique social environment of online games is often framed in relation to being a new "third place" (Steinkuehler & Williams, 2006). A term coined by Oldenburg (1999), a "third place" is an informal social environment where individuals can create and enhance social relationships. A traditional third place would be the fictional neighborhood pub *Cheers* from the television show of the same name. *Cheers* is a place where everyone is welcome, everyone knows your name, and it is a home away from home. Online gaming spaces fulfill this same function. As discussed by Steinkuheler and Williams (2006), online video games are structurally similar to "third places" in terms of their informal sociability and ability to generate social capital (see Table 1.2). While the research of Steinkuheler and Williams (2006) specifically focused on the ways in which Massively Multiplayer Online Role Playing Games (MMORPGs) function as "third places," the development of online video games over time has established a thriving social environment no longer limited by genre.

| Characteristic | Definition |
|---|---|
| Neutral Ground | Individuals are free to come and go as they please with little obligation or entanglements with other participants |
| Leveler | An individual's rank and status in the workplace or society at large are of no import |
| Conversation is the main activity | Conversation is a main focus of activity in which playfulness and wit are collectively valued |
| Accessibility & Accommodation | Easy to access and are accommodating to those who frequent them |
| The Regulars | A cadre of regulars who attract newcomers and give the space its characteristic cool |
| Low Profile | Characteristically homely and without pretension |
| The Mood is Playful | The mood is generally playful and market by frivolity |
| A Home Away from Home | They exhibit rootedness, feelings of possession, spiritual regeneration, feelings of being at ease, and warmth |

Table 1.2 Oldenburg's (1999) Eight Characteristics of "Third Places."

It is worth noting that online games are a particularly unique third place because friendship bonds between players are "emotionally jump started" through a series of rapid, stressful, trust-building situations (e.g., killing a difficult enemy), allowing players to choose to befriend those who have already demonstrated their trustworthiness through the course of in-game actions (Yee, 2002). This is in contrast to traditional friendships in which individuals are unable to determine whether others can be trusted until a significant period of time has passed.

The social environment of online gaming spaces are also unique in relation to other online social spaces (such as chat rooms or online forums) because of their integration of a playful space in a socially accommodating environment. The game itself is socially accommodating because it provides a shared activity. This takes the forefront of attention and can largely guide the content of the conversation, as well as mediate the pace (Kowert, 2015). Online gaming spaces also provide visual anonymity and asynchronous communication, which can provide greater control over social self-presentation and impression formation than one would have in by face-to-face communication (Walther, 1996; Walther, et al., 2018). Lastly, online video games allow for the ability to manipulate one's physical presentation through the customization of avatars. This sense of control can mediate social anxieties associated with a lack of social control by allowing for the strategic (and potentially idealized) presentation (Leary & Kowalski, 1995; Segrin & Kinney, 1995).

## Real Versus Virtual World: A False Dichotomy

When discussing online video games, a distinction has been made between "real" and "virtual" worlds. The real world is the one we engage in face-to-face, whereas the virtual world refers to the interactions that take place within video games. The shift in gaming content and cultures from offline to online has blurred the lines between the real and virtual to the point where the dichotomy of off- and on-line is no longer black and white. This false dichotomy is more than just a technicality: understanding the fluidity of the real (offline) and virtual (online) world is imperative to understanding the role that video games have come to play in the daily lives of their players.

For example, video game play is often thought of as a solitary activity, making it one is that is "less valuable" in a variety of ways to "real world" interactions. It is erroneously pigeonholed as an isolating environment that is unable to foster meaningful relationships, among other things. The stereotypically isolated and lonely gamer is completely outdated and no longer applies to the vibrant social space video gaming has become (Kowert et al., 2012, 2013). Video games are highly social spaces where individuals can foster new meaningful social relationships as well as support pre-existing ones (Kowert, 2016; Steinkuehler & Williams, 2006;

Williams, 2007). They are socially accommodating spaces for individuals with social difficulties (Kowert, 2015, 2016) and fantastic tools for learning a range of social skills and behaviors, such as teamwork and leadership (Ducheneaut & Moore, 2005; Yee, 2007).

Failure to understand the fluidity between the real and virtual world can be pitfall for parents, educators, and clinicians. It is important that the role that video games play in an individual's life begin to be recognized as something beyond a leisure activity. Its role as a multi-faceted and integrated part into our daily (social, work, and leisure) life needs to be acknowledged. Video games are places to have fun, meet new people, play with old friends, engage with a global community, a place to learn, a place to socialize, a "third" place.

The faster that the interchangeability of "real" and "virtual" environments begins to be acknowledged, the sooner we can start to conceptualize the virtual world as an extension of the non-virtual world, particularly in relation to video games.

# References

Aoyama, Y., & Izushi, H. (2003). Hardware gimmick or cultural innovation? Technological, cultural, and social foundations of Japanese video game industry. *Research Policy, 32*(3), 423–444.

Apperley, T. H. (2006). Genre and game studies: Toward a critical approach to video game genres. *Simulation & Gaming, 37*(1), 6–23.

Barreto, M., & Ellemers, N. (2000). You can't always do what you want: Social identity and self-presentational determinants of the choice to work for a low status group. *Personality and Social Psychology Bulletin*, (26), 891–906.

Bean, A. M. (2018). *Working with video games and game in therapy: A clinician's guide*. New York: Routledge.

Bessiere, K., Kiesler, S., Kraut, R., & Boneva, B. (2012). Longitudinal effects of internet uses on depressive affect: A social resources approach. *American Sociological Association*. Philadelphia, PA.

Bogost, I. (2011). *How to do things with videogames*. University of Minnesota Press.

Branscombe, N. (1998). Thinking about one's gender group's privileges or disadvantages: Consequences for well-being in women and men. *British Journal of Social Psychology*, (37), 167–184.

Branscombe, N., & Wann, D. L. (1991). The positive social and self concept consequences of sports team identification. *Journal of Sport and Social Issues*, (15), 115–127.

Capcom. (2017). Capcom Annual Report. Retrieved April 18, 2019, from http://www.capcom.co.jp/ir/english/data/pdf/annual/2017/annual_2017_01.pdf

Caplan, S., Williams, D., & Yee, N. (2009). Problematic internet use and psychosocial well-being among MMO players. *Computers in Human Behavior, 25*(6), 1312–1319. https://doi.org/10.1016/j.chb.2009.06.006

Chen, M. (2009). Communication, coordination, and camaraderie in World of Warcraft. *Games and Culture, 4*(1), 47–73.

Cole, H., & Griffiths, M. D. (2007). Social interactions in massively mul-tiplayer online role-playing games. *Cyberpsychology and Behavior,* *10*(4), 575–583. https://doi.org/10.1089/cpb.2007.9988

Ducheneaut, N., & Moore, R. (2005). More than just 'XP': learning social skills in massively multiplayer online games. *Interactive Technology and Smart Education, 2*(2), 89–100.

Entertainment Software Association. (2018). *2018 sales, demographic and usage date. Essential facts about the computer and video game industry.*

Ghuman, D., & Griffiths, M. D. (2012). A Cross-genre study of online gaming: Player demographics, motivation for play, and social inter-actions among players. *International Journal of Cyber Behavior, Psychology, and Learning, 2*(1), 13–29.

Griffiths, M. D., Davies, M., & Chappell, D. (2003). Breaking the ste-reotype: The case of online gaming. *Cyberpsychology and Behavior,* *6*(1), 81–91.

Hussain, Z., & Griffiths, M. (2009). The attitudes, feelings, and expe-riences of online gamers: A qualitative analysis. *Cyberpsychology and Behavior, 12*(6), 747–753.

Jakobsson, M., & Taylor, T. L. (2003). The Sopranos meets EverQuest: Social networking in massively multiplayer online games. In *2003 Digital Arts and Culture (DAC) conference* (pp. 90–91). Melbourne, Australia.

Jansz, J., & Tanis, M. (2007). Appeal of playing online first person shooter games. *Cyberpsychology and Behavior, 10*(1), 133–136.

Joinson, A. (2001). Self-disclosure in computer-mediated communica-tion: the role of self-awareness and visual anonymity. *European Journal of Social Psychology, 31*, 177–192.

Kaye, L. K., Kowert, R., & Quinn, S. (2017). The role of social identity and online social capital on psychosocial outcomes in MMO play-ers. *Computers in Human Behavior, 74*, 215–223.

Kim, E., Namkoong, K., Ku, T., & Kim, S. (2008). The relationship between online game addiction and aggression, self-control, and narcissistic personality traits. *European Psychiatry, 23*(3), 212–218. https://doi.org/10.1016/j.eurpsy.2007.10.010

Kowert, R. (2015). *Video Games and Social Competence*. New York: Routledge.

Kowert, R. (2016). Social outcomes: Online game play, social currency, and social ability. In R. Kowert & T. Quandt (Eds.), *The Video Game Debate: Unraveling the Physical, Social, and Psychological Effects of Digital Games* (pp. 94–115). New York: Routledge.

Kowert, R., Domahidi, E., & Quandt, T. (2014). The relationship between online video game involvement and gaming-related friendships among emotionally sensitive individuals. *Cyberpsychology, Behavior, and Social Networking*. https://doi.org/10.1089/cyber.2013.0656

Kowert, R., Festl, R., & Quandt, T. (2013). Unpopular, overweight, and socially inept: Reconsidering the stereotype of online gamers. *Cyberpsychology, Behavior, and Social Networking*, *17*(3), 141–146. https://doi.org/10.1089/cyber.2013.0118

Kowert, R., Griffiths, M. D., & Oldmeadow, J. A. (2012). Geek or chic? Emerging stereotypes of online gamers. *Bulletin of Science, Technology & Society*, *32*(6), 471–479. https://doi.org/10.1177/0270467612469078

Kowert, R., & Oldmeadow, J. A. (2014). Seeking social comfort online: Video game play as a social accommodator for the insecurely attached. *Computers in Human Behavior*. https://doi.org/10.1016/j.chb.2014.05.004

Kowert, R., Vogelgesang, J., Festl, R., & Quandt, T. (2015). Psychosocial causes and consequences of online video game involvement. *Computers in Human Behavior*, *45*, 51–58. https://doi.org/10.1016/j.chb.2014.11.074

Leary, M., & Kowalski, R. (1995). *Social Anxiety*. New York: Guilford Press.

Lemmens, J., Valkenburg, P., & Peter, J. (2011). Psychological causes and consequences of pathological gaming. *Computers in Human Behavior*, *27*(1), 144–152. https://doi.org/10.1016/j.chb.2010.07.015

Lo, S., Wang, C., & Fang, W. (2005). Physical interpersonal relationships and social anxiety among online game players. *Cyberpsychology and Behavior*, *8*(1), 15–20. https://doi.org/10.1089/cpb.2005.8.15

Lucas, K., & Sherry, J. (2004). Sex differences in video game play: A communication-based explanation. *Communication Research*, *31*(5), 499–523.

McKenna, K., & Bargh, J. (2000). Plan 9 from cyberspace: The implications of the Internet for personality and social psychology. *Personality and Social Psychology Review*, *4*(1), 57–75. https://doi.org/10.1207/S15327957PSPR0401_6

Moore, R., Ducheneaut, N., & Nickell, E. (2007). Doing virtually nothing: Awareness and accountability in massively multiplayer online worlds. *Computer Supported Cooperative Work*, *16*(3), 265–305.

NewZoo. (2018). *Global Games Market Report*.

Oldenburg, R. (1999). *The Great Good Place: Cafés, Coffee Shops, Community Centers, Beauty Parlors, General Stores, Bars, Hangouts, and How They Get You Through The Day*. New York: Marlowe & Company.

Peters, C., & Malesky, A. (2008). Problematic usage among highly-engaged players of massively multiplayer online role playing games. *Cyberpsychology and Behavior*, *11*(4), 481–484.

Segrin, C., & Kinney, T. (1995). Social skills deficits among the socially anxious: Loneliness and rejection from others. *Motivation and Emotion*, (19), 1–24.

Shen, C., & Williams, D. (2010). Unpacking time online: Connecting internet and massively multiplayer online game use with psychological well-being. *Communication Research*, *20*(10), 1–27. https://doi.org/10.1177/0093650210377196

Smyth, J. (2007). Beyond Self-Selection in Video Game Play. *Cyberpsychology and Behavior*, *10*(5), 717–721.

Statista. (2018). *Distribution of computer and video gamers in the United States from 2006 to 2018, by gender*. Retrieved from https://www.statista.com/statistics/232383/gender-split-of-us-computer-and-video-gamers/.

Statista. (2019). *PC online game market value worldwide from 2011 to 2020 (in billion U.S. dollars)*. Retrieved from https://www.statista.com/statistics/292516/pc-online-game-market-value-worldwide/.

Steinkuehler, C., & Williams, D. (2006). Where everybody knows your (screen) name: Online games as "Third Places." *Journal of Computer-Mediated Communication, 11*(4), 885–909.

Suler, J. (2004). The online disinhibition effect. *Cyberpsychology and Behavior, 7*(3), 321–326.

Tajfel, H. (1970). Experiments in intergroup discrimination. *Scientific American, 223*(2), 96–102.

Tajfel, H. (1974). Social identity and intergroup behaviour. *Social Science Information, 13*, 65–93.

Tajfel, H. (1978). The achievement of group differentiation BT - Differentiation between social groups. Studies in the social psychology of intergroup relations. In *Differentiation between social groups. Studies in the social psychology of intergroup relations.* (pp. 77–98). London: Academic Press.

Tajfel, H., & Turner, J. C. (1979). An integrative theory of intergroup conflict BT - The social psychology of intergroup relations. In W. G. Austin & S. Worchel (Eds.), *The Social Psychology of Intergroup Relations* (pp. 33–47). Monterey: Brooks-Cole.

Tajfel, H., & Turner, J. C. (1985). The social identity theory of intergroup behavior BT - Psychology of Intergroup Relations. In S. Worchel & W. G. Austin (Eds.), *Psychology of Intergroup Relations.* Chicago: Nelson-Hall.

Turner, J. C. (1984). Social identification and psychological group formation BT - The social dimension. In H. Tajfel (Ed.), *The social dimension* (Vol. 2, pp. 518–538). Cambridge: Cambridge University Press.

Vorderer, P., Hartmann, T., & Klimmt, C. (2003). Explaining the enjoyment of playing video games: the role of competition. In *Proceedings of the second international conference on Entertainment computing.*

Walther, J. (1996). Computer-mediated communication: Impersonal, interpersonal, and hyperpersonal interaction. *Communication Research, 23*(1), 3–43.

Walther, J., Kashian, N., Jang, J.W., Shin, S.Y, Dai, Y., & Koutamanis, M. (2018). The effect of message persistence and disclosure on liking in computer mediated communication. *Media Psychology*, 21(2), 308 – 327.

Whitty, M., & Gavin, J. (2001). Age/Sex/Location: Uncovering the Social Cues in the Development of Online Relationships. *Cyberpsychology and Behavior*, 4(5), 623–630.

Williams, D. (2007). The impact of time online: Social capital and Cyberbalkanization. *Cyberpsychology and Behavior*, 10(3), 398–406.

Wolf, M. J. P. (2002). Genre and the video game. *The Medium of the Video Game*.

Yee, N. (2002). Befriending ogres and wood-elves - Understanding relationship formation in MMORPGs. *Nickyee.Com*. Retrieved from http://www.nickyee.com/hub/relationships/home.html

Yee, N. (2007). Motivations of play in online games. *Journal of CyberPsychology and Behavior*, 9(6), 772–775.

Zimmerman, E. (2002). Do independent games exist? In L. King (Ed.), *Game on: The history and culture of video games*. New York: Universe Publishing.

# Video Games: The New Mythology

**Anthony M. Bean, PhD**

**2**

Archetypes are considered to be images with universal meanings attached to them (Stein, 1998). They are a widely used and beloved way of experiencing and discussing life, but also one of the most difficult ideas or motifs to conceptualize due to the intangible existence they represent. The conceptual idea of these psychologically abstract and literal interpretations of our lives is usually associated with Carl Jung (2014) or James Hillman (2004) as the creators and identifiers of these themes. Archetypes are everywhere, yet have to be conceptualized from a metaphorical, symbolic, and non-literal approach to be used in therapy and commonplace life.

What constitutes archetypes are the similarities in which they are presented; they create an analogous thematic form of what is common between multiple scenarios, ideas, behaviors, objects, and images. For example, a shield is symbolic of protection of one's self or a group, while a sword represents an attack. Similarly, the color blue is considered to be conceptually cold while red is hot. Apply these pictures and ideas to almost anything and the person viewing them can understand the representation quite simply.

Commonly, we find most archetypes in books, stories, fairytales, and myths (Hillman, 2004; Jung, 2014). These examples are considered to be the primary places to find them in varying cultures across the world. These narratives do not just tell a story, but allow readers and experiencers to experience the journey and gain insight from them. Mythological stories give people ideas about who we are, lessons we can learn, and help to transform our cognitions within a learning experience (Hillman, 2004).

New generations have begun to create new mythologies and narratives within video games that younger generations can relate to through the use of archetypal characters and experiences. Archetypes can be experienced by individuals across varying cultures and identities. This is what makes archetypes so powerful and outstanding experiences; they are commonly experienced across the world through the playing of video game avatars even though they are virtual (Bean, 2015, 2018). Only by viewing them from this point of reference does one begin to see the importance of how they are intertwined with everyday life, therapy, and psychology for our clients.

## Video Game Avatars

The video game avatars being played act as constellated behavioral patterns and are considered to be archetypes in a literal interpretation or format of existence. They require a watchful eye to understand what the avatar may represent for the player. This is where the second part, and definitely the harder portion, comes into existence. An observer, the clinician, has to *think* about what the avatar and storyline represent and symbolize, beckoning us to understand an instinctual need of the person playing them. They must almost reverse engineer the behavior back to the archetypal idea.

Individuals unconsciously identify with video game archetypes on a deeper and more personal level. Most of the time, video gamers are unaware of the resonance with the archetype(s) they are personifying, but with a critical eye, a clinician will be able to draw the conclusions necessary for clinical intervention (Bean, 2018, 2019b). These archetypes are neither good nor bad, but are justly present as a form of energy people feel, experience, and are directed by (Johnson, 1986; Jung, 2014; Stein, 1998). To place a distinction of negative or positive would be a projection of our opinion upon the archetype(s).

To be clear, archetypes can influence us in healthy and unhealthy, adaptive and maladaptive, functional and dysfunction manners, behaviors, and views compared to the world around us (Bean, 2018, 2019a). These views may be considered to be socially dependent and derived. When the views are considered to be bad or socially deviant, an identification is placed upon the archetype narrowing the idea, literalizing the energy, and inherently destroying the experience itself through a negative viewpoint. However, when the archetype is seen as positive, society tends to swing to the other extreme of idealizing and idolizing the archetype to a point where it becomes unhealthy. In each of these cases, a polarization effect has occurred and disallowed the archetype to be seen for its own purpose or being.

However, it is important to note while archetypes may sound beautiful and noble, they have both light and dark (or positive and negative) sides. In the Eastern traditional perspective, every archetype has a yin and a yang, both are needed to be whole. We, as humans, strive to be in the light or positive side, but occasionally fall into the dark, or negative side. In order to find wholeness or completion, we must find the balance between both. Without the acceptance of our dark side or shadow, we fall prey to it and tend to act out in our different environments usually spelling out disaster.

## Video Games & Archetypes

Video games bring a different perception and experience for the hero's story as *the video gamer is able to direct and play as the hero*. This establishes a substantial motive for why individuals enjoy the video game realms so abundantly. While playing, they are instinctively being able to participate in the myth of the hero, not just watching, reading, or observing it. In this logic, the playing of the video game is an exceptionally important action for the player as they become part of the story. However, when the story becomes stale or stagnant, we usually see a decline in the participant's play and enjoyment of it, regardless of the medium (Bean, 2018).

What makes video games unique, compared to mythological archetypes, is their conceptualization of archetypes in a literalized visual format, rather than relying on the imagination and interpretation of the reader as in literature or a board game. This creates a projection upon the character and an interactional effect between the gamer and the avatar (Bean, 2018, 2019a). Video games take archetypes even a step further than a visual medium like movies because the archetype becomes an interactive experience to be played. Video games literalize the archetype played by the video gamer choosing to interact as one of them. The video game character or avatar itself is a literalized representation of the archetype created by the video game developer. The image of the archetype represented in the avatar gives it life, but the *playing* of the character gives it meaning. The character is only a character comprised of pixels. Without the video gamer to interact, move, and have the character explore, it would not exist past the pixelated stage. By playing as the character, the video gamer brings meaning and life to the existence of the pixels and provides narrative meaning for the created virtual character. The storyline in which the avatar is played, whether chosen through a linear path or open world fantasy, is as, if not more, important to the image of the archetype. It helps us create a specific narrative for the projection onto the character that may represent internal manifestations of our own personality. Projection upon video game characters further enhances our experiences and understanding of real world problems, solutions, and behaviors by which to handle difficult situations we encounter.

## Psychological Projection

Conceptually, projection refers to a phenomenon of an individual taking a part of themselves and thrusting it upon an external object or person. Usually this occurrence is completed unconsciously – similar to most video game players. The concept is derived from Freud and Jung (1916/1960) and suggests that everyone projects outward onto one's surroundings in all aspects of life. While this may be seen as a beneficial action, it additionally can have destructive consequences, such as loss of friendships, intimacy, or even social aspects of life. When one projects onto their surroundings, they meet other psychic projections from others which collide with one another. If one is not aware of the projections and cannot reclaim them, then they can lead to difficult interpersonal problems which require support and can cause significant disruption.

However, while one is playing a video game, one is constantly projecting onto their character. The player takes on their avatar's characteristics just as the avatar takes on their players. It helps individuals create a specific narrative for the character which may represent internal manifestations of our own personality. These instances of the video gamer finding meaning are extremely rich and important to the video gamer and their thoughts and behaviors. As the video gamer concludes battles, quests, and storyline, the character – and player – grow stronger, and the opportunity of taking back that newfound strength survives when the immersion concludes and the projection is reclaimed. This means that playing video games can provide the player with growth opportunities which may not otherwise be found in society and offer that important development we all seek in ourselves through immersion within video games (Bean, 2018, 2019b).

## Immersion

Immersion is a key factor in working therapeutically with a video gamer population. It is about being immensely and intensely present with an activity, yet engaged wholly encompassing all of one's attention. Immersion is similar to Csíkszentmihályi's (2009) state of flow, but in reality, provides a step beyond the Flow concept suggesting Flow may be more of a stepping stone or schema on the path to immersion.

One must have a schema on which to build to become immersed. The state of Flow is considered a basic schema through which one learns new cognitions and repeated encounters. As video gamers create and build the basic schemas for different video games and genres, they utilize the concept of Flow to create and absorb the building blocks of the game play. However, once the schema has been created, Flow is no longer needed to create the satisfaction and immersion takes over when the video gamer picks up a controller. The gamer has already acquired the basic schemas to understand the video game, console controller, and movements therefore immersion is achieved rapidly again once the game begins anew.

Inherently, this means that the video gamer becomes captivated into the game, narrative, visual pictures, and actions being taken in the game itself via immersion. The video gamer is not just playing the game any longer, they are living it through projecting upon their character different aspects of themselves as well through a narrative journey of The Seven Paths of Valor (See Figure 2.1).

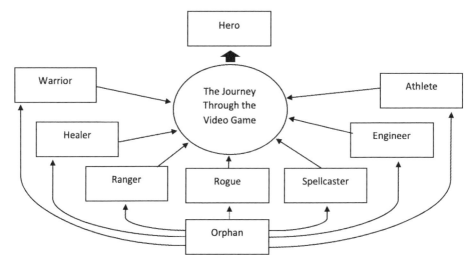

Figure 2.1 The Seven Paths of Archetypal Valor; Adapted from Bean, 2018.

## Clinical Case Study

The present Clinical Case Study describes a case study of "Dean," a Caucasian 16-year-old adolescent who came into the office for complications of socializing with others, asking for help, mood difficulties, and communicating with people at school. He had not been diagnosed with any mental health disorders from a professional clinician previously and was attending weekly therapy sessions due to his parent's report of "mood difficulties, trouble with friends, and low grades at school." Dean socially had a couple of close friends at school, was having trouble in his classes due to his disposition, lack of focus, not completing his assignments, and a low sense of self-worth.

Dean's parents expressed their concerns about his excessive game playing, difficulties with attention, anxious behaviors around others, and depression symptomology at home and school. His parents felt as if he were breaking apart from the family and they could not "reach him." In fact, Dean was socially isolating himself at home and in school withdrawing from his parents resulting in an "Orphan Archetype" experience – one that he was creating unconsciously for himself.

As a result of his current life experiences and feelings of isolation, Dean became interested and immersed with the video game worlds, specifically *World of Warcraft,* a popular Massively Multiplayer Online game (MMO). He would play the game or discuss his conquests as he got home from school, when he had any additional free time, or when he was with his friends. His father had significant difficulties with his game time playing and "did not understand why he even played the game."

The clinician suggested that his father should play the video game with Dean to build closeness in their relationship, help Dean understand the world and consequences, observe and learn from Dean about his preferred activity, and also to monitor the game time being played after the initial intake therapy session. Dean's father was hesitant, but agreed he would attempt to play the game with him. This intervention provided a place for Dean to instruct his father on how to play the game and inherently made Dean the leader in his family system. This helped bridge the relationship gap between him and his father.

Within a session, great amount of rapport had to be built quickly with Dean as he was exceptionally mistrustful of the therapeutic process. This hesitancy quickly dissipated during the course of the second session once Dean found out his therapist knew substantial information about the video game world and the games he played. He reported feeling more comfortable working with a therapist who understood his world and "did not look down" on him for playing these video games as his parents had done. The clinician at first attempted to talk about mood symptoms and how to manage them in session in an attempt to engage Dean, but Dean was primarily interested in discussing the preferred topic of video games and he would bring the conversation back to video games. As a result, the clinician allowed Dean to talk more about his gaming habits and what psychological meaning the games meant for him.

At the end of the second therapy session, the therapist suggested Dean continue to play video games with his father to help Dean explain the video game world to his father and so his father could help Dean process and overlay character qualities upon Dean's life difficulties that his father was observing. This involved Dean immersing himself into the characters played and questioning why he played defined roles, chose in-game identities, and how he could relate these characteristics back into his life experiences with his father further building their relationship.

In the virtual world he was a fearless conqueror of enemy bases, laying waste to rival lands with multiple individuals in his personal clan and others bowing to him. Other less powerful warriors would avoid him out of fear of being destroyed and the enemy tended to retreat when he arrived at an in-game conflict occurring in the video game. Yet, this was not the true reason he played. He did not crave power, but the feeling of being more powerful than how he saw himself in real life.

His friends in school were his companions in the virtual world and together they helped save the virtual lands from many different foes with Dean as their leader. They would run into battle protecting the innocent players in the game, storm the enemy's lair, and even stop other players from causing bullying issues online. Dean felt powerful and important in the game, but significantly less so outside the game. He was a shy and introverted adolescent with self-esteem issues when talking to others face-to-face – even with his friends. He had difficulties talking to other people, classmates, teachers, and even his parents at times avoiding them at all costs. He felt weak and powerless in in-person social situations which impacted his self-esteem even further leading him to avoid the stressful situation.

However, in the game, he was courageous, talked to everyone he could, was well-liked, respected, and a guild leader. Players would reach out to him for help and he would respond, talk to them with ease, and lead them on a journey to complete their quest without a second thought. It appeared that Dean had contradicting and polar opposite views of himself. He viewed himself as weak and powerless in real life, but a strong leader in the video game world. The therapeutic difficulty lay with transferring his online self-esteem to his real life self.

Dean would become animated and excited about discussing his

accomplishments and experiences within his virtual worlds. He was powerful and could withstand multiple attacks, but still be able to hold out and win the area or level by his determination. He further expressed how he was able to play the video game because it provided a cathartic experience for him and helped create positive and helpful coping styles for him. These coping styles, as identified by Dean, consisted of thinking of how to handle a new situation, dealing with social anxiety, helping people in need, and being rewarded for caring behaviors.

After discussing his attributes and leadership skills for a couple weeks in sessions, we made the connection he felt inferior in real life compared to his character in the game. His warrior character held a rich backstory: He was from a noble family, but cursed because an evil warlord had taken his father's strength by poisoning him and taken over the kingdom. Dean was then forced to leave and told to never return. He was questing using the hero's journey in the video game to end the evil warlord's grip on his kingdom with hopes of attaining great power and courage. With his companions, he was able to survive and accomplish feats impossible alone. This was a key point in working with him on the transferring of his character's qualities and archetypal elements onto his real life experiences.

Dean's in-game character had made personal choices he could only fantasize about and play through the character – because they were not available to him in real life. This made him bold, daring, and even courageous because of the powers he attained by leveling up and working with his friends to defeat the virtual monsters. In a way, he was facing his personal fears through the virtual character and talents chosen, he just needed the analytical and psychological push to make the connection. Once made, he was able to realize the potential he had in the real world and began to incorporate his character's ideals and powers into his own self-concept.

The video game appeared to be allowing him to experience different methods in which to handle difficult scenarios for himself across his lifespan and different peer circles. He expressed an importance of his characters and how they were specifically chosen for qualities he felt needed to be represented in the virtual world as he saw these same qualities in himself. He believed the narrative journey found across the lore of *World of Warcraft* was resonant with his life experience - and built upon it with his character back stories.

As Dean and the clinician continued to talk about the video game, class points (ability points specific to the character being played which gave them special and powerful abilities) and the linear storyline, Dean was able to see the progression of the characters he chose to play. He selected to play as an in-your-face melee brawler (Warrior Archetype; his primary choice of character) or a ranged sniper (Ranger Archetype; his secondary choice of character) during this play-through of the games. However, it was discovered, Dean continually played the same characters or avatars within his guild, suggesting some standardization of avatar building, itemization, and playability.

Through examination of Dean's conscious thoughts, choices within the videogame, and experiences outside of the videogame, the clinician and Dean were able to work on his own personal heroic journey found within. Dean chose to work as a hero saving everyone he could, including other non-player characters whom he did not believe deserved it. He stated it was because they asked for his help. Through this application of the hero's motif and journey, Dean was able to relate it to his personal experience, including his mood difficulties, to the video game characters.

Dean and the clinician discussed the heroic journey he had to go through in each of the different areas of the video game and how he experienced them. Through playing these zones he was able to understand why he was drawn to certain characters and overlaid their qualities upon his real life as well.

For example, the clinician and Dean discussed how in certain situations with his peers, Dean decided to take a spectator approach in the conversation or playing when he felt he did not have anything to contribute or his self-esteem was low. However, in other situations he would jump right in, participate, and become very excited at the different prospects when his self-esteem was higher. These were very symbolic with his character development within the virtual worlds as well with his sniper (Ranger Archetype - observing) and melee character (Warrior Archetype – jumping into the conversation). Dean and the clinician further discussed the possibilities of him choosing his characters he played as because they *represented him* in the video game itself. Further, by playing as a part of himself in the video game, he was able to work through his feelings and concerns with the implementation of his coping skills and further helping him understand the video game world as well. Dean then became more thoughtful and further engaged with his character as an archetypal and mythological form of himself.

Later in the therapy sessions, Dean mentioned he was interested in a girl in his school but was unable to find the courage to ask her out. Dean discussed how he imagined his warrior would ask her out and he humbly replied "courtesy and treating her as an equal." We used imagery and role playing to figure out what he could say when he approached her. The clinician additionally suggested he use his companions to help with his ideas. Not surprisingly, a couple of weeks later, his mother mentioned he had been seeing a girl in his class on occasion during the week and appeared to be happier than before. When the clinician and Dean discussed this in the weekly therapy session he blushed and admitted he had found the courage to ask her out. Furthermore, Dean reported he had talked to his teacher about his grades and, to her surprise, asked for extra help. He began seeing the teacher after school for tutoring; an action he credited to his video game character. He additionally attributed his newfound confidence to asking his new girlfriend out on a date. He reported he would have never found the courage to ask for help without thinking about his character and the positive qualities found within himself.

Dean's father additionally was noticing change with his son during this time and that he was interacting more with friends and family again. His father had additionally mentioned he had been enjoying playing the game with his son due to him "feeling like I can connect with him again." His father joined his son's guild and crept up the ranks similar to how Dean did and even was found helping others in need – similar to how Dean was with his in-game persona. By having the father play with his son, the game play Dean was experiencing was given new life and sustenance from the fact he was able to enjoy it with his father and was no longer feeling ostracized. In fact, he was eating dinner with his family more, interacting and spending time offline with his father, completing his homework, and helping around the house with chores.

Overlapping these new distinctions of archetypal play within the video game of *World of Warcraft* for Dean provided differential insight into his videogame play and how he could approach his own difficulties in life. Overlaying the general concepts found within the videogame to his actual life experiences and self-esteem, Dean was able to see how he had found and developed his own personal hero and his anxiety and depression was his villain.

Incorporating the hero's journey into the therapeutic process appeared to be crucially helpful in allowing Dean to overcome his difficulties and increase his confidence. The literature on the concept of the heroic journey suggests every individual undergoes multiple personal and heroic journeys throughout their lifetime (Campbell, 2008). For Dean this was an important part of his life that in turn, he came to realize was an important feature of himself.

Parental involvement was also critical to Dean's success, particularly his at-home and school behaviors. His father worked with him and allowed Dean to teach him how to play the game which gave Dean a sense of purpose and power. Overall, this created a broader and more accepting support network in which Dean quickly thrived and succeeded at home and was able to be transferred to his school work as well. His father immersed himself in the video game Dean was playing and therefore was able to answer questions and provide guidance when necessary or queried in real life encounters mirrored in the video game world. Parental involvement is considered to be key in any therapeutic process, and thus should be considered a first line of defense/offense when working with this population. Parents need to be engaged in the process, be willing to help outside of the therapy room, show interest, provide time, and help to reduce additional stressors for their children in times of need.

Our work continued for a period of time and Dean, of course, still played his character and overlaid the qualities of his warrior upon his own self to much success in other communication and personal relationship areas. He made many new friends, online and offline, which he kept in touch with and had begun to show leadership qualities in his classroom, much to his mother's surprise and enjoyment.

Video games hold immense potential to work with many clinical disorders and to help many heal through post-traumatic growth. A clinician simply needs to be willing to jump into the journey with their client and learn more about their virtual and internal worlds. Dean's improvement over multiple sessions illustrates the progress of one adolescent using video games, archetypes, and the heroic myth to help with his emotional difficulties. Had an addictive perspective been utilized instead of the immersive/Jungian approach focus, this would have concentrated upon the removal of video games from Dean's life, possibly damaging the clinical relationship along with his personal growth. He would not have been able to practice a new narrative through his video game play. As outlined through this case study, a narrative and mythological approach to video games, video gamers, and games in therapy are more suitable for clinical cases like this to help improve client's well-being and are useful tools for engagement within the realm of therapeutic practice.

# References

Bean, A. M. (2015). Video gamers' personas: A five-factor study exploring personality elements of the video gamer (Doctoral Dissertation). Retrieved from ProQuest Digital Dissertations. (AAT 3726481).

Bean, A. M. (2018) *Working with Video Gamers and Games in Therapy: A clinician's guide.* New York, NY: Routledge.

Bean, A. M. (2019a). *The Archetypal Attraction.* In A. M. Bean, (Eds.), *The Psychology of Zelda: Linking Our World to the Legend of Zelda Series* (pp. 79-102). Dallas; TX: BenBella.

Bean, A. M. (2019b) Working therapeutically with video gamers and their families. *Journal of Health Service Psychology.*

Campbell, J. (2008). *The hero with a thousand faces.* Novato, CA: New World Library.

Csikszentmihalyi, M. (2009). *Flow: The Psychology of Optimal Experience.* New York: Harper and Row.

Hillman, J. (2004). *Uniform edition:1.* Putnam: Spring Publications.

Johnson, R. A. (1986). *Inner Work: Using Dreams and Active Imagination for Personal Growth.* San Francisco: Harper & Row.

Jung, C. G. (2014). *The Archetypes and the Collective Unconscious.* London: Routledge.

Jung, C.G. (1960). General aspects of dream psychology. *In Collected Works vol.8.* New York, NY: Bollingen. (Original published in 1916.)

Stein, M. (1998). *Jung's Map of the Soul: An Introduction.* Chicago: Open Court.

# The Integration of Play Within Video Games in Clinical Practice

# 3

Jessica Stone, PhD, RPT-S

Psychology is a broad field that includes many different theoretical foundations, models, and belief systems. The components of these fundamental tenets inform how a clinician conceptualizes and approaches a wide array of concerns that people bring into the office. Clients are best served by practitioners who have explored, and been adequately trained in, various theories and have a solid understanding regarding what and why they are doing anything in session.

Psychological theories provide "a model for understanding human thoughts, emotions, and behaviors" (Cherry, 2019, para. 7). Primary theories include, but are not limited to: psychoanalytic, psychodynamic, behavioral, cognitive-behavioral, and humanistic. Each has basic tenets that describe behavior, define pathology, and inform the process of interaction which can elicit change. A clinician can subscribe to one clinical paradigm of thought exclusively or an amalgamation of multiple theories. Therefore, the interventions held sacred can be exclusive to one theory or applicable to many.

The inclusion of video games in psychotherapy provides an intervention that is applicable across multiple theories. The therapeutic use of video games, and their relevant platform(s), benefit the therapist and client by providing a mechanism to 1) build rapport, 2) gain valuable information, insight, and understandings about the client, 3) allow for intervention both within and outside the game play, and 4) allow for acquired skills to be integrated into day to day life.

## Theory Specific Tenets

Psychology currently includes numerous theories and foundations for clinicians to explore, conceptualize, and adopt. A clinician's theoretical underpinnings define every aspect of the treatment process. Understanding how any intervention, including video game play, is incorporated into the fundamental theoretical approach gives the process therapeutic value. Psychoanalytic, behavioral, and humanistic theories provide examples from the theoretical cornerstones and briefly illustrate some key tenets that a clinician would use to include video game play in session with a solid theoretical base.

*Psychoanalytic*

The basic tenets of Psychoanalytic theory include the importance of working with repressed and unconscious material, predominately regarding aggression and sexuality, which manifest in emotional and physical ways (Brill, 1949). According to Dr. Sigmund Freud, this material can present in therapy through projection, transference, and defensiveness (American Psychoanalytic Association, no date). Through a process of self-exploration and catharsis, Dr. Freud believed a patient undergoing psychoanalysis could benefit greatly. Over time psychoanalysis has evolved, however, and a few of the tenets are quite applicable today, in general and in therapy involving video game play. For example, self-exploration, catharsis, projection, transference, and defensiveness can all be exhibited within the play and interactions, providing the therapist with a plethora of important information. In particular, the game play can frequently include scenarios in which a player would include elements of psychoanalytic tenets within interactions with other players.

*Cognitive Behavioral*

Cognitive behavioral therapy (CBT) focuses, as the name implies, on the cognitions and behaviors of the client. Stemming from the mechanics of behavior and behavioral therapy, CBT constantly reevaluates conceptualizations of the client's difficulties. Precipitating factors and patterns of behavior are evaluated in terms of cognitive analyses of problematic behaviors (Beck, 2011). Collaboration and active participation within the session are important components of the therapist and client working as a team to approach mechanisms of change. The work is very problem-focused and goal-oriented (Beck, 2011), just as working toward a goal or quest could be within video game play. A therapist utilizing CBT could find a number of parallels between the game-play patterns, problematic behaviors, and approaches to problem solving within the video game play and the client's day to day difficulties.

*Humanistic*

Self-actualization and an inherent belief in the good in people are the cornerstone tenets of Humanistic psychological theory. Humanistic theory was born predominately in response to the psychoanalytic and behavioral foci of the mid-twentieth century. For humanist psychologists, psychoanalysis focused too much on pathology, and behaviorism focused too heavily on the mechanics of behavior. Humanistic theory focuses on assisting people with achieving their full potential and living their best lives. The basic tenets include: the whole person is more than individual components; to understand a person one must look at their micro and macrocosms; people are conscious, have free will, and seek meaning and connection (Cherry, 2018). Video game play, particularly cooperative or team-oriented games, inherently includes scenarios and situations for a therapist to witness and experience how these components affect the client and the difficulties s/he is experiencing.

Different types of video game play will elicit different actions, reactions, and approaches from clients of all ages. Clinicians can learn more about games that psychologically pull for certain qualities based on their type, purpose, structure, and gameplay. Appropriate therapeutic incorporation of particular video games can be made wherein the in-game interaction, the metaphoric aspects, and generalizability of insights, skills, and experiences can be made. Understanding the qualities of the different types of video games can assist the therapist and client with psychological needs, while utilizing an engaging, highly motivating medium (Ceranoglu, 2010). A solid theoretical base can help structure the therapeutic conceptualizations and help the client achieve his/her treatment goals.

## Initiating Use of Video Games in Clinical Practice

The discussion and/or inclusion of video games is often initiated by clients who have interest or familiarity with the game(s). Other times the therapist can initiate the discussion and inclusion of video games as an intentional, more directed intervention. Playing video games is a great way for many people to become immersed in an alternate or parallel world, create a character like themselves with components of self and other, or even explore one's internal psychological world (Bean, 2019; Przybylski, et al., 2012). Additionally, clients can practice everyday skills, understand the importance of teamwork, and improve interpersonal communication and creativity (Jackson & Games, 2015; Stone, 2019a).

Speaking the client's language and utilizing the tenets of the therapeutic powers of play along with an identified theoretical foundation, will pave the way to appropriate video game use in clinical practice (Stone, 2019b). Understanding the various genres of hardware and software will allow the therapist to make sound decisions regarding the use of video games and digital tools in mental health treatment. When a clinician can tailor the interventions to the treatment goals through theory and foundation, compliance and engagement will be higher and the treatment will be more successful.

## Digital Platforms

For those who are not familiar with technology platforms, this will serve as a very brief introductory overview. Further searching will yield a plethora of information one can incorporate into clinical practice.  Typically, phones and tablets are used to play app-based games and programs. PlayStation, Xbox, and Nintendo consoles are used to play cartridge-based games or downloadable content. Computers tend to play both disc or downloadable content, and virtual reality games use downloadable content with a head-mounted display (HMD) unit.

Specific to video games, Bean (2018, 2019) has both delineated the historical research regarding video game genres and narrowed down a list of seven categories. Understanding these categories can assist the therapist in choosing and playing video games within therapeutic interactions. Bean's categories include: action, adventure, action-adventure, role playing (RPG), simulation, strategy, and other (Bean, 2018, p. 31-36; 2019, p. 96). The following tables were adapted from Bean's book, *Working with Video Gamers and Games in Therapy* and can serve as a guide when learning about and choosing video games for integration into clinical practice.

| Action | |
|---|---|
| *The gamer is often under time pressure and combat can be one player at a time; turn taking combat* | |
| Challenges the gamer in: | • Tests of physical skill<br>• High reaction speeds<br>• Superior hand-eye coordination |
| Includes activities not considered to be central to the game play | • Puzzles<br>• Races<br>• Mazes<br>• Challenges<br>• Exploration demands |
| Examples | Overwatch, Super Mario Brothers, Super Smash Brothers, Call of Duty, Donkey Kong |

Table 3.1 Types of Video Games and Play; Adapted from Bean, 2018.

| Adventure |
| --- |
| *Player assumes a role as a protagonist within the game storyline via the narrative drive gameplay* |
| Originally began with computer text adventures using keyboard arrows |
| Challenges and action are not a focus or part of the game play like in action games |
| The player goes through a linear and plot-driven narrative with the singular focus of completing the adventure |
| One will explore and encounter multiple obstacles and barriers in place which will remain until a tool or similar item is used to work through the obstacle/barrier |

| Examples | Haunted House, Heavy Rain, King's Quest, The Longest Journey |
| --- | --- |

Table 3.2 Types of Video Games and Play; Adapted from Bean, 2018.

| Action-Adventure |
| --- |
| *Hybrid – Consist of elements found in both action and adventure games* |
| Began as players became bored with pure adventure games |
| To progress in the game, one typically obtains a tool or other in-game items to overcome obstacles, etc. and includes smaller obstacles requiring navigation, combat, gathering, and simple to complex puzzle solving in order to progress |
| Reflex skills are relied upon during parts of combat to dodge or advance on an enemy |
| Puzzles are more common than combat, requiring a constant cognitive process to think through the conniving riddles |
| Storyline is linear and goal driven |
| Tend to focus on exploration and item gathering to level up |
| Typically clear delineation of enemy, hero, and populace to be rescued or saved |

| Examples | Minecraft, Assassin's Creed, Resident Evil, Half Life, Portal, Legend of Zelda |
| --- | --- |

Table 3.3 Types of Video Games and Play; Adapted from Bean, 2018.

| Role-Playing Game (RPG) | |
|---|---|
| *Player specializes in a specific set of skills and role for group or solo adventuring* | |
| Ancestry – Dungeons and Dragons | |
| Immersion is quite common in this genre | |
| Layout of the virtual world well defined character composition storyline solo and group play | |
| Progression to higher levels, acquiring experience points, and obtaining improved gear | |
| Character development is the main focal point of the game | |
| Different than the action games, RPG combat is in "real time" with players both in action at once – not turn taking | |
| Quests, story progression, and development | |
| Examples | World of Warcraft, Diablo, Final Fantasy, Runescape, and Pokémon |

Table 3.4 Types of Video Games and Play, Adapted from Bean, 2018.

| Simulation | |
|---|---|
| *This diverse category attempts to replicate real life.* | |
| Games include nurturing games, tending to farms, family simulation | |
| Virtual Reality simulating job training, medical training, role playing, creative arts, world creation, environment experiences | |
| Examples | Sims, Farm Story, FIFA, Rollercoaster Tycoon, Goat Simulator, Flight Simulator |

Table 3.5 Types of Video Games and Play; Adapted from Bean, 2018.

| Strategy |
| --- |
| *The player creates, manages, and/or controls items within the world to achieve victory.* |
| Focus on careful, methodical, skillful planning to win |
| Use in game mechanics to their advantage to plan a series of actions using the game system bonuses to add to their chance of victory |

| Strategy sub-genres | • Real-time strategy (RTS)<br>• Turn-based strategy (TBS)<br>• Turn-based tactics (TBT)<br>• Real-time tactics (RTT)<br>• Multiplayer online battle arenas (MOBAs)<br>• Tower defense |
| --- | --- |
| Examples | Civilization, Age of Empires, Starcraft, Warcraft, Clash of Clans, League of Legends |

Table 3.6 Types of Video Games and Play, Adapted from Bean, 2018.

| Other |
| --- |
| Includes games which do not fit into the aforementioned categories |

Table 3.7 Types of Video Games and Play; Adapted from Bean, 2018.

## Play

The therapeutic inclusion of play can take many forms and utilize a wide variety of tools. Over time, some tools have become mainstays – such as Playmobil, Legos, puppets, sand trays, and art supplies. Tools have varied with the trends, advancements, and interests of the clients. The last decade has brought with it great interest in digital tools (Pew, 2019). This area has been showing significant breadth of topics, interests, and engagement with rich materials, interactions, understandings, and interventions for use within the mental health therapeutic setting.

*Speaking the Client's Language*

One critical component of mental health treatment is the importance of speaking the client's language (Stone, 2015, 2018, 2019a). Each generation has its trends and foci. Clients often bring in, or at least speak of, the current toys, games, or music that they are interested in and passionate about. At the core of the therapeutic milieu is the importance of understanding and valuing each other's experiences and needs based on expressed language (verbal and non-verbal). It is fundamental that providers understand what is important to their client, how they are expressing themselves, how they identify their self-objects, and therefore the best ways to be personally seen, heard, and known. Clients express this within the language of their interests; therefore, it is imperative that providers incorporate these interests in powerful, informed, and therapeutic ways.

Since the use of digital devices is so prevalent in the current era, and many children are digital natives, it is logical that mental health providers find ways to appropriately incorporate the digital language into therapeutic work. By systematically applying a structure, in addition to a fundamental theory, by which the therapist can evaluate the therapeutic value of the digital tool and language, client interests can be incorporated into sessions appropriately. This structure can assist with fundamental conceptualization, communication with collateral contacts, and writing of clinical notes.

*Therapeutic Powers of Play*

Charles Schaefer, Ph.D. authored a book entitled "The Therapeutic Powers of Play" in 1992 and updated the work with a second edition, co-authored with Athena Drewes, Ph.D. (2013). The Therapeutic Powers of Play include four main categories and "20 core agents of change" (Schaefer & Drewes, 2013). The main tenets of this approach believe that play is essential for promoting normal development and that therapy requires both a therapeutic relationship and a medium of exchanging of ideas, desires, and projection into the play (Drewes, 2001). As a direct result, the therapeutic powers of play have been used as an answer to professional desire to further understand the curative factors of play. These capacities provide a much needed structure to apply to the use of video game play in therapy.

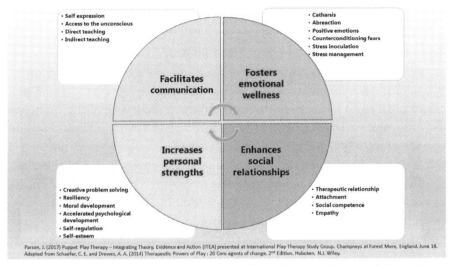

Figure 3.1 Therapeutic Powers of Play from Parson (2017); Adapted from Therapeutic Powers of Play, Schaefer & Drewes, (2013).

The outcome components of the therapeutic powers of play are categorized by Schaefer into four quadrants: Facilitates Communication, Fosters Emotional Wellness, Increases Personal Strengths, and Enhances Social Relationships. These four main elements encompass change agents that have been identified as fundamental to the aspects of play which are therapeutic in nature. Understanding these elements, and the identified change agents, provides the necessary structure for therapists to identify, understand, utilize, and discuss what is happening in the therapeutic process with their clients. When using tools such as video games therapeutically, this structure and the elements included provide the practitioner with ways to conceptualize and address identified concerns within any theoretical foundation.

If we look at the twenty core agents of change, we can see that they are all powerful components of working with clients, particularly children and teens.  For instance, utilizing a video game in session, or discussing the use of a video game, can assist with a number of therapeutic change agents, (see Figure 3.1 for reference). Often, a clinician can identify one or more from each quadrant and highlight those agents of change in their communications.

## Clinical Case Example

Marie was a seven-year-old, highly gifted, third grade student who presented for play therapy treatment regarding her difficulties with frustration tolerance, social interaction skills, and anxiety concerns. She had a strong need to be correct and in control, was unforgiving of the mistakes of others, and had difficulties truly integrating the concept that her mind works differently than many of her peers. She frequently experienced imposter syndrome (a belief that she was less capable than others believe and she would be found to be a fraud) and intense bouts of perfectionism, which greatly affected all aspects of her life.

The designation of giftedness is much more complicated than a particular intelligence quotient score (IQ). Rather, being gifted is a capacity for increased and accelerated breadth and depth of exploration and conceptualization. The potential clinical implications and impacts of this way of thinking are far reaching, such as: an increased ability to identify the underlying goals of interventions and discussions, greater concerns about whether or not the therapist can be helpful, and insecurities regarding any experienced difficulties, thereby creating a strong need to mask and/ or overcompensate that must be respected (Stone, 2019b).

Marie strongly desired positive interactions with others, particularly peers and authority figures, but she had difficulty navigating and balancing her belief systems, her own needs, and the needs of others. She wanted to be seen as competent, and even superior in some senses, quite possibly in an attempt to hide any difficulties she experienced. Her need to maintain these lofty presentations impacted her willingness to try new things. She had fears regarding exposing her vulnerabilities and ultimately this resulted in an avoidance of anything that would chance failure. She constricted her involvement to activities that would not threaten her ability to maintain this appearance.

Upon entering the office, Marie would initially tend to gravitate toward activities that allowed her to feel in control, knowledgeable, and secure. Utilizing a primarily non-directive approach to treatment, wherein the activities are chosen and initiated by the client and not the therapist, Marie was able to explore the office and decide what she wanted to do.

For the first four sessions, Marie chose activities that emphasized and reinforced her desire to utilize her strengths, thereby increasing her sense of security and safety. This initial non-directive approach can contribute greatly to the rapport building process. Allowing the child the ability to explore the office at her own pace, without challenging her needs as defined above, created a safe space and a solid initial therapeutic relationship.

After this initial positive, trusting relationship and alliance between Marie and the therapist was established, it appeared less threatening to introduce the use of a therapist-chosen activity. This is not always necessary, however. To challenge the system Marie adhered to, it would be necessary for her to use items with which she was less comfortable. This was an unlikely direction that she would choose on her own. Knowing that the family did not typically engage in play with technological tools, this was identified as an area where Marie would not feel as competent as she typically desired. Therefore, the Nintendo Switch was planned to be presented as a possible activity by the therapist in the fifth session. A discussion with her parents, without Marie present, included the therapeutic relevance of such an activity within the session. It was important for her parents to understand the goals regarding the use of technological tools within therapy, particularly since they held strong familial views regarding general use of such devices. The novelty of the use, along with some potential for high motivation (i.e., the use of a typically taboo but social relevant device), had a high probability of engaging Marie in activities where she could not maintain her typical stance. Marie still had the ability to decide whether or not she wanted to use this in the session.

Thankfully, Marie was quite excited about the introduction of the Nintendo Switch. This met the "highly motivating activity" criteria for the intervention along with the need for a novel, unknown process. If her need to use and engage with the device was high enough, she would most likely endure the difficulties of the learning curve of the Switch use and the unknown components of the game play.

Clinically, the Switch is used as a team effort within these sessions. The basic Switch console consists of a handheld tablet device with two removable controllers, one on each side. The controllers, or joy cons, are removable (if desired) so the center tablet can be propped up for easy view by the therapist and client, and the controllers can be used together by one person (one in each hand) or they can be used separately. Removing the controllers increases the cooperative nature of the play drastically. To increase cooperative play within some games, particularly games that traditionally utilize a single player format, the controllers are separated, and the client and therapist each have one. This increases the need to communicate and establish and/or negotiate goals, increases empathy for the opponent's tasks, and supports the team approach to therapeutic Switch use.

Utilizing this therapist-client cooperative controller game play approach allows for a different experience of the play. Whereas an individual would control all aspects of movement, decision making, and overall gameplay if playing alone, now the therapist and client team have to share what the individual needs and desires are in order to do simple tasks such as movement within the game, and more complex tasks such as completing quests. Sharing needs and desires, along with compromising to support the team approach, can be very difficult tasks. Much trust must be placed in the partnership in order to advance in the game with this approach.

The Legend of Zelda, Breath of the Wild (BOW; Nintendo, 2017), game was specifically chosen for this task and was introduced to Marie for the first time in the fifth session. She was intrigued by a funny story of being able to use a chicken to glide safely instead of a glider and she really wanted to play with the Switch. She was not familiar with the BOW game or the Legend of Zelda game series.

The Legend of Zelda BOW game falls within the action-adventure genre of game play and was released in 2017 (Nintendo, 2017, para. 1). The original Legend of Zelda game was released in Japan in 1986 and has developed in many directions and generations since then (Fandom, n.d.a). The main character and protagonist, Link, is the eternal hero in each installment in the series (Fandom, n.d.b, para. 1). He explores a variety of landscapes, defeats monsters, navigates challenges and quests, collects items, and helps others. Breath of the Wild is an entirely open-world game where players explore Hyrule with the goal of defeating the evil Ganon and can complete tasks in any order desired (Cooper, 2017, para. 3). Ganon has been locked away in the Hyrule Castle with evil plans for the future, and it is Link's task to save Hyrule.

Marie was very excited to play the game and explore this "chicken gliding experience." Despite suggestions that practicing her controller features would benefit her play, Marie jumped in and began to move Link all over in sporadic, confusing ways. She quickly became frustrated with the controller, herself, and with the therapist, but she still wanted to play. She began to yell at the therapist regarding movements she was making, fully externalizing the blame and frustrations regarding her own inability to instantly master this activity. She was either unaware of her contribution to this frustration, unwilling to admit her contribution, or both.

A quick pause of the game allowed for some conversation about her dysregulated state, some ways to help her re-regulate, and a discussion about the necessity of playing as a team. As stated earlier, in this team approach modality of using the Nintendo Switch, it is imperative that the two people play while communicating needs, desires, expectations, and concerns, or the game play will not be successful. A monster's attack or a fall off a cliff will surely cause Link's demise if the team is not working together.

The game was un-paused and game play resumed. Once re-regulated after the break and discussion, Marie was able to hear and integrate the information about the importance of working together and the mechanics of such. A safe place in a village was found and she independently explored the features of her assigned left controller. The features of the therapist's right-hand controller were also demonstrated and a strategy was formed for working together as a team to move outside of the village. She was able to discover, through the process of playing Zelda in a safe, therapeutic environment, the importance of making decisions while regulated, the exploration of new and novel stimulus, and the need for practice, communication, trust, and teamwork.

In Marie's case, the introduction of this new game play allowed for further exploration of her difficulties in environments outside of the office. If she had remained in her comfort zone she would not have become dysregulated and the patterns displayed and demonstrated coping skills (and lack there-of) would not have become apparent in the therapist-client interactions. Demonstrating these struggles, within a highly motivating interaction, motivated her to work through them to achieve a more satisfying interpersonal exchange and game play experience.

After the teamwork skills became more comfortable for Marie, parallels were made between the Zelda play dynamics and what she experiences outside of the office. Marie had a history of difficulties in situations where she needed to rely on others. The demonstration of more beneficial interaction skills during the video game play, and the experience of the difference in employing them, can made within interactions, allowed her to experience and practice these skills in a safe environment. Relying on others included situations at home, at school, and with same-aged peers. For instance, when her mother asked her to bring her glasses to school, Marie did not trust that her mother was correct. She didn't know the overarching goal of bringing her glasses to school, and she didn't trust that her mother had any agenda beyond the typical "nagging" she often perceived. She concluded that she didn't need to bring her glasses. After school she learned she had an eye doctor appointment and needed her glasses, which she did not have with her. Within session this situation was revisited and analyzed. Marie was able to identify that she and her mother should have worked as a team, with her mother communicating the overarching goal and Marie trusting that her mother had a valid reason for Marie to bring her glasses to school. Communication and trust were two powerful lessons Marie learned from the Nintendo Switch therapist-client cooperative controller game play experience.

In another example, emphasis was placed on how Marie's tendency to have her anxiety and rigidity enter into social interactions effects the dynamic between her and other people. Parallels drawn between her initial frustrated response to the novel BOW/Switch experience and her responses to her peers at school allowed Marie to realize some of her contributions to the degradation of peer interactions. Although this is a process and often not a quick resolution, Marie's ability to gain insight regarding how her own behaviors and needs affect her ability to make and keep friends is imperative. Achieving such insights will move her in a positive direction and can be built upon in future sessions.

Curative factors activated within these sessions of video game play include self-expression, stress management, counterconditioning of fears, and positive emotions under the *facilitates communication* and *fostering emotional wellness* categories from the therapeutic powers of play. Other curative factors employed within the video game play are: attachment, therapeutic relationship, and empathy under   *enhancing social relationships*; and self-esteem, self-control, resiliency, and sense of self under *increasing personal strengths*. Identification of these factors will structure and enhance the understanding of the therapeutic process and clinical direction.

## Conclusion

Video games are phenomenally rich in content, process, and possibilities. The application of a theoretical foundation enhances the therapeutic value of the inclusion of video games in sessions. Utilizing them within one's clinical practice to speak the client's language, identify areas of need, and implement a variety of interventions can enhance and advance the treatment in ways not previously possible. The integration of video games, a solid theoretical foundation, and the application of a structure with which to understand the therapeutic value of the games into clinical practice incorporates many of the basic tenets one must consider when using any intervention within the mental health treatment process. Video games can be a powerful therapeutic tool.

# References

American Psychoanalytic Association. (N.D.). *Psychoanalytic terms and concepts defined*. Retrieved from: http://www.apsa.org/content/psychoanalytic-terms-concepts-defined

Bean, A. M. (2018). *Working with video gamers and games in therapy: a clinician's guide*. NY: Routledge.

Bean, A. M. (2019). I am my avatar and my avatar is me: utilizing video games as therapeutic tools. In J. Stone. (Ed.), *Integrating technology into modern therapies* (pp. 94-106). NY: Routledge.

Beck, J. (2011). *The basic principles of cognitive behavior therapy*. Retrieved from: https://pro.psychcentral.com/the-basic-principles-of-cognitive-behavior-therapy/

Brill, A. A. (1949). *The basic principles of psychoanalysis*. Retrieved from: http://www.institutobios.org/catharsis.pdf

Ceranoglu, T. A. (2010). Video games is psychotherapy. *Review of General Psychology*, *APA*, *14,* 141-146.

Cherry, K. (2018, May). *Humanistic psychology: definition and history*. Retrieved from: https://www.explorepsychology.com/humanistic-psychology/

Cherry, K. (2019, May). *10 Types of Psychological Theories*: *How theories are used in psychology*. Retrieved from https://www.verywellmind.com/what-is-a-theory-2795970

Cooper, D. (2017, January). *The Legend of Zelda: Breath of the Wild – Everything We Know So Far*. Retrieved from https://gamerant.com/legend-zelda-breath-of-the-wild-wiki/

Drewes, A. A. (2001). The possibilities and challenges in using play therapy in schools. In A. A.

Drewes, L. J. Carey, & C. E. Schaefer (Eds.), *School-based play therapy* (pp. 41–61). NY: Wiley.

Fandom (n.d., a). *History of the Legend of Zelda series*. Retrieved from https://zelda.fandom.com/wiki/History_of_the_Legend_of_Zelda_series

Fandom (n.d., b). *Link*. Retrieved from https://zelda.fandom.com/wiki/Link

Jackson, L. A & Games, A.I. (2015). Video games and creativity. In G.P. Green & J. C. Kaufman (Eds.), *Video games and creativity* (pp. 3-38). London: Elsevier.

Nintendo (2017). *The Legend of Zelda Breath of the Wild: Nintendo Switch*. Retrieved from    https://www.nintendo.com/games/detail/ the-legend-of-zelda-breath-of-the-wild-switch/#game-info

Parson, J. (2017). Adapted from Schaefer, C.E. & Drewes, A. A. (2014). *Therapeutic powers of play: 20 core agents of change, (2)*. NJ: Wiley.

Pew Research Center (2019, June). *Internet/broadband fact sheet*. Retrieved from: https://www.pewinternet.org/fact-sheet/ internet-broadband/

Przybylski, A. K., Weinstein, N., Murayama, K., Lunch, M., & Ryan, R. M. (2012). The ideal self at play: the appeal of video games that let you be all you can be. *Psychological Services, 23*(1), 69-76.

Schaefer, C.E. (1992). *Therapeutic powers of play (1)*. New York, NY: Jason Aronson.

Schaefer, C. E., & Drewes, A. A. (2013). *The therapeutic powers of play: 20 core agents of change*. Hoboken, NJ: Wiley.

Stone, J. (2015). Board games in play therapy. In K.J. O'Connor, C.E. Schaefer, & L. Braverman, (Eds.), *The Handbook of Play Therapy, Second Edition* (pp. 309-323). NJ: Wiley.

Stone, J. (2018). Play therapy needs the baby and the bath water. *Play Therapy, 13*(3), 16.

Stone, J. (2019a). Connecting gifted people: utilizing technology in mental health to speak an intellectually gifted person's language. In J. Stone (Ed.), *Integrating technology into modern therapies* (pp. 149-165). NY: Routledge.

Stone, J. (2019b). Digital Games. In J. Stone & C.E. Schaefer (Eds.), *Game Play*, (3). NJ: Wiley.

# Dungeons and Dragons

# Introduction to Dungeons & Dragons

# 4

**Joseph Lasley, PhD**

Dungeons & Dragons (D&D) has seen a dramatic rise in popularity and an increase in its use as a therapeutic interaction and intervention since the early 1990s (D'Anastasio, 2017). This has created a two-fold need for clinicians to understand D&D, the context around D&D, and its potential use in broader therapeutic settings. People of all ages may relate to the characters created and storylines within the game, making it a topic of interest for therapists who want to relate to clients (D'Anastasio, 2017). Additionally, there is therapeutic potential in playing D&D that can be leveraged by clinicians to deliver therapy in a group setting via playing the game. Therapeutic work is already being done by clinicians around the world within D&D group settings and has shown promise working with social skills, identity development, and autism (Granshaw, 2018). Clinicians hoping to benefit from the knowledge of and use of D&D first need to learn about the recent rise in popularity, what the game entails, some relevant context of the game, the psychological impact in the game, and critiques of power and exclusion inherent in both the cultural context and structural history of the game. One can begin by understanding that D&D is just one of many tabletop role-playing games.

## Tabletop Role-Playing Games

There are many individual titles for games that are considered examples of tabletop role-playing games (TTRPG) including, Dungeons & Dragons, *Call of Cthulhu, Vampire: The Masquerade,* and *Pathfinder,* to name a few. Many editions of D&D have been published that each feature a different variation of rule systems and various iterations of lore. The most recent and popular edition of D&D is the fifth edition (D&D 5e). The game is popular despite the publication of long rule books and each game of D&D is inherently unique because the way in which the rules are applied can vary from group to group. For example, some players use strict literal applications of "Rules as Written" (RAW) while others avoid constantly looking up exact wording by adjudicating rules in whatever way they agree best serves the story (a highly useful approach when working clinically with individuals). D&D also highly encourages the use of homebrew content (rules, abilities, items, etc. that are original creations by players). Even among the many varying playstyles and groups, there are basic rules and experiences that are common across groups.

## Rise in Popularity

Dungeons & Dragons, initially published in 1974, is the first formalized game of this type and is perhaps the most widely recognized name. The game is experiencing an unprecedented surge in popularity, with record sales each year and famous celebrities speaking publicly about their love for the game (Weiss, 2018). The recent rise in popularity is refreshing given that D&D was falsely blamed and associated with suicide, homicide, and occult worship in the 1980s (Laycock, 2015). Numerous live-play D&D podcasts and internet video streaming sites have emerged in recent years which are also connected to increasing interest. Popular titles include *Critical Role, Adventurers Inc., Girls Guts Glory, Dice Camera Action, Drunks and Dragons, Misscliks, High Rollers,* and *Dragon Friends. Critical Role* is one of the best-known D&D streams. *Critical Role* published its first live-recorded episode in March 2015, the 100th episode aired in June of 2017, and a successful Kickstarter campaign on March 4, 2019 raised over

$6 million in two days, ending at $11 million. The success of *Critical Role* and similar shows indicates they are being used as an example of D&D for many players. Each episode of *Critical Role* is around four hours in length and is recorded in a live web broadcast on a weekly basis on Twitch.tv/criticalrole. The cast is comprised of a group of friends who have careers as voice actors outside of *Critical Role*. Tens of thousands of viewers watch the stream live each week and the episodes, which are later published on YouTube and accrue hundreds of thousands more views each.

Fans of *Critical Role* call themselves "Critters." Throughout the rise of the show's popularity, numerous reports surfaced of people feeling inspired by their relationships with the show and experiencing transformation in their games and other areas of life, including work, relationships, and personal well-being. Players have reported benefits of TTRPGs including transformational learning, community building, and identity development (Bowman, 2010; Cover, 2010; Daniau, 2016). These benefits have been the subject of research and illustrate that people are being drawn to D&D while using shows as models in their own games (Lasley, 2017). The impact of these shows involves parasocial interaction but also helps a wider audience gain access to D&D by increasing its popularity and reducing barriers to entry. Newly interested players can learn about the game by watching these shows. Shows like *Girls, Guts, Glory, The Sirens,* and *Misscliks* provide representation of diverse identities, joining D&D celebrities like TJ Storm and Satine Phoenix, which helps reduce historical barriers associated with stereotypes about gamers being smelly white men in their parent's basements. With an easier, more accessible understanding of the game, more people from more diverse backgrounds gain confidence in starting their own or joining existing gaming groups and experiencing the benefits of playing D&D for themselves.

## Dungeons & Dragons

In a game of D&D, players act as characters that (usually) work together to complete quests and achieve both character and game objectives within the imaginary world. The designers of D&D state that adventure is the heart of the game and is made up of three pillars: exploration, social interaction, and combat (Mearls & Crawford, 2014). Exploration is about creating and discovering an imaginary world. Social interaction focuses on interacting with characters and objects in the imaginary world. Combat is a structured contest in which characters strategize to defeat opponents. Each of the three pillars of adventure come together to contribute to the overall adventure experience and form a story.

D&D games typically involve 4-8 players, one of whom is designated in a facilitator role often called a Dungeon Master (DM) or Game Master (GM). Dungeon Master is a title specific to the D&D brand while Game Master or Storyteller are titles shared more generally by other games and gamers. This person serves as a narrator, author, facilitator, and referee among other roles while the remaining players take on the roles of specific characters. The dungeon masters (DMs) who facilitate these games use many leadership abilities that are useful in other areas of life, including facilitation, problem solving, and leading collaborative creativity (Cover, 2010; Daniau 2016). Creative context is important because the environment shapes the willingness of people to engage in creative problem solving (Kasof, 1995). Some conceptions of creative work outside the gaming context acknowledge that creativity is often social and relies on collegial relationships (Abra, 1994). Likewise, individuals with professional facilitation or teaching skills incorporate them into how they take up the role of a DM with their friends, students, and clients (D'Anastasio, 2017; Garcia, 2016).

DMs are directly involved in the variations between TTRPG experiences through their use of variable game design elements in their leadership role. Dungeons & Dragons *5th Edition*, for example, is intentionally customizable and encourages DMs to modify or create their own styles, game designs, and stories. The therapeutic potential of TTRPGs could be associated with various design or facilitation elements that might impact the use and development of creativity in TTRPG experiences. Design elements such as facilitation, play style, length of sessions, and frequency of sessions may all play a role in how or to what extent groups engage in creative activities. The psychological environment, including perceptions of psychological safety, established when playing these games may also impact creative experiences similar to how psychological safety has been shown to mediate creativity in work groups (Williams et al., 2006).

In D&D, a group of characters (role-played by the players) embark on a quest. Each character has their own background, motivations, personality, and unique abilities that they use to work together to overcome obstacles (fighting goblins, sneaking past monsters, and persuading guards) and interact with other characters on their journey. The human players are each responsible for creating, improvising, and role playing as one character (except the dungeon master, who acts as a facilitator and narrator). General plot elements are determined in advance by the dungeon master. Some gamers create their own settings and stories while others use published adventure modules written specifically for D&D 5e.

Since there is not a complete script to follow, players are afforded agency to improvise and interact as they feel their character would respond to the various situations that arise. D&D players are driven by various motivations, using multiple strategies to relate to a mental concept of their character held in their subjective experience (Banks et al., 2017). The dungeon master is responsible for preparing and role playing as the non-player characters (NPCs; like a guard, villain, or bartender) and other elements of the environment or setting such as describing the landscape or culture of the fictional populace. As the game and story progresses, players build onto their characters' personalities to account for the improvised experiences that unfold (a character may develop a fear of water after almost drowning during a mission) and also add abilities to the character's repertoire (ex. a wizard will learn more powerful spells as the game goes on).

A common routine of gameplay might begin with the dungeon master narrating to explain a setting and situation. Players can then interact with NPCs, each other, or fixtures of the environment (ex. talk to the bartender, open the door, check for traps, attack the goblin) by describing their character's actions to the group. The dungeon master adjudicates outcomes of the players' actions using dice according to the rules of the game. Rolling higher numbers helps convince the bartender to tell you some secrets or makes it more likely a player will defeat the goblin, while lower numbers will bring less favorable or even detrimental results. Each action is then followed by a description of the outcome and more choices for how the players might respond and proceed. Eventually, the story unfolds through a combination of functions: the players reach some predetermined plot points (completing objectives or overcoming obstacles), the outcomes of player actions and dice rolls create unforeseen outcomes, and players improvise scenes while interacting with each other role playing as their characters. Together, the players achieve game objectives while also creating a story. In doing so, they make meaning from the experience for both themselves and their characters.

## Social Interaction

Humans innately learn by playing, a skill we have from childhood. Learning through role playing has been widely observed in children as they shift roles unconsciously. Evidence is documented of the benefit of using tabletop fantasy role-playing games as an activity to perform social work with children (Zayas & Lewis, 1986). Children naturally imitate social roles when they play (in and out of TTRPGs) to learn about the social world (Vygotsky, 1978). As adults, we take up multiple roles in defining a sense of self; the process is not unique to role-playing games (Williams et al., 2006). In this way, people of all ages can learn in different ways through social role playing.

One key element of D&D experiences is the reliance on social interaction in creating the play experience. D&D games are traditionally played through social interactions around a table. The advancement of technology has allowed virtual versions (e.g. Google Hangouts, Roll20.net, Dndbeyond. com) of such games to be played though the premise remains the same. A group of people gather to role-play characters in a game in which the set of rules and objectives is moderated partly by pre-existing rules and partly by players as they play rather than solely by the premeditated computer coding in video games. Virtual TTRPG interactions are not always face to face and can be considered computer mediated communication. However, it is the epistemology of the rules which is within the players' agency in TTRPGs in contrast to rules being solely executed by computer programming in video games. TTRPG players have agency over the rules, while video games only allow player agency within the rules and choices already programmed into the game's code.

The social nature of D&D also drives the narrative of the story and increases decision making affordances within a fantasy world. Fantasy represents a genre of games that involve imaginative creation of alternate realities and narratives with themes that often utilize science fiction or settings similar to the works of J.R.R. Tolkien to visualize content (Cover, 2010). D&D is considered a classic example of fantasy, sometimes called sword and sorcery, drawing heavily from Tolkien. The nature of the fantasy genre favors the use of imagination and human processes, such as small group communication, as the basis of the game experience. Tilton (2019) observed that small group processes including groupthink and nonverbal communication subsidized or even replaced decision-making logic in social deception games. Similarly, in D&D, players' social interactions and dynamics constitute the primary processes that mediate the creation and management of an imaginary game environment.

## Role-Playing

Role playing, or using imagination to shift roles, is a major component of social interaction and communication in role-playing games, including D&D (Bowman, 2010). When children play, they imitate actions that are beyond their own capabilities (Vygotsky, 1978). Adults are capable of more advanced forms of play (Winnicott, 1989). In playing, individuals can imagine themselves to embody a role both similar and different from roles they have in life and will obey the constructed rules of the imagined role (Vygotsky, 1978). The continuum from reality to fantasy is a powerfully salient aspect of games (Pavlas et al., 2009). The rules of imagined roles in TTRPGs are subject to the agency of the players and the facilitator, making them suitable for crafting therapeutic experiences by therapists and coinciding imagined roles with reality (Vygotsky, 1978; Winnicott, 1989). The use of imagination and role playing in TTRPGs is partly a deliberate act of creating role-play situations that could be crafted by a therapist but also involve discovering unforeseen aspects of the self through improvisation.

Improvisational play in the context of tabletop fantasy role-playing games is unique, as it is non-instrumental and can be fully immersive (Toles-Patkin, 1986). Experiences in role-playing games can allow players to experientially further their understanding of complex roles and relationships with overlapping boundaries on the continuum from fantasy to reality. While in a game experience, players develop shared, concrete narrative fantasies (Blinka & Smahel, 2007). These concrete narratives can be utilized as objects for reflection on gaming experiences that are real for players.

Role playing and creativity in TTRPG experiences can be linked to development. Development can be thought of as a creative act in which a new understanding of self and reality is formed through experimenting with relatedness to others in a state of play (Winnicott, 1989). In this view, adults engage in advanced forms of play in order to exercise creativity and develop. Winnicott's (1989) model situates the therapist as a guide in facilitating this process with an individual similar to Vygotsky's (1978) notion of a more experienced other that guides development through the zone of proximal development. This framework, when applied to TTRPGs, could be used to facilitate TTRPG interactions that are forms of role-play intersecting with an individual's zone of proximal development and can foster therapeutic learning, creative capacity, and development.

## Psychological Impact

There is a need to understand the concepts of rules, possibilities, narrative ideology, social impact, and psychological impact of fantasy role-play before deciding whether to use D&D for good or judge it as harmful. The origins of the concern about D&D provided some useful lessons underneath the overall damage to public opinion. One case report, which serves as a cautionary tale, detailed obsessive distraction as a result of a game of D&D among psychotherapy patients. This report shows what could happen if professionals who are not familiar with or trained in how to utilize the therapeutic modality of D&D encounter patients who relate strongly with D&D. In this case, problematic personality traits were amplified with clear connections to the game and subsequently relieved upon termination of the game (Ascherman, 1993). There was also a lack of leadership and a new director in the treatment center. The absence of effective leadership may have allowed problematic gameplay to exacerbate existing issues. The therapists also lacked an understanding of the game and may have been limited by their ambivalence toward the game.

To the contrary, therapeutic potential can be sought by relating to game experiences in a therapy session or by using direct in-game experiences conducted by a game facilitator also acting as a therapist who has experience with D&D. Blackmon (1994) reported a case of psychotherapy enabled by the patient's experience in an ongoing game of D&D. Role playing served as a safe displacement of emotions as the patient became comfortable working with and gaining mastery with those feelings (Blackmon, 1994). The game served as a waking fantasy that gave form to a person's internal fantasies and their life. The game experience was used as a therapeutic tool to help the individual work through psychological issues, build self-efficacy, become familiar with emotions and relate emotions to the therapist (Blackmon, 1994). Role-play seems to reveal actual characteristics of the players which means a troubling trait could be exacerbated just as positive work could be done. This emphasizes the importance of qualified facilitation and knowledgeable therapists.

Players identify with their characters as a part of their personality, sometimes partially driven by the unconscious (Blinka & Smahel, 2007). This complexity highlights the role of therapists as crucial to effectively navigating the psychological potential of some gaming experiences. Facilitators are needed to help with conflict resolution too. Social conflict in games has been reported when players experienced role confusion between relationships in and out of the game (Bowman, 2013). Gamers were reported to rely heavily on facilitators to navigate emotional experiences in role-playing games, even if the facilitators were not therapists and therapy was not an intentional part of the game (Bowman, 2013). This suggests that gamers may be eager to work with a therapist as a game facilitator to help guide therapeutic aspects of role-playing games.

The psychological safety and agency created in a tabletop role playing environment has potential for avoiding outside challenges, similar to work avoidance, and is also necessary for creating safe learning environments. This evidence suggests a need for qualified facilitation to ensure productive gameplay, or at least being able to recognize any significant problems and subsequently ending the game experience. Knowing the difference between necessary separation and avoidance depends on understanding how people play, learn, and develop.

## Authority and Facilitation

Critical theory is necessary in understanding and utilizing D&D as a system of social interaction for human development. Garcia (2017) found, in a critical analysis, that power structures in D&D rules were historically problematic in how they regarded marginalized identities (race and gender) and have improved in recent versions. Knowing the importance of the facilitator or DM role in facilitating these experiences carries a responsibility like that of a teacher or therapist (albeit less imperative) to understand the impact one can have on others. In fact, best practices of the DM role have been applied as advice for teaching in a traditional classroom (Garcia, 2016).

Formal authority in D&D is mainly manifest in the role of the Dungeon Master, who is given a great deal of power and control over the players, as the determiner of rules' application and outcomes. This role was initially an embodiment of patriarchy drawn from the male creator's original use of his children as players to test and create the game. While problematic authoritarian language describing the DM role has given way to more inclusive facilitation and advice, the systemic power of the DM role remains inherent in the rules and carries with it a responsibility to promote distributed leadership and healthy group dynamics. Advice for facilitating and debriefing group dynamics in game settings is helpful for creating a constructive learning environment (Hermann, 2015).

The authority of the Dungeon Master in D&D games cannot be denied, but it is also essential in creating a learning environment and successfully guiding collective creativity and growth. This makes the DM role suitable for integration with therapist and teaching roles. A competent facilitator will acknowledge the authority structure inherent in D&D and be able to manage how they embody such a role to be inclusive and empower the development of players. Likewise, a responsible clinician is specially trained, licensed, and knowledgeable about their methods, including knowledge of D&D's popular context and critical awareness of D&D as a social system.

# References

Abra, J. (1994). Collaboration in creative work: An initiative for investigation. *Creativity Research Journal, (7)*, 1–20.

Ascherman, L. I. (1993). The impact of unstructured games of fantasy and role-playing on an inpatient unit for adolescents. *International Journal of Group Psychotherapy, 43*(3), 335–344. https://doi.org/10.1080/00207284.1993.11732597

Banks, J., Bowman, N. D., & Wasserman, J. A. (2017). A Bard in the hand: The role of materiality in player–character elationships. *Imagination, Cognition and Personality*, https://doi.org/10.1177/0276236617748130

Blackmon, W. D. (1994). Dungeons & Dragons: The use of a fantasy game in the psychotherapeutic treatment of a young adult. *American Journal of Psychotherapy, 48*(4), 624–632.

Blinka, L., & Smahel, D. (2007). "Role-playing" games in the context of analytical psychology. *Ceskoslovenska Psychologie, 51*(2), 169–182.

Bowman, S. L. (2010). *The functions of role-playing games: how participants create community, solve problems and explore identity.* Retrieved from http://public.eblib.com/choice/publicfullrecord.aspx?p=517013

Bowman, S. L. (2013). Social conflict in role-playing communities: An exploratory qualitative study. *International Journal of Role-Playing, (4)*, 4–25.

Cover, J. G. (2010). *The Creation of Narrative in Tabletop Role-Playing Games.* Retrieved from http://public.eblib.com/choice/publicfullrecord.aspx?p=547921

D'Anastasio, C. (2017, May). Therapists are using dungeons & Dragons to get kids to open up. *Kotaku.* Retrieved from https://kotaku.com/therapists-are-using-dungeons-Dragons-to-get-kids-to-1794806159

Daniau, S. (2016). The transformative potential of role-playing games: From play skills to human skills. *Simulation & Gaming, 47*(4), 423–444. https://doi.org/10.1177/1046878116650765

Garcia, A. (2016). Teacher as dungeon master. In A. Byers & F. Crocco (Eds.), *The Role-Playing Society: Essays on the Cultural Influence of RPGs* (pp. 164–183). Jefferson, N.C.: McFarland & Company.

Garcia, A. (2017). Privilege, power, and dungeons & dragons: How systems shape racial and gender identities in tabletop role-playing games. *Mind, Culture & Activity, 24*(3), 232–246. https://doi.org/10.1080/10749039.2017.1293691

Granshaw, L. (2018, May). How Tabletop Games like Dungeons & Dragons can be Therapeutic for Players. *Syfy Wire*. Retrieved from https://www.syfy.com/syfywire/how-tabletop-games-like-dungeons-Dragons-can-be-therapeutic-for-players

Hermann, K. (2015). Field theory and working with group dynamics in debriefing. *Simulation & Gaming*. https://doi.org/10.1177/1046878115596100

Kasof, J. (1995). Explaining creativity: The attributional perspective. *Creativity Research Journal, 8*(4), 311.

Lasley, J. (2017) Fantasy in real life: Making meaning from vicarious experience with a tabletop role-playing game webcast (unpublished pilot study). University of San Diego, San Diego, CA.

Laycock, J. P. (2015). *Dangerous Games: What the Moral Panic over Role-Playing Games Says about Play, Religion, and Imagined Worlds* (1). Oakland, CA: University of California Press

Mearls, M., & Crawford, J. (2014). *Player's Handbook*. Renton, WA: Wizards of the Coast LLC.

Pavlas, D., Bedwell, W., Wooten, S. R., Heyne, K., & Salas, E. (2009). Investigating the attributes in serious games that contribute to learning. *Proceedings of the Human Factors and Ergonomics Society Annual Meeting, 53*(27), 1999–2003. https://doi.org/10.1177/154193120905302705

Tilton, S. (2019). Winning through deception: A pedagogical case study on using social deception games to teach small group communication theory. *SAGE Open, 9*(1), 2158244019834370. https://doi.org/10.1177/2158244019834370

Toles-Patkin, T. (1986). Rational coordination in the dungeon. *The Journal of Popular Culture, 20*(1), 1–14. https://doi.org/10.1111/j.0022-3840.1986.2001_1.x

Vygotsky, L. S. (1978). *Mind in society: the development of higher psychological processes* (M. Cole, ed.). Cambridge, Mass: Harvard Univ. Press.

Weiss, J. (2018, March). Dungeons & Dragons had its biggest sales year in 2017. Retrieved March 9, 2019, from SYFY WIRE website: https://www.syfy.com/syfywire/dungeons-Dragons-biggest-sales-year-2017

Williams, J. P., Hendricks, S. Q., & Winkler, W. K. (2006). *Gaming as Culture: Essays on Reality, Identity and Experience in Fantasy Games*. Jefferson, N.C: McFarland & Co.

Winnicott, D. W. (1989). *Playing and Reality*. London; New York: Routledge.

Zayas, L. H., & Lewis, B. H. (1986). Fantasy role-playing for mutual aid in children's groups. *Social Work with Groups*, *9*(1), 53–66. https://doi.org/10.1300/J009v09n01_05

# Tabletop Role Playing Games in Therapy

# 5

Megan Connell, PhD, Elizabeth D. Kilmer, PhD,
& Jared N. Kilmer, PhD[1]

Five kids sit in the waiting room. One draws their favorite characters from Steven Universe, another chats with friends on Discord, two more work on a house in Minecraft, and a final sits quietly with their mother. The challenges of the week weigh them down, as they try to navigate the stressors of high school, work through anxiety, and look for the place they fit in. All of that melts away as they enter into the group room and take their places around the table across from their therapist and Game Master. They temporarily transform as they don the mantle of heroes adopting a new perspective on themselves, other people, and the world. Through rolling dice and creating a story together, they learn to forge friendships and how to stand up for themselves.

30 years ago, at the height of the satanic panic, few would have believed that Dungeons & Dragons (D&D) would become a tool used in therapy. Yet therapeutic D&D groups are running weekly in offices from Washington to North Carolina. Participants in these groups include children, adolescents, and adults, dealing with concerns related to autism spectrum disorder, lagging or atrophied social skills, anxiety, depression, and posttraumatic stress disorder. The following is a brief discussion on

---

[1] All authors contributed evenly to this chapter and are considered to be first authors.

becoming a therapeutic Game Master (GM) and theories of change regarding applied tabletop role-playing games (TTRPG).

## On Becoming a Therapeutic Game Master

Running TTRPGs as a therapeutic intervention is more than simply calling your sessions "therapy" and/or hoping for growth in your players (Connell, 2017; Game to Grow, 2018, 2019). It is important to view TTRPGs as a therapeutic tool. The right tool in the right hands can act as an implement for growth and self-discovery. However, the same tool can harm a person if misused or misapplied, even when the GM is well-intentioned (American Psychological Association [APA], 2017; Boccamazzo, & Connell, 2019). A Therapeutic GM must have three distinct skill sets to be an effective TTRPG therapist: a clear understanding of the game system they use, formal training as a mental health practitioner, and a willingness to play (Boccamazzo & Connell 2019). As these groups can be seen as a system of play layered on top of a therapy group, Therapeutic GMs need to be able to synthesize skills across these domains in order to be successful.

## Game System

The most successful GMs embody their title; they have a mastery of the game, the mechanics, and the story. Therapeutic GMs need to be well versed in the mechanics of the game system, requiring minimal effort when employing the rules of said game (Boccamazzo, & Connell, 2019). A therapeutic GM is likely to miss important events occurring around the table if they are continually looking up or preoccupied with the rules. Knowing all the ins and outs of the gaming system might not be feasible, but having a basic mastery of the way you want to run your games is necessary. In TTRPGs, the rules are mostly seen as guidelines; at any time, the GM may change rules or alter them to fit the story they are telling (Crawford et al., 2014). As long as the therapeutic GM is comfortable making rulings as they go along, they do not need to have the rules memorized. As a generality, rules are best broken when done with intention and after mastery of the rule set (i.e., understanding both the rule and the rationale for the rule).

In many ways, being a therapeutic GM is comparable to being a jazz musician. Jazz is, in many ways, built around breaking the rules of music. An expert jazz musician will have a deep understanding of the rules of music and know when and how to break them to the best musical effect (Skoler, personal communication, 2001). Indeed, having rules that alter slightly from game to game offers therapeutic benefits for some treatment populations. For example, when working with clients with rigid thinking patterns, typically seen in those diagnosed with autism (American Psychiatric Association, 2013), one of their treatment goals may include increased flexibility in thought processes. When done with intention, having a rule set that changes can help such clients practice cognitive flexibility (Honomichl & Chen, 2010; Rubinstein et al., 2001; Towse et al., 2000; Qu & Zelazo, 2007).

Before becoming a Therapeutic GM, an individual should have experience with the game system in a non-therapeutic, social context. This can be especially helpful to practice the game system's mechanics and GM skills without the added complexity and responsibility of a client population. With the increasing popularity of TTRPGs, there are a multitude of in-person and online opportunities to gain exposure with the gaming system of choice. When first learning, it is wise to observe how a game is played and/or play the game for oneself (Boccamazzo & Connell, 2019). Once one gets an understanding for how the game is played, it is educationally important to try running games for friends before attempting to run therapeutic games. Having experience with the gaming system is paramount. One would not run a manualized therapy program without specialized training in the treatment area, understanding of the research, and training in the manualized program itself. Further, one would not use a psychological assessment measure without training in administration, scoring, and interpretation of the measure. When using a TTRPG therapeutically, one must treat the gaming system the same as other therapeutic tools and techniques.

## Formal Training

To be a successful a Therapeutic GM, one needs to be a trained clinician. It is the weaving together of therapeutic training and the gaming system that allows for the therapeutic benefits of role-playing games to become evident. One must be competent at running therapeutic groups, as well as successful at running games. The game experience must transcend the structure of the gaming system being used. The primary jobs of any therapist running a group are to maintain the safety of group members and to manage the therapeutic needs/goals of the group (Yalom & Leszcz, 2005). The medium used for the group, whether it is a game or a structured group protocol, needs to take as little of the therapist's focus and concentration as possible. To have the ability to do this, any therapeutic group facilitator needs to be familiar with group dynamics and have proper training in the facilitation of group therapy (APA, 2017; Yalom & Leszcz, 2005).

Those running games therapeutically will need to be aware of the theoretical concepts of change and how change occurs in TTRPGs. Therapeutic TTRPG groups most closely mirror process-type groups in that the therapeutic themes that arise might be unexpected, and while some can be planned, the facilitator/GM needs to be able to work with the emotions and themes that arise during play (Kilmer & Kilmer, 2019). Additionally, these groups utilize the players as a powerful source for change. Over time, the players become a team, and the group develops its own norms that can influence behavior change (Yalom & Leszcz, 2005). The players give and receive direct feedback regarding how actions of other players affect their characters. As such, training in psychoeducation or didactic style groups is less applicable to this intervention (Kilmer & Kilmer, 2019).

Group therapy can be a powerful vector for change through the utilization of group members' strengths and challenges, and a well-run therapeutic TTRPG group is no exception (Kilmer & Kilmer, 2019; Yalom & Leszcz, 2005). In addition to managing group dynamics, the Therapeutic GM will need to develop goals for the group on both the individual and group level. The GM needs to be able to identify target skills and processes (e.g., impulsivity, emotion regulation, conflict resolution) and design the group to address these goals. Additionally, a therapeutic GM works with the group to reflect and process therapeutic themes and personal reactions that arise during the session (Boccamazzo & Connell, 2019; Connell, 2018a; Game to Grow, 2018; Kilmer & Kilmer, 2019).

Just as it is helpful to have experience running games in a non-therapeutic context, it is valuable to have experience running non-TTRPG groups. As with any mental health treatment, supervision or consultation when beginning this work is an important part of best practice for treatment (APA, 2017). Further, once competency in this modality is firmly developed, ongoing consultation and continuing education are valuable resources and support for mental health professionals (Rousmaniere et al., 2017).

## Willingness to Play

We define play as an activity that is done for its own sake (Connell & Dunlap, 2020).

Play may feel particularly challenging as a mental health professional, as it may be seen as a threat to the 'expert' role (Bowman & Lieberoth, 2018). If a GM is able to conceptualize growth and recovery as a collaborative, client-centered process, this role may feel less threatening (Boccamazzo & Connell 2019). Additionally, the GM may find it helpful to consider the healthy functions of play and the benefits of an expert modeling such behavior.

Vygotsky believed that play is the most important activity in which children engage (Bodrova, & Leong, 2015). Play can be planned in advance or manifest spontaneously. Though play is often seen as fun it can be a socially complicated activity for adults (Bowman & Lieberoth, 2018) and children with social anxiety (Ginsburg et al., 1998; Hearn et al., 2017; Pickard et al., 2018). In western culture, it is often viewed as a transgression from the norm when adults engage in play (Bowman & Lieberoth, 2018). Thus, it is common for those engaging in play to experience self-critical or self-conscious thoughts about participating in the activity. These thoughts can be present whether one is playing a video game, trying a new activity (e.g., dancing), or role playing a character.

Role playing is a risk; it requires one to step out of their comfort zone and practice new perspectives and behaviors, often unfamiliar to the role player. Such behavior is unusual in our day-to-day interactions and carries with it the risk of judgment for acting outside social norms. This judgment may originate internally or externally, regardless of whether or not the perception of judgment is accurate. As the one running the game, the GM sets the stage for what behaviors are expected and acceptable around the table (Connell, 2018b). If the GM is not willing to model appropriate behavior, get into character, and be animated, excited, or invested in the story, the players will not either.

The GM is also responsible for modeling interpersonal boundaries and norms around the table. For example, should a player start making fun of the GM's acting, it is up to the GM to correct the player's behavior. If left unaddressed, the player's problematic behavior is likely to be directed towards the character acting of fellow players. As such, it is the responsibility of the GM to show what topics are acceptable and how to correct behaviors. How this is handled will vary depending upon the GM, the players, the agreed-upon group norms, the treatment goals of the group, and the specific grievance. For example, a player says, "Wow, you really suck at doing voices!" to a GM voicing a character. In a group focused on teaching social skills to children on the autism spectrum, this might offer a teachable moment about appropriate comments and differing perspectives. In contrast, modeling how to stand up for yourself might be the more appropriate reaction in a group focused on social anxiety and issues related to empowerment.

If one cannot engage in play, the effectiveness of running therapeutic TTRPGs is reduced. Thus, enjoying one's role of GM or clinician is vital for an effective therapeutic intervention. Much of being a GM is being an actor or performer (Boccamazzo & Connell, 2019). Many are not comfortable being the center of attention, and that is okay! Just as being a researcher or clinician is not a good fit for every psychologist, being a therapeutic GM is not right for everyone. Being a therapeutic GM involves weaving together one's theoretical orientation, the therapeutic needs of the group, game mechanics, and the goals/objectives of the group into a unified whole. At the end of the chapter, resources will be provided for building skills as a GM.

## Fine's Frame Theories of Change

The most in-depth study on TTRPGs to date is Gary Alan Fine's 1983 study of D&D players. Fine sought to understand what was occurring during games of D&D and if the players were in touch with reality or if, as many feared, the game produced identity confusion and psychosis (Fine, 1983). Fine found that those who played TTRPGs operated within three different perspectives, which he described as "frames," and later on became the basis for his Frame Theory.

The first frame is of the here and now, or **the player as a person**. To be successful in this frame, a player has to know who they are, where they are, what is occurring with the other players at the table, and what was going on in their physical environment (Fine, 1983).

Fine (1983) found that play became impossible if the players did not utilize a uniformly agreed-upon rule system leading to his second frame: **gaming mechanics**. The players need to be aware of the rules of the game they are playing. Without an agreed-upon set of rules, a game cannot be played. Any disagreement of the rules between users creates confusion and makes having a shared gaming experience difficult, if not impossible.

The third frame adopts the **perspective of the character**. The player has to keep in mind that their character has a different and unique frame of reference – because the character is playing in the imaginary world. Their character is not aware of the player controlling them nor the mechanics of the game being played.

In a typical TTRPG session, players will seamlessly switch between the three frames. Consider the following three statements:

1.  Bondro looks through the room trying to see if there are any traps.

2.  I rolled a 17.

3.  Nadia, can you pass the chips?

The first statement concerns character action and is an example of frame three. The second statement is in reference to game mechanics and relates to frame two. Finally, the third statement is a player's request for food and is a reflection of frame one.

Playing the game becomes difficult, if not impossible, when a player struggles to define and understand which frame they are working within. For example, a GM's response to a request for information about the game world would vary depending on the perceived frame of reference (i.e., the player or the character). Further, a player may exhibit a tendency to misinterpret actions taken against their character as actions taken against them personally. A character may be randomly targeted by the attack of a monster, but perceive the event as a personal attack. Groups quickly become disjointed when players exhibit confusion around frames of reference, resulting in diminished joy, engagement, and therapeutic potential. The ability to distinguish between different frames is a skill that can develop or atrophy depending on the frequency with which it is practiced.

## Frame Confusion and Bleed

On occasion, problems may originate when there is confusion between different frames of reference. A common type of frame confusion occurs when a player perceives events that are happening to their character as actually happening to them (confusion between frames one and three). Frame confusion is disrupting to the individual, the gaming table, and the flow of play overall. It can occur for a multitude of reasons, most readily when the motivation behind another character's action is unclear and a player becomes negatively impacted by their interpretation of that action. For example, Sally's character helped an NPC by donating part of her earnings from her last adventure. Meanwhile, Harry, another player at the table, had their character rob the same NPC. Sally became angry, feeling betrayed by Harry, who she had considered a close friend up until this point. Thus, frame confusion can transform tension between characters into tension between players.

Another example of frame confusion can occur when players misinterpret the motivations behind others' actions, such as when a player misattributes how another *character* feels about their character with how that character's *player* feels about them as a person. Such examples of frame confusion can influence and sometime lead to *Bleed*. While frame confusion refers to a blurring of boundaries between different frames of reference, Bleed refers to the emotional exchange between the player

and character, and vice versa (Bowman, 2013). Bleed occurs bi-direc-
tionally, resulting in players experiencing either bleed-in or bleed-out.
Bleed-in occurs when a player's emotions impact their character (Bowman
& Lieberoth, 2018), while bleed-out occurs when a character's actions
impact its player (Bowman & Lieberoth, 2018; Lankoski & Järvelä, 2012;
Leonard & Thurman, 2018).

To elaborate on the aforementioned example, the NPC becomes angry
with Harry's character for robbing him, and Harry now inaccurately perceives that the GM is angry with him. The players, Harry and Sally, are
now experiencing emotions that are congruent with their characters',
blurring the boundaries between frame one and frame three. This blend
of frame confusion and bleed-in offers a prime opportunity for process
and discussion in therapeutic games. The GM can pause the game to help
address frame confusion and work to help strengthen a concept known as
theory of mind, one's ability to understand that others have a unique and
different perspective from oneself.

While the disruptive nature of frame confusion is sometimes unde-
sired in a game, the emotional crossover of Bleed is not inherently unhelpful. Bleed can be leveraged as an opportunity for clients' learning and
growth by a competent therapist to adaptively shift individual and group
perspectives (Boccamazzo & Connell, 2019; Kilmer & Kilmer, 2019).
Indeed, having corrective emotional experiences through the character
is one of the most important tools for the therapeutic GM (Boccamazzo &
Connell, 2019; Kilmer & Kilmer, 2019).

Bleed is one of the greatest agents of change available to the therapeutic GM (Boccamazzo & Connell, 2019). Bleed-out allows a player to
have a corrective emotional experience through play. Individual players
may experience bleed-out when they feel the rush of emotion that can
accompany one's character defeating a difficult villain or solving a complex
puzzle (Bowman & Lieberoth, 2018; Lankoski & Järvelä, 2012; Leonard
& Thurman, 2018). Examples include when players: learn to speak up
for themselves, feel pride in the actions of their character, or have one's
character act in kindness and continue to provide support to their group,
despite being personally frustrated. Further, bleed-out can also entail
the communal experience of victory that can manifest around the table.

Frame confusion and Bleed elicit multiple perspectives from the player. Although this can result in a person experiencing unwanted emotions, such as anger or fear, the empathy engendered from alternative perspectives is generally considered an adaptive and pro-social trait. Learning how to make space for and work through such emotions is a common goal of TTPRG therapy. Further, allowing oneself to experience unwanted emotions in a safe and controlled environment can help foster growth and learning (Boccamazzo & Connell, 2019; Kilmer & Kilmer, 2019). Consider the following case example.

Mia had been verbally and emotionally bullied by someone she had considered a friend in school. One of her goals in her therapeutic D&D group was to learn what positive supportive friendships look like. Throughout the campaign, the group had been working to stop an evil god from being summoned to the world. They identified the green dragon responsible for this plot and were able to ambush it. The group's forethought, planning, and use of resources led them to victory. When the group was told of their victory, they burst into tears, and Mia was able to articulate why. She simply said, "Look what I can do when I'm with my friends." The experience of victory was shared between those who supported one another. The experience of heroic victory felt by Mia's character allowed for bleed-out to occur and for Mia to understand what friendship can feel like.

In the above example, Mia learned that the girls around the table were her friends and while in real life they did not fight Dragons, they were stronger and better together. It was through the emotional experience of her character that this lesson was driven home for her. Mia's growth and experience are understood from an applied TTRPG perspective through the fourth frame.

## The Fourth Frame

Fine's Frame Theory has been reiterated upon by Boccamazzo and Connell (2019), who posited the existence of a fourth frame - the therapeutic frame. This occurs when TTRPGs are used therapeutically. Traditionally, a therapist leverages their therapeutic orientation to understand the needs of their individual clients while collaborating to generate appropriate treatment goals. Once goals are established, the therapist monitors progress through measurement (e.g., self-report measures, verbal feedback, behavior change, etc.) and documentation. In doing so, they can design in-game interventions that allow clients to vicariously experience scenarios that move them towards their treatment goals and promote growth.

TTRPGs give the therapeutic GM powerful tools to combat societal and personal struggles when viewed through the fourth frame. Placing fictional avatars in a fantastical setting allows for the therapeutic GM and players to discuss important or difficult topics with emotional distance. For example, one or more group members may struggle with bullying and would benefit from focusing on that topic. Therapeutic GMs can provide player characters an opportunity to interact with NPCs experiencing similar issues, allowing for opportunities to address bullying in a covert and less threatening context. This allows the players to practice skills in a setting where the risk of failure is small. Further, when failure inevitably occurs, it is the character, not the player, who experiences the consequences. Within frame theory, this shifts the failure from occurring in frame one to frame three. Thus, players are provided increased opportunities to challenge maladaptive beliefs and practice new behaviors (i.e., social risks) within the context of the game, allowing for therapeutic growth not readily found without the aid of the game.

Consider the following example. Sydney has been diagnosed with social anxiety. One of their goals was to practice self-advocacy, as Sydney reported difficulty with confrontation and speaking up for themselves. The GM created opportunities in the narrative for Sydney's character to advocate for themselves and the group. Further, the GM took a direct approach by stating, "Your character's warnings are being ignored by this NPC," and asking Sydney, "How do you think [your character] would react to this?" In this example, the GM could then deliberately contrast their question with, "How would *you* react to this?" Thus, forcing a different frame upon the event.

Such language from the GM helped to moderate the distance between the thoughts and behaviors of Sydney and their character, providing a scaffold for Sydney to master the skill of flexibly differentiating between perspectives (frames) and associated behaviors. This facilitated Sydney's ability to engage in desired behavioral changes, initially through their character and ultimately in their everyday life. In this case, Sydney experienced less anxiety and self-doubt as they worked towards their treatment goals through their avatar.

## Therapeutic Orientations as Applied to TTRPG Therapy

*Acceptance and Commitment Therapy (ACT)*

A therapeutic GM operating from an Acceptance and Commitment Therapy (ACT) perspective will enact change by leveraging the six core processes of the hexaflex. In ACT, pathology is believed to be the result of being psychologically inflexible. Psychological flexibility is considered to be the result of the six core processes working in conjunction (Boccamazzo & Connell, 2019; see Figure 5.1).

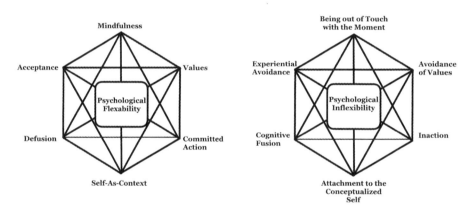

Figure 5.1 The Six Core Processes of Psychological Flexibility and Inflexibility.

From an ACT perspective, pathology has the potential to develop if rigidity is found in any one of the six core processes.

When playing a character, a player is able to examine the character's thoughts, feelings, and actions without being fused with the character. Group members are provided opportunities to develop skills analyzing their character's areas of flexibility and rigidity. Further, these analyses can occur at the group level, as the whole group works together to analyze individual and group behaviors. This process allows the player to make decisions about what the character should do next, based on the character's values or what is best suited to the situation, independent of the character's thoughts and feelings. Additionally, the GM can design the game environment to promote mindfulness and create opportunities for values consistent action. Through TTRPG therapy, the player can test and develop skills such as observing thoughts and feelings of their character without being rigidly tied to them, which can then be applied to their life outside the game. TTRPG therapy allows players to observe, understand, and develop challenging shifts in thought and behavior in a safe space where the natural consequences (and therefore motivations for change) are clearly apparent. A player can apply their own values to a character and act based on these, however this is not necessary. Simply practicing how one is able to act flexibly and consistently with any set of values is sufficient for increasing insight and developing these skills.

*Cognitive Behavioral Therapy (CBT)*

From a traditional Cognitive Behavioral Therapy (CBT) perspective, distress is often related to unrealistic and unhelpful automatic thoughts/ beliefs (Beck & Beck, 2011). These thoughts influence feelings and behavior, which can ultimately influence subsequent thoughts. This triad of thoughts, feelings, and behaviors is called the cognitive model and is a core concept in CBT. Shifts in thoughts and behaviors can lead to changes in feelings. Traditional CBT treatment involves identifying, evaluating, and challenging unrealistic and unhelpful beliefs, as well as developing new patterns of behavior in line with the client's goals.

In game sessions, the GM can introduce situations and provide space to identify and challenge unrealistic and unhelpful beliefs. For example, a player who has the belief, "I'm a bad person," could be exposed to a situation in which their character has the opportunity to save a child with no direct benefit (i.e. a monetary reward). If the player character saves the child, the GM can ask questions to further challenge this belief (e.g. "How does this action line up with your character's beliefs about themselves?"). TTRPGs also allow space for players to test out new patterns of behavior in a safe space. The reality-mirroring nature of the game allows players to practice behaviors in a space where they can observe the possible outcomes of the behavior, but are sheltered from consequences that might be experienced from trying out a behavior at work or school for the first time.

*Humanistic Therapy*

From a humanistic perspective, individual suffering stems from incongruence between one's ideal self and their actual self (Maslow, 1973; Rogers, 1951). Several basic assumptions pervade humanistic therapy. First, individuals have free will (personal agency) and must take personal responsibility for their choices and the associated consequences (e.g., self-growth and fulfillment versus stagnation). Second, people are inherently good and possess an innate drive to overcome hardship, reach their maximum potential (self-actualization), create, and improve the world around them. Third, all individuals are assumed to view the world from unique, yet equally valid, perspectives. Furthermore, an individual's subjective, conscious experience (i.e., perception and interpretation) is more important than objective reality. To create change in humanistic therapy, the client works toward increased understanding of their own worldview while developing self-acceptance. Consistent with humanistic therapy's basic assumptions, the therapist promotes change through unconditional positive regard for the client, empathy, and genuineness, while treating the client as the expert of their experience.

When utilizing this orientation in TTRPG therapy, a GM takes a less directive role, allowing players to fill a greater role in world building and story direction. Furthermore, the narrative of the game creates a controlled space that provides opportunities for players to move towards self-actualization. During game play, the GM would expect and encourage players to make the best decisions for themselves, with an emphasis on understanding their characters' and their own viewpoints, while developing a positive and consistent sense of self. Finally, in accordance with the assumption that subjective experience is more valuable for personal growth than objective reality, a humanistic GM perceives lessons learned vicariously through simulated experience (play) as equally valuable to lessons learned outside of the game.

*Group Therapy*

According to Yalom (2005), change in group therapy occurs through multiple mechanisms, primarily dependent on the group itself. Yalom identifies eleven factors that promote healing and change in psychotherapy: instillation of hope, universality, imparting information, altruism, corrective recapitulation, socializing techniques, imitative behavior, interpersonal learning, group cohesiveness, catharsis, and existential factors. Instillation of hope and universality occur early on in a group therapy - clients start to understand that they are not alone in their struggles and begin to gain hope for change. For these factors to work, clients need not all have the same diagnoses, nor do diagnoses and problems need to be explicitly discussed in group. Imparting information occurs in multiple ways in TTRPG groups. For example, players may offer advice about game mechanics (such as which die to use or how a spell works) or about how to handle a particular situation in-game (e.g., recommending a conflict-resolution strategy), with the latter advice translating to out-of-game skills. Similarly, TTRPG therapy groups offer an ideal setting for the modelling and imitation of adaptive behavior changes. Altruism occurs when group members have opportunities to help each other, as well as NPCs in the game. Through these experiences, players can build confidence and cohesion, as well as challenge negative self-image.

Throughout the game, the players will set norms for the group, which may or may not be explicit (i.e. party rules), and begin to act more cohesively. This becomes apparent through game play, as players transition from relying on the GM as a guide and authority, to using each other as game and social references. Socializing techniques and interpersonal learning happens throughout the group on both a conscious and unconscious level. Much of this is set through group norms and can be driven through the facilitation of giving and receiving direct feedback from group members. Group cohesion and interpersonal learning supports the ability of the group to provide corrective recapitulation experiences.

Corrective recapitulation leverages current group relationships to challenge maladaptive lessons learned in previous important relationships. Many players may have negative, self-directed thoughts that stem from unfulfilling or hurtful prior experiences with important individuals in their lives. Having new experiences and hearing different feedback from group members can help to challenge and correct these prior experiences. Similarly, catharsis allows group members to express and work through previously suppressed emotions. The fantasy setting and variable psychological space between player and character can promote the expression and resolution of previously repressed emotions. Finally, existential factors speak to the concept of understanding that one exists as a small part of a larger system, a system that will continue to move and change regardless of the player's wishes. Players learn to experience emotions and the changes of life without becoming tied to or stuck in a particular moment or emotion. Though some of Yalom's 11 therapeutic factors are differentially present at the beginning, middle, or end of a group, they can be leveraged by the GM to meet the needs and goals of the group as a whole.

## Conclusions

TTRPGs are powerful therapeutic tools when used by a trained professional. Regardless of therapeutic orientation, TTRPG therapy allows for direct observation of the player's response to social interactions around the table, as well as to "real-world" problems encountered in the game. Traditionally, therapists are limited by a client's insight and the behavior exhibited in the therapy room when working with an individual. The addition of a TTRPG in a group setting allows for more direct observation of experiences that can mimic real world problems. This can be particularly useful when working with a client to better understand and intervene in the moment with behavior that may be harder to directly observe in a traditional therapy room such as impulsiveness, conflict resolution, avoidance, and creative problem solving. Although research into the therapeutic application of TTRPGs is ongoing within multiple disciplines, the field is still in its infancy. The theories and practices of mental health professionals will continue to evolve as this area of research develops.

# References

American Psychiatric Association. (2013). *Diagnostic and Statistical Manual of Mental Disorders (DSM-5®).* American Psychiatric Pub.

American Psychological Association. (2017). *Ethical Principles of Psychologists and Code of Conduct.* Washington, DC: American Psychological Association, https://www.apa.org/ethics/code/.

Beck, J. S., & Beck, A. T. (2011). *Cognitive therapy: Basics and Beyond* (2nd ed.). New York: Guilford press.

Boccamazzo, R., & Connell, M. (2019, November). The Applied Use of TTRPGs. *Gamehole Con.* Seminar conduced from the Aliant Energy Center Exhibition Hall, Madison, WI.

Bodrova, E., & Leong, D. J. (2015). Vygotskian and post-Vygotskian views of children's play. *American Journal of Play, 7,* 371-388.

Bowman, S. L. (2013). Social conflict in role-playing communities: An exploratory qualitative study. *International Journal of Role-Playing, 4*(4), 4-25.

Bowman, S. L., & Lieberoth, A. (2018). Psychology and role-playing games. In J. P. Zagal & S. Deterding (Eds.), *Role-Playing Game Studies* (pp. 245-264). New York: Routledge.

Connell, M. [G33kslikeus]. (2017, October 17). Tips for DM's/GM's Psychology at the Table Introduction. Retrieved from https://www.youtube.com/watch?v=eKZ5Ymwa8Wg&list=PL2IRUzcSUyX0y-CWc4P2nyOvgvdwFPl8HM&index=2&t=1s

Connell, M. (2018a, April 16). Dragon Talk: Dr. Megan Connell. Retrieved from https://www.youtube.com/watch?v=aipShIh_UvU

Connell, M. [G33kslikeus]. (2018b, July 31). Tips for GMs/DMs Psychology at the Table; Leadership. Retrieved from https://www.youtube.com/watch?v=lIPmGVZtYZs

Connell, M., & Dunlap, K. (2020). You are the one foretold: The hero's journey. In R. Kowert (Ed.) *Video Games and Well-Being: Press Start* (pp. 125-140). New York: Palgrave.

Crawford, J., Wyatt, J., Schwalb, R. J., & Cordell, B. R. (2014). *Player's Handbook.* Wizards of the Coast. Renton, Washington.

Fine, G. A. (1983). *Shared Fantasy: Role-Playing Games as Social Worlds*. Chicago, IL: University of Chicago Press.

Game to Grow. (2018, December). PAX Unplugged Panel | Roll for Healing: Therapeutic Game Master Round Table. Retrieved from https://www.youtube.com/watch?v=iT__GioqnGA

Game to Grow. (2019, February). Therapeutic game master round table | PAX South Panel 2019. Retrieved from https://www.youtube.com/watch?v=uIUx7W7DbUw&t=15s

Honomichl, R. D., & Chen, Z. (2010). Relations as rules: The role of attention in the dimensional change card sort task. *Developmental Psychology, 47*, 50-60.

Kilmer, J. N., & Kilmer, E. D. (2019, June). Utilizing role-playing games as treatment: Basics for clinicians. Training presented at Dallas VA Medical Center, Dallas, Texas.

Lankoski, P., & Järvelä, S. (2012). An embodied cognition approach for understanding role-playing. *International Journal of Role-Playing, 6*, 18-32.

Leonard, D. & Thurman, T. (2018). Bleed-out on the brain: The neuroscience of character-to-player spillover in LARP. *International Journal of Role-Playing, 9*, 9-15.

Maslow, A. H. (1973). Self-actualizing people: A study of psychological health. In R. J. Lowry (Ed.), *Dominance, Self-Esteem, Self-Actualization: Germinal papers of A. H. Maslow* (pp. 177-201). Monterey, CA: Brookes/Cole Publishing Company. (Original work published in 1950).

Qu, L., & Zelazo, P. D. (2007). The facilitative effect of positive stimuli on 3-year-olds' flexible rule use. *Cognitive Development, 22*, 456-473. doi: 10.1016/j.cogdev.2007.08.010

Rogers, C. (1951). *Client-Centered Therapy*. Cambridge Massachusetts: The Riverside Press.

Rubinstein, J. S., Meyer, D. E., & Evans, E. (2001). Executive control of cognitive processes in task switching. *Journal of Experimental Psychology, 27*, 763-797. doi: 10.1037//0096-1523.27.4.763

Towse, J. N., Redbond, J., Houston-Price, C. M. T., & Cook, S. (2000). Understanding the dimensional change card sort: Perspectives from task success and failure. *Cognitive Development, 15*, 347-365. doi: 10.1016/S0885-2014(00)00021-6

Yalom, I. D., & Leszcz, M. (2005). *The theory and practice of group psychotherapy* (5th ed). New York: Basic Books.

# Dungeons, Dragons, and Social Development    **6**

Adam Davis, MA Ed. & Adam Johns, MA

Dungeons & Dragons has shown to be a fantastic tool for helping youth develop in numerous ways. In fact, playing Dungeons & Dragons in childhood and adolescence aligns with and may help overcome the struggles within Eriksonian stages of psychosocial development. Many of the benefits of Dungeons & Dragons are incidental, and simply playing the game with a guiding and therapeutic hand may contribute to positive outcomes. Youth may experience benefits in academic outcomes related to literacy and mathematics simply from playing and engaging within the fantasy world. Additionally, the interactional nature of the game provides an environment to enrich social skills and connectedness. While these benefits are accessible to any child, game masters have the opportunity to use Dungeons & Dragons intentionally to harness the game's potential to maximum benefit, especially for populations that are in need of additional support, such as those on the autism spectrum.

## Staging Developments

Erik Erikson was an important and influential psychotherapist throughout the 1900s, and one of his many important contributions to the field of psychology was his psychosocial stages of development. Erikson posited that development was based in unconscious challenges that occur at various stages of life. The challenges at each stage is a conflict between two important concepts that require the individual to navigate their understanding of the world.

For example, Erikson's first stage of development, from birth to around 1-year-old, states that the child is struggling with trust and mistrust (Erikson, 1982). During this period of time the child must learn to navigate what and who they can trust in order to shape their concepts of those two ideas. A child that learns trust learns that the world is generally good and trustworthy, whereas a child that learns mistrust takes away the opposite. In either case, the child decides their belief about the world and their loved ones, and then uses that as a building block in their next areas of development. However, the two stages centered on pre-teen and adolescent development are most applicable to exploration in Dungeons & Dragons: Industry versus Inferiority (ages 6-11), and Identity versus Role Confusion (ages 10-20).

In the Industry versus Inferiority fourth stage of development, children direct their energy and focus into mastering skills and a wealth of new experiences. In this way they are often enthusiastic about learning, questioning the world, and understanding that it is possible to be good and bad at different tasks. This stage of development is a struggle between feeling rewarded for one's efforts, seeing oneself as skilled, capable and industrious, or feeling arrested by one's failures and internalizing a sense of inferiority.

Dungeons & Dragons and other role-playing games are relevant to this fourth stage of Eriksonian development because they contain the aspect of role playing as a hero and not just being skilled as an individual, but being an important part of a heroic team. In Dungeons & Dragons, players play characters that are usually very capable and able to fight monsters and save the day from ultimate disasters. Few players seek to play characters as bumbling shopkeepers or as incompetent farmers! In Dungeons & Dragons, individuals must use various sources of feedback in order to see oneself as successful and capable. Such feedback can come from one's own appreciation of a job well done, the praises of a teacher or parent, or through a clear measure that one's skills allowed for the success of a task. Dungeons & Dragons provides many opportunities to see oneself as successful and capable through the successes of their character. As the player's character is successful in the game, the player can reinforce the view that they have of themselves as industrious rather than inferior, supporting them to continue to take risks and attempt new skills in the future.

In Erikson's fifth stage of development, Identity vs Role Confusion, adolescents aged 10-20 are tasked with discovering and understanding their role within the world around them. This stage is a crucial period for adolescents to learn what their job and career paths could be, but in many ways the stage is much more than that. It is a stage of development where individuals figure out who they are and the roles that they want to play within the society around them. Individuals who receive the proper opportunity, feedback, and support, are able to successfully discover career paths, personal identity, sexual identity, and even a sense of personal morality throughout this stage.

There are clear parallels to these important developing skills in any role-playing game. The nature of role-playing games is that the character's roles are asymmetric, where each character is good at and bad at different things. The rogue may be quick and dexterous but is rarely strong, the barbarian might be strong but not intelligent, and the wizard may be intelligent but socially inept. Each player selects a combination of class, fantasy race, equipment, attributes, and even personality that help sort their characters into skilled and unskilled areas. As choices are made, the player creates, and often explores, a role for their character in the group dynamics at the table. There are many ways to observe, view identity exploration, and role discovery at a Dungeons & Dragons table. There is a dynamic of the player's discovery of interacting with new peers at a table, of experience and knowledge of the game itself, and of character roles within the game. All of these give opportunity for Dungeons & Dragons to help foster a player through their livable period of personal identity exploration. When well-fostered by a group of supportive peers and game master, this gives many opportunities to explore the kind of role that an adolescent might look for or enjoy in their own life.

## Rolling for Mathematica and Literacia

Like many games, role playing games offer an opportunity for building academic skills that is enhanced by the fun and engaging experience of the game itself. With regard to academics, there are obvious opportunities that games like Dungeons & Dragons present for building skills. Whenever a player rolls dice for a check or an attack roll, they are building an understanding of statistics, basic math, and numeracy skills. While when a child has to look up rules or monster statistics they're building literacy skills as they learn how to quickly and effectively navigate the rulebooks. A player is much more likely to double check the math on an attack roll when they know that it may mean the difference between missing their target and dealing the final blow against the rampaging skeleton or fiend.

For many students in the US, math classes are the bane of their early education experience, and for many teachers, creating engagement in math concepts is a difficult task. Studies have shown that, in the US, many students' enjoyment with math classes decreases as they progress through education (Dossey et al., 1988). A possible reason for the challenge in mathematic engagement is the lack of clear correlation to real-world application. However, once the correlation is made more apparent learning is facilitated easily. For example, one study done with a group of third graders gave them the option to decide how they wanted to learn, and they picked Dungeons & Dragons, bringing in much better engagement in the elementary classroom and applied mathematics skills (Carter, 2011).

Of course, in many ways it makes sense to apply such an engaging and rich hobby for teaching math and numeracy skills. The utilization of Dungeons & Dragons to add to those skills and create a curriculum for deeper and more integrated mathematics understanding is simply a matter of modifying the game to purposefully foster, teach, and encourage the specific skills or knowledge that a teacher is highlighting. For instance, shooting a bow in an arc could be a simple dice roll with a bonus, or could require a greater level of specific parabolic arc calculation in order to be a successful attack.

As in mathematics, Dungeons & Dragons' opportunity for improving literacy is rooted in the fun and engagement of the game. Learning reading comprehension skills is difficult when a student does not care or connect with the material itself. In a role-playing game like Dungeons & Dragons, the players' understanding of the rules has a direct correlation to their success in understanding the game. Further, it gives an opportunity for the player to connect to their experiences through a story that they are helping to define. A study by Stephanie Kaylor (2017) found that

> "[P]articipants felt that playing TTRPGs improved at least one literacy skill and that greater depth and breadth of TTRPG experience helped some participants to surmount real or perceived difficulties with reading or speaking" (p. 5).

One participant of the study reported that the fun and engagement of role-playing games helped them to overcome challenges related to dyslexia:

> "His love of the game motivated him to read the rulebooks, which in turn improved his ability to read." As he said, "That's what D&D did for me. I was invested. I needed to learn these rules in order to play the game, so I had to sit there with a 60-page book and read it" (Kaylor, 2017, p. 22).

Utilizing Dungeons & Dragons for academic improvement certainly requires a shift in teacher mindset and a creative examination of the way in which academic goals are presented to students, but it also provides a great opportunity for students to find a new form of engagement with material that they may have found difficult to approach in the past. Students who might not be as interested in reading through great works of history or important works of fiction, may find that their motivation is improved when they are acting out their interaction with Marie Antoinette to convince her to change her stance on the ongoing revolt of the people of 18th-century France.

## Social and Group Bonding

The development of social skills correlates with many clinical positive outcomes later in life, and measurements of social connectedness show significant reductions in many adverse outcomes including depression, substance abuse, and other clinical concerns (Steiner et al., 2019). Many young children identified as needing services to support the building of social skills receive skills in the form of play-based groups, though when they reach adolescence, they have less access to play-based interventions. Additionally, many youths are not identified as needing social support until they reach late adolescence, which can hamper their own interpersonal and social development. Because teachers, parents, and therapists acknowledge this truth and seek to support the social outcomes in childhood and adolescence, many youths are enrolled in social skills groups or social skills instruction programs. These groups have shown to improve overall social competence and friendship quality in research studies (Reichow et al., 2013).

Children with autism are often the clients identified as needing supplemental services to assist with socialization (Rose & Anketell, 2009). Dungeons & Dragons and similar games provide a framework for a fun, play-based social skill intervention strategy that empowers youth to build social skills and social connectedness in a semi-natural setting that can be easily generalized into other environmental settings.

## Vignette: Kit'zar's Speech

*Shannon is enthusiastic but extremely under-socialized. Pervasive medical conditions result in frequently lengthy hospital visits, and have prevented her from attending a regular school setting. She is excited to have a social group, but extremely hesitant to speak up. As her performance deficit is based on anxiety, she often freezes up when she is put "on the spot." Her quiet nature and hesitancy has made it difficult for her to build positive relationships with the other members of the group. Shannon is playing a noble dragonborn fighter named Kit'zar, a descendant from a royal bloodline. The adventuring party has discovered that a horde of undead monsters is marching toward a nearby town, searching for a powerful magic artifact that will make their evil army unstoppable. The party knows that they cannot defeat the horde without aid and travel to neighboring kingdom to ask the king to rally his armies against the undead invasion.*

*Knowing that Shannon struggles with conversational exchange and self-advocacy, the game master encourages her practice of skills by establishing that the king is a haughty dragonborn who refuses to converse with anyone who is not of royal blood, which means that Kit'zar is the only character who can address the king directly. When the characters are in the king's chamber, the game master makes sure that the King only responds to Shannon's in-character statements, but lets the other players offer her suggestions or help so long as those suggestions are not overwhelming or unwelcome. Shannon's nervousness and anxiety makes speaking as her character challenging, but the game master gives Shannon the option to describe Kit'zar's voice and stance as confident and noble even when she is not able to present herself this way in real life. At the end of the encounter the king agrees to share a battalion of troops—under Kit'zar's command—due to the nobility and confidence shown by Kit'zar in the request.*

In this example, Shannon was struggling to compose herself with a calm and confident demeanor. She did not need to be *taught* how to conduct herself, but needed an opportunity to practice and receive feedback on her presentation and affect in order to build skills. In Shannon's case, her struggle was not in learning appropriate pro-social behaviors, but in utilizing them effectively. Most of the social learning in this case occurred through the prompting and shaping of behaviors. She had been taught, in other social groups and from parents, what a confident and calm disposition looked like. However, she lacked the opportunity to practice social interaction in an environment in which it was safe to practice and generalize skills.

Because Shannon's social struggles were based on her anxiety and low self-efficacy, the challenge was adjusted to Shannon's individual needs as a player. The game master made sure to provide a role-play challenge, but not one that would be an impossible task for Shannon. Shannon experienced the reciprocal success of her character and the resultant rewards of practicing her skills, all while receiving guidance from her peers and the game master on the best way to demonstrate confidence through body and voice.

## Vignette – Zombardo's Fireball

*Tim is playing as a wizard named Zombardo. Tim has been very focused on personal success and often struggles to allow his team- mates to be a resource or help for him. He frequently fails to include teammates in his planning. The game master designs an encounter where Zombardo's party must surprise and ambush a group of bandits robbing a bank vault. Zombardo, without consulting the rest of the group, decides that he will step into the open and use the powerful fireball spell to incinerate the bandits single-handedly.*

*Since the game master understands Tim's performance deficit around effective communication and because Tim has used this strategy in the past, the GM has planned ahead and equipped the bandits with necklaces that make them immune to the damage of the fireball spell. The bandits are unaffected by the spell and quickly overwhelm Zombardo. The characters played by Tim's fellow play- ers come to Zombardo's aid and are faced with a challenging fight because their teammate Zombardo is badly injured.*

*In the midst of the battle, Tim finally role-plays as Zombardo, telling the rest of the team about the protective necklaces and sug- gesting that stealing the necklaces might help him be more effec- tive. Listening to Zombardo's (and by proxy Tim's) suggestion, the rest of the team focuses on taking the necklaces from the bandits instead of trying to defeat them directly. Once they do so, Tim joy- ously announces that Zombardo will launch another fireball for maximum impact, ultimately defeating the bandits.*

*At the end of the session the players gave compliments to each other. Tim stated that he appreciated how the team helped him out, and the other players stated that they appreciated how Zombardo (and by proxy Tim) shared the information with them and asked for their help.*

In the above example, much like the vignette above featuring Shannon/Kit'zar, the game master enabled skill practice both at the table and through *in-character* interactions. The game master designed the in-game scenario to target Tim's real-world areas of social growth such that he would practice the desired skill while role playing his character. Because Zombardo's use of the skill was instrumental in achieving a desired game outcome, the encouragement and reward for skill practice were built into the game and required minimal additional prompting and reward by the group facilitator. What made this scenario especially effective for the group was the opportunity for the players to reflect on and appreciate each other for the specific ways in which they worked collaboratively to find success. Tim's use of the pro-social behavior was heavily reinforced both through the in-game outcome and the social encouragement from his peers.

When designing in-game scenarios to prompt and shape social behaviors and build social capacity, the game master needs to ensure the story of the game is compelling to the player so that the players will be motivated to use the skills as their characters. The game master's responsibility is then to support the acquisition of the skill by rewarding its use and providing feedback as necessary, and by facilitating an environment where the pro-social behaviors are safe to practice and supported by peers.

## The Roles We Play

Shannon and Tim had learned many of their skills for social interaction through direct instruction, though of course not all behaviors learned by children are taught to them directly. According to Bandura's (1977, 1986) social learning theory, behaviors are naturally learned by observing others in a relational context. When indirectly learning a behavior from another, an individual notices the other using the behavior and observes the outcome. The individual then, on their own, uses the modeled behavior and experiences their own degree of success in achieving the outcome. Over time, an individual will have enough practice and feedback to improve the skillfulness with which they can use the behavior. In an ideal natural context, desirable prosocial behaviors are modeled, observed, and imitated by children. In an ideal environment, children have the opportunity to both learn appropriate behaviors and, through a process known as vicarious punishment, learn how *not* to behave. If they see a peer use a behavior and receive a punishment, they will ideally learn not to use the same behavior.

There are many reasons why children do not learn and use positive prosocial behaviors. Children may not have access to an environment that provides appropriate modeling and feedback, if at all, and thus do not have the opportunity to learn from peer modeling. Some children (because of complexities related to autism, sensory processing challenges, etc.), are not able to sufficiently translate observed behaviors into effective social skill practice. A child with challenges integrating observed behaviors and who lives in an environment with insufficient modeling will be especially susceptible to challenges in building a repertoire of effective social skills. Regardless, understanding the natural context in which children integrate behaviors provides game masters who are using role-playing games to support youth the framework for how to structure the environment and game sessions to maximize social outcomes.

It is important to remember when working with individuals to help them flourish socially that discrete observable behaviors are only one small piece of the puzzle. The discrete behaviors in one's toolbox are an individual's social *skills*. Once social *capability* refers not only to one's learned skills but also to the individual's desire and capacity to use them effectively in the appropriate context. It is a mistake to assume that a youth struggling to build social connections need be explicitly taught appropriate social skills, as there are many reasons why a youth may not use positive prosocial behaviors.

The two cases above are a clear example of this. In DeMatteo et al.'s (2012) analysis, three types of deficits emerged: knowledge deficits, performance deficits, and fluency deficits. While the types of deficits are not entirely discrete, specific intervention strategies should be used to address the different types of deficits, and games like Dungeons & Dragons provide a powerful tool to assess and address the different types of deficits. Because each type of social deficit compels a different type of intervention, it will be important for game masters using Dungeons & Dragons or other role-playing games to understand what type of deficits a child has in order to best support their development of a social skill repertoire and thus build their social capability. The game master has the opportunity in the context of a role-playing game to subtly prompt the use of a behavior in a natural context either at the table with peers or through character interactions within the narrative context of the game. Observing whether or not a skill is utilized provides the game master the opportunity to assess for deficits and thus strategize an appropriate intervention (see Table 6.1).

| Deficit | What it Means | How to Respond |
| --- | --- | --- |
| Knowledge Deficit | They don't know the skill. | Teach the skill. |
| Performance Deficit | They choose not to use the skill. | Incentivize the use of the skill and reward the use, no matter how well it's used. |
| Fluency Deficit | They use the skill, but ineffectively. | Provide opportunities for practice, constructive feedback, and repetition. |

Table 6.1 Skill Deficits.

When a youth does not utilize a social skill because they never learned it, the resulting knowledge deficit requires that they are taught the skill directly or provided the clear opportunity to observe and reflect on the skill's use by a peer or model. The child must learn not only the specific skill, but also the context in which to use it. A child who has just learned a brand new behavior will still most likely have a performance or fluency deficit.

Performance deficits arise for many different reasons, such as an individual's belief that a skill is ineffective or a lack faith in their own capacity to use it effectively. Individuals may also have a lack of desire to achieve the outcome of a skill or have a strong avoidant fear of the outcome of using a skill ineffectively. It is possible that a child previously attempted to use a skill but was not successful, such that they were punished by the environment and learned to avoid using the skill in the future for fear of a similar outcome. Shannon from the above vignette struggled with confidence and as a result rarely performed the skill without strong encouragement while Tim had used the same tactic repeatedly and required divertive help. Many children with performance deficits will need initial encouragement to perform the skill and then be provided rewarding reinforcement to continue to practice it, regardless of their initial skillfulness.

A child with a fluency deficit "knows" social skills and attempts to use them, though lacks the capacity to use them to successfully achieve a desired outcome. In this case, the child does not need encouragement to use a skill or direct instruction on the performance and context for a skill, but needs constructive feedback and coaching on how they use the skill. The child will the opportunity for repeated practice in order to integrate the skill and feedback on how to improve as they practice.

As mentioned above, the types of skill deficits are not wholly discrete, i.e., an individual may have more than one deficit and may require interventions to address multiple deficits simultaneously. Additionally, deficits in one area of social skill may be wholly unrelated to capacity in another area of social interaction, e.g., a child may be knowledgeable and skilled at the ability to start and maintain a conversation, but may struggle giving and receiving compliments, making clear requests to others, following instructions etc.

A game master attuned to the social experiences of the players will be able to identify lagging social skills and harness the inherent potential of the game to intentionally encourage prosocial behavior development. The process for naturally reinforcing social skills using a role-playing game is to observe when a skill should ideally be prompted and assess for the type of deficit when a skill is or is not utilized. If a skill is not used in a social setting, the game master should keep track in order to provide modeling, instruction, and reinforcement.

# References

Bandura, A. (1977). *Social Learning Theory*. New York: General Learning Press.

Bandura, A. (1986). *Social Foundations of Thought and Action*. Englewood Cliffs, NJ: Prentice-Hall.

Carter A. (2011) Using Dungeons & Dragons to integrate curricula in an elementary classroom. In: Ma M., Oikonomou A., Jain L. (eds) *Serious Games and Edutainment Applications*. Springer, London

DeMatteo, F. J., Arter, P. S., Sworen-Parise, C., Fasciana, M., & Paulhamus, M. A. (2012). Social skills training for young adults with autism spectrum disorder: overview and implications for practice, *National Teacher Education Journal, 5(4)*, 57-65.

Dossey, J. A., Mullis, I. V. S., Lindquist, M. M., & Chambers, D. L (1988) *The Mathematics Report Card: Trends and achievement based on the 1986 National Assessment*. Princeton: Educational Testing Service.

Erikson, E. (1982). The life Cycle Completed. New York: W. W. Norton.

Kaylor, S, L. (2017). Dungeons & Dragons and literacy: The role tabletop role-playing games can play in developing teenagers' literacy skills and reading interests. *Graduate Research Papers*. 215. https://scholarworks.uni.edu/grp/215

Reichow, B., Steiner, A.M. & Volkmar, F.R. (2013) Cochrane review: Social skills groups for people aged six to twenty-one with Autism Spectrum Disorders (ASD). *Evidence-Based Child Health, 8*(2), 266-315. doi: 10.1002/ebch.1903.

Rose, R. & Anketell, C. (2009). The benefits of social skills groups for young people with Autism Spectrum Disorder: A pilot study. *Child Care in Practice, 15*(2), 127-144. doi:10.1080/13575270802685377

Steiner, R. J., Sheremenko, G., Lesesne, C., Dittus, P. J., Sieving, R. E., & Ethier, K. A. (2019). Adolescent Connectedness and Adult Health Outcomes. Pediatrics, 144(1), e20183766. doi:10.1542/peds.2018-3766

# Why Older Adventurers Can Beat a Lich: How Dungeons & Dragons Empowers Older Adults

# 7

Joseph F. Atanasio, PsyD

Dungeons & Dragons uses a combination of shared storytelling, dice rolls, puzzle-solving, and strategical game play to facilitate a unique experience, usually for a group of anywhere between two and six players. While it has recently grown in popularity with younger Millennial and Gen-Z audiences due to its use in popular culture, Hollywood productions, and video-game media, it has a surprisingly much older history. Its original baby-boomer and Gen-X players, who once played in their teens and 20s, are entering into their older adult years. It might seem a bit off or eccentric to see a group of geriatric residents and patients playing a game based heavily on imagination, pretending to be heroes and magic wielders. But this generation is the original adventuring party that grew up reading the wildly fantastical pages of Tolkien's *Lord of the Rings or Jules Verne's Journey to the Center of the Earth*. Accessing these types of fantasy adventures through the new 5th Edition of Dungeons & Dragons can have a powerful nostalgic effect for many.

One may initially believe that Dungeons & Dragons only caters to the child inside of us. So much of the game is spent in the imagination, utilizing childhood tropes such as searching for long lost treasure or having underdog heroes fight an uphill battle against powerful magical villains. The exploratory and adventurous themes of tabletop games such as Dungeons & Dragons may even seem destined, at times, to be utilized therapeutically with children and adolescents. These games tend to promote all of the necessary skills that help adolescents navigate through the socially demanding and stressful learning environments of home and school. Teamwork, verbal communication skills, conflict management, boundary setting, empathy, problem solving, and other solution-focused behaviors are integral to a healthy growth pattern of social development in children and adolescents (Beauchamp & Anderson, 2010). Tabletop games such as Dungeons & Dragons engage the imagination and growing minds of youth, challenging them in cognitive and social skills that will be necessary for healthy functioning as adults (Carter, 2011).

How then does a clinician integrate such an imagination-based intervention into therapy with an older adult/geriatric population, a group that is in a completely different stage of life with vastly different cognitive, emotional, and social needs? Perhaps while differences exist between adolescence and older adults in the nuances and details of their needs and life experiences, there are a plethora of similarities to be found. The cognitive building skills that Dungeons & Dragons has to offer its players can technically be of benefit to any age cohort, but are especially impactful with older adult and geriatric populations. The same skills that teens need to navigate through new dynamics of adolescent social life are the very skills that can promote increased happiness and daily positive functioning in the lives of older adults who find themselves living in independent senior housing, senior centers, physical rehabilitation facilities, or even nursing homes (Williams & Kemper, 2010).

## The Wizard's Mind: Cognitive Impact of the Aging Process

It is first helpful to understand how a tabletop game such as Dungeons & Dragons can address the clinical and cognitive challenges of older adults. The game fosters a vast number of executive functions and cognitive skills within its gameplay, skills that are essential to the possible pre-vention of age-related cognitive disorders such as dementia (Tse et al., 2018). Planning, organization, behavioral inhibition, regulating one's own behaviors, and evaluating others' all are incorporated into the role playing narrative of tabletop games. The group may need to tactically plan out a battle before engaging enemies to reduce casualties, or perhaps another challenge entrusts a player to act diplomatically with a disagreeable and not entirely truthful non-player character in the story (role played by the Dungeon Master). Understanding how to regulate one's words, tone, and social skills within this role play could be critical to gaining useful information or aide in a quest.

As we age, our minds become vulnerable to a trending decline in various cognitive abilities. Often our fluid intelligence (process-based abil-ities such as problem solving, reasoning, and working through unfamil-iar tasks) is initially affected by the ageing process. As we age further, our crystallized intelligence can then become eroded; this is the type of knowledge that we have accumulated over longer periods of time such as academic facts or learned skills. Our memory is also impacted as we age, with our short-term memory being most diminished; this leads to greater problems in attention, encoding, and recall (Luo & Craik, 2008; Williams & Kemper, 2010). Cognitive decline may be more noticeable to some older adults than others. Tabletop games such as Dungeons & Dragons can incorporate memory-based puzzles and traps that the players must nav-igate through, testing and exercising these vulnerable cognitive abilities in older age. Some studies have shown how brain training games can have a positive impact on the improvements in memory-related tasks for older adults (Carle, 2007). One example may be to test a group of players on memorizing a sequence of glowing magical runes in order to get through that part of the dungeon to the next room.

One could imagine that recognizing a decrease in these abilities may lead to concern, frustration, and even sadness or depression, in some cases. These innate abilities that we often take for granted gradually change over time, which can impact our self-perception, mood, and sense of autonomy. Luckily, cognitively challenging games such as D&D and additional socially interactive activities such as art therapy allow an indi-vidual to practice and strengthen these skills, and potentially prevent rapid cognitive decline (Andel et al., 2005; Herholz et al., 2013).

Research has shown that engaging in skills-based activities that exercise these vulnerable cognitive abilities can help prevent their decline and loss due to both the aging process, as well as biological diseases such as dementia and Alzheimer's Disease, in participant self-reports (Papp et al., 2009) and empirical research (Nguyen et al., 2019; Robertson, 2013). These studies have supported the idea that despite cognitive decline in older adults, certain skills can be preserved through cognitive training programs. Cognitive training program may include play therapy or training in particular tasks that encourage the use of working memory, abstract thought processing, spatial awareness, and decision-making strategies. Tabletop role-playing games (TTRPG's) implement many of these similar skills-based cognitive functions through narrative storytelling, recall of relevant information to utilize your character's abilities, puzzle solving, and even utilizing map-based visual aides to strategize an in-game battle with models and figurines. To date, some studies question whether specific cognitive training with a single program or game can transfer the benefits and effects to other untrained tasks and daily living skills (Owen, 2010; Papp et al., 2009). These studies have supported the findings that playing a cognitively challenging game only improves the used cognitive function within the practice of that specific game rather than broadly increasing its strength across multiple tasks or challenges. From a clinical and therapeutic perspective, however, playing D&D may also help older adults regulate common mood disorders found when living in a nursing home, and assist them in answering a common question that arises when they are thrust into life transition due to a loss or changes in health or living environment: *Who am I now?*

## The Fighter's Uphill Battle: Common Clinical Issues within Older Adult Populations

Depression is a prevalent mental health diagnosis found in older adults living in nursing homes or retirement facilities – and even appears to be a cross-cultural experience, as shown through international studies (Chuang & Kuo, 2018; Wang et al., 2014; Bohlmeijer et al., 2010).

Many older adults, even outside of assisted living environments and in the absence of mental health issues, will likely benefit from the playing of TTRPG's. Gary Gygax began the formal creation of his Dungeons & Dragons game in his adulthood, inspired by childhood experiences and readings that influenced his imagination and sense of adventure. Many older adults are around the age that Gary would be at the time of this book's publication, and many may even remember reading the same fantasy or science fiction publications and novels that he based his story telling game design after (Kelly, 2014-2015). Authors such as Edgar Allan Poe, Poul Anderson Robert E. Howard and Ray Bradbury greatly influenced a generation of adolescents, including Gary Gygax, enthralled with mystery and fantastical adventure. Works such as *Conan the Barbarian* and *Three Hearts* and *Three Lions* likely became the scaffolding for many of the narrative and even structural aspects of Gygax's tabletop creation (Johnson, 2017). These are further experiences and wonderful memories to be shared within a therapeutic narrative and expansion upon the group therapy model.

Group therapy via Dungeons & Dragons can become a powerful tool in helping older adults overcome depressive symptoms including isolation, hopelessness, and personal loss of meaning (Agronin, 2009). Group members become aware that the mental and physical health symptoms they experience on a daily basis are often shared by others in the group, leading to a sense of solidarity and commonality in and out of the game. In groups, similarly aged peers can connect with each other, share life experiences, and even grow a sense of belonging as they help each other navigate through life experiences and present challenges. Within the group there potentially develops an overall sense of usefulness and helpfulness towards one another, a source of pride that is often lost when one begins to age and depend on the aide of professional staff for basic tasks and functions (Rachel and Turkot, 2014). Bringing older adults together to form a team challenges them to interact and exercise their social skills, leading to many emotional benefits (Chuang & Kuo, 2018). Such groups assist them with breaking down feelings of cognitive stagnation and even relational despair that often are related to older adult depression in long-term care settings. Group therapies utilizing Dungeons & Dragons can also assist with other common emotional difficulties when managing living changes due to aging including shame, guilt, loneliness, and a lack of purpose (Chuang & Kuo, 2018; Bohlmeijer et al., 2010; Wang et al., 2014).

The narrative portion of TTRPG's allows older adults to reminisce and share their life experiences in meaningful, fun, and sometimes surprisingly innovative new ways via the Dungeons & Dragons experience. They begin to build a sense of accomplishment and positive self-perception (Chuang & Kuo, 2018; Wang et al., 2014). A prime example of this comes from one group member who played the character of a bard, a magical entertainer who uses an instrument to cast magical spells. The patient was a long time blues enthusiast, and he would lift the group's spirits by bringing his harmonica to session and playing it every time he casted a spell. This not only created a more immersive effect for the gameplay and group, but it introduced a talking point of excitement between group members as they shouted out different songs for him to play. This immersion brought group members closer together and became a catalyst for discussing deeper life issues. Topics such as pain management, loss of support systems from family or friends, and even complaints about facility food quality, all began to be discussed and emotionally processed and through the shared storytelling experiences in the Dungeon and Dragon's group. At one point, the group members feasted at a high-end tavern after a long battle in the game, where every member got to choose the best meal they ever had, bringing more smiles to their faces than perhaps the underwhelming, over-served, and questionable chicken piccata coming up for dinner in the facility. The narrative of their in-game choices reflects back to them a staunch reminder of who they are and what meaningful values they hold onto, no matter their living environment.

## A Druid's Therapeutic Manual: Utilizing Dungeons & Dragons in Group Therapy for Older Adults

Picking the right Dungeons & Dragons game module to play for a geriatric population group will be essential in having a seamless and cohesive experience for players, especially those new to TTRPGs. The new-player friendly starter sets, such as *Lost Mine of Phandelver* (Mearls et al., 2014) or *Dragon of Icespire Peak* (Crawford et al., 2019), are perfect sandbox storylines that allow new players to get used to the rules of the game while also feeling a moderate sense of freedom in the places they choose to explore or the quests they agree to take on. The simple narratives of these stories may be more relatable to an older adult population with little to no experience of the Dungeons & Dragons world, than a complex and lengthy storyline that could potentially take years to complete (yes, some games take years to get to the end of the adventure!). When working with older adults, a clinician may want to consider changes with members' inpatient status, health concerns, doctor's appointments, and overall cognitive functioning or physical mobility. Setting up a storyline for a realistic number of sessions, whether an established publication or made up (homebrew) story, will keep members from being overwhelmed. A weekly session that runs for an hour and a half over the course of 10 weeks may be a good starting place for a closed group where accommodations for older adults can be considered.

Perhaps the most difficult part of utilizing Dungeons & Dragons in a clinical setting is that as a therapist, one is ascribed two roles and responsibilities: that of the clinician supervising the therapeutic process of the group, and that of the dungeon master ensuring a fun, interactive, and immersive experience for the group players. These two roles are at times difficult to manage at the same time. Each has unique challenges and requirements that can sometimes come into conflict with each other. It is therefore important to have a set of guidelines that can be used and modified (depending upon the type of group) to ensure the clinical progress and safety of your members. It is noteworthy that many state laws consider older adults, ages 65 and up, to be a potentially vulnerable population to work with and certainly an underserved clinical population that need specialized care, knowledge, and clinical skill to work with. Despite these challenges, older adults can also provide some of the most clinically rewarding experiences and some of the most unexpected narrative choices in your tabletop therapy game and interventions.

As one is taking on the role of a Dungeon Master (DM), the primary role must be as a clinician. The group therapist should work towards ensuring the functionality of the group on a clinical and therapeutic level. As a dungeon master, it is important to consider how to homebrew (create your own adventures outside of the manual) and write in some challenges within a storytelling narrative which complement the therapeutic need and milieu of each group member. If one group member tends to have challenges asserting themselves, perhaps they are the ones asked to give a rallying cry speech before a battle. Or maybe an isolated group member is given consequences when always trying to scout ahead alone. There will be times when some of these technicalities of being a DM/therapist may require more attention and focus than making clinical observations during a group. For example, teaching rules of the game to new players even during play, clarifying questions players have of the storyline, and putting in narrative detailed descriptions of the world that is being played through to enhance immersion can take up a lot of attention from the leading clinician that is acting as a DM. This is just one of many reasons why it can be very helpful to co-run the group with another clinician. This would be structured similarly to groups run in Dialectical Behavioral Therapy (DBT) as established by Marsha Linehan (2015).

As within DBT groups, a focus upon skill-based learning and psycho-education is a must within the D&D groups, and can be especially impactful while working with geriatric populations. Tabletop games often have complex rules and parameters which are not as initially intuitive to learn as simple board games that only use a six-sided die to determine movement. This can be a challenge while teaching older adults with limited tabletop gaming experience and who may have attention, focus, or even eyesight difficulties, which make reading a character sheet, game rules, or the smaller numbers on 20-sided die. A two-clinician-led group can assist with these challenges. While one clinician teaches and manages the flow of the group from a practical game running perspective, the co-runner can focus more on clinical concerns while they observe, take notes, and give feedback on how members have been processing various emotional and cognitive discoveries.

Likewise, a D&D tabletop therapy group benefits from a separation of clinical roles between a two-clinician-led group. The DM can focus on keeping the game running (essential for clients with attention or focus difficulties), prompt responses or engagement for depressed or socially anxious members, and deliver an immersive experience that incorporates clinical and therapeutic challenges for the members. If the goal for an inpatient group member is to practice pain management through their narrative, the primary clinician acting as the DM can take the members through a therapeutic guided body-scan exercise after a significant battle where the group may have suffered some injuries. This creates an in-game experience consistent with narrative, that may also be an essential coping skill and tool that clients utilize outside of group. The DM can focus on helping the group members play out this experience through immersive guided imagery and story description while the co-runner clinician has the choice of just observing and taking clinical notes or prompting reflections from the players after the exercise. The co-clinician is therefore able to pay more attention to emotional reactions, cognitive patterns, strengths, and needed areas of growth for individual group members. Feedback and ways to address these observations can be shared with the DM and prepared for next session.

Structure and format of the group is malleable and can fluctuate in clinical focus per session depending on the goals. It may be helpful to begin many groups with a 15 minute "check-in," assisting group members emotionally and cognitively warm up for the game. This is especially important when working with older adult populations who may be excited to utilize this time to share with each other highlights or difficulties of their week as social interactions can sometimes be limited within hospital or nursing home settings, exacerbated by clinical issues such as depression or physical disability. It may also be common for group members to trickle into the start of the group due to difficulties with mobility, or if conducting an inpatient group, the limited patient transportation that is available to bring each group member from their room to group. A "check-in" will allow group members to trickle in without missing the main parts of the narrative storyline and game engaging activities.

During a check-in, each member gets a turn to share about their week without going into much processing. This individual check-in would only last a few minutes to ensure other members know what they may encounter in terms of each player's mood and general engagement. Many things can be disruptive in a nursing home or rehabilitation center setting. Health issues, inpatient facility policy stressors, financial loses, and even peer or family deaths can all be prominent contributors to changes in depression and anxiety levels for older adult group members. Sometimes, the group's bard won't want to sing their songs of magical inspiration, and the healer of the group may be frustrated to be designated as such if they are at health risks themselves. The check-ins allow the group to prepare for any new challenges group members may have faced during the week. "Check-outs" can also be enveloped into the end of sessions, allowing group members to debrief, reflect on the highlights of the session, and maybe even acknowledge how the session emotionally impacted them. Suggestions and criticisms should also be a part of the check-out to help the DM navigate changes that can be made to the narrative, or help the co-runner catch unhelpful group interactions or behaviors.

While engaging in role play and pretending to be one's best self can be relieving, it is important as a clinician to observe how narrative can emotionally impact our group members. Many older adults have experienced and survived multiple traumas and/or losses. It would be advisable to be aware of these histories and find an appropriate level of adult-themed narrative without it becoming triggering. Narrative therapy can be a fantastic way for individuals to work through and process their trauma, and games like D&D are a fantastic opportunity for clinicians to help individuals role-play out successful stories of trauma survival. However, this can be talked about with each individual group member prior to sessions and the beginning of group, and it should be done at the member's own pace rather than forced upon an individual for the purpose of the group's enjoyment.

It can have more clinical impact to let a group member have a 1:1 in-game encounter with an NPC that represents a possible former real-life abuser rather than get the whole group involved with a giant battle that downplays the significance of this NPC towards a single member's back story. There is nothing more empowering that seeing a group member achieve emotional catharsis for standing up to a representation of their trauma and then get the full support from the rest of the group members after the encounter. For instance, in one group run a member had been placed inpatient for physical rehabilitation and a general failure to thrive as physical conditions had worsened due to inability to care for himself independently. While inpatient for an extended period of time, the client lost his home due to inability to pay rent and began to lose his eyesight from an ocular stroke. This severely impacted the client's emotional stability as he became emotionally traumatized from multiple areas of loss. This client incorporated his disability and loss into his game character, a blind, wandering monk that utilized heightened skills of perception through smell and hearing to scout ahead for the group. The client took the trauma from age-related struggles and reframed them into empowering strengths that could assist his group in game.

## A Monk's Focus and a Bard's Song: Ways to Incorporate Coping Skill Building into Narrative Play

Another clinical focus that can be implemented into game therapy with the geriatric population is the practice of particular skills and everyday difficulties both in and outside of the group. For instance,   there are many clinical considerations when your group is older in age. Pain management can greatly impact session attendance, with some members finding it difficult to get to the group due to arthritis, neuropathic pain, or general immobility issues. Sometimes gastrointestinal issues and incontinence can be an emotional factor that prevents members from attending due to embarrassment (Kurniawan & Kolopaking, 2014). Other times group members just want to learn skills on how to manage their symptoms so that they can enjoy the social aspect of group. Sessions can have story-driven themes attached to them on a weekly basis; one week the story may focus on the experience of loneliness and how empowering social engagement and teamwork can be, while another week's game can examine how to process grief, loss, and existential themes of death or dying, a frequent occurrence in a nursing home setting. The 15-minute check-in's can be alternatively used to teach basic coping skills, which then can be prompted to be utilized in-game. Successful use of these skills in-game can then result in in-game rewards such as magical equipment, improved reputations with story-line factions, or free dice rerolls, often called inspiration points in D&D game play (Cordell et al., 2014). Learning how to use deep breathing, mindfulness, "I" statements, or thought-stopping skills can all be part of psycho-education and narrative. During one session, before going into a large battle, the group's player monk guided the group in a deep breath mindfulness exercise to strengthen each other's focus and prepare for the fight.

Another consideration is that depending on the group, some members may have cognitive limitations that impact their ability to navigate through the adventure or play their character in a cohesive manner. There are many rules to tabletop games such as D&D, and at times there may need to be compromise on how to simplify or provide supporting material for players who have attention/focus difficulties, memory impairment, and other cognitive limitations. A player may be attracted to the idea of playing a wizard but find it tedious to remember the extensive amount of available spells to them, a classic feature of this type of character in most TTRPGs. It can be helpful to guide the player to a general idea of the types of spells they imagine casting, with the DM picking their spells for them and providing a brief annotated written explanation: "'Polymorph' - Turn someone into an animal!" Or "'Fireball' – Blow stuff up!" Patience in teaching complicated tabletop games is something that not all dungeon masters enjoy doing or have mastery in. Grab plenty of pencils, and a bunch of extra character-sheets that players can build and create their character on to help players avoid feeling judged if they make mistakes.

Additional therapeutic interventions can integrate into a tabletop group for older adults. These various activities can assist with feelings of stagnation and lack of emotional expression. Firstly, journaling can be a fantastic complementary coping skill that has both in-game practical uses and emotional insight-building skills (Smyth et al., 2018). Members can write a weekly journal about sessions, note parts of the narrative that might be important for solving a puzzle, and exercise the puzzle-solving cognitive skills to help manage memory loss or attention difficulties. Journaling has also been particularly helpful in facilitating positive attitude towards health conditions and medical related anxiety (Smyth et al., 2018). This may be a particularly effective intervention to utilize within an inpatient geriatric population. Group members can also emotionally reflect on their weekly session experience, building insight into how their mood changes based upon their participation and furthering their therapeutic experience.

A complementary therapeutic enhancement is to combine elements of art and music therapy into the experience. Certain tabletop games can be played with small figurines and characters that can be painted. Group members imagine their character's appearance – this can be a powerful way to reflect their inner vision of themselves. The therapeutic process of art can assist with emotional expression and overall depression reduction (Kim et al., 2016; Stephenson, 2013), strengthening the overall therapeutic narrative in addition to helping clients practice the visual-spatial and emotionally-expressive skills promoted with model painting. Music has also shown to be an effective therapeutic intervention with older adults (Norman, 2012; Schmid & Ostermann, 2010). If a bard is in the group, (a character often focused on casting magic spells with music and song), encourage them to sing their favorite rock or blues songs from sentimental musical eras – this can bring the group together. DMs could even enhance the game by playing the actual tune and integrating battle music.

## An Adventuring Case Study

*"Go ahead, just throw another fireball and set everything on fire again, just like the last time. It'll be great, we've already got the town angry at us."*
— Strider, Human Ranger

In the particular adventure quoted above, Strider is being played by one of five 50+ aged residents in a nursing home and physical rehabilitation facility. There was a lot of banter and sarcasm coming from Strider towards his fellow nursing home resident and friend who plays in the game as the elven sorcerer, Sakorah. The two residents had always been at odds in personality and strategy, trying to overcome these differences in a game that often rewards teamwork and cooperation. The dungeon-delving party consisted of five older adults ranging from their 50s to their 70s had been exhaustingly out of options while fighting two trolls in the game, who snuck their way into the local inn for a midnight snack. Some bickering between players ensued, magical fireballs were cast and thrown, and the team ran off laughing into the night, away from disgruntled townsfolk waiving pitchforks at the adventuring party for indeed burning their town down.

The creation of this therapy group was part of a trial intervention to see if having an older adult population engage in a structured cooperative game could enhance sociability and cognitive functions while addressing some clinical symptoms of anxiety and depression. The most prominent symptom that all the players exhibited was severe isolation behaviors and limited interactions with fellow residents along with a general loss of interest in hobbies or activities they once found enjoyable. The group members had been clinically diagnosed with mental health disorders ranging from depression, generalized anxiety, trauma related disorders, and chronic pain. In addition, a multitude of physical diseases and disabilities all contributed to their severe isolation behaviors while residing in a long-term care and rehabilitation facility. For these clients, the role-playing tabletop game of Dungeons & Dragons had brought them a myriad of positive and hopeful new beginnings that changed their lives over the three-month group adventure and beyond. It alleviated their hopelessness and assisted them in building coping skills, but most importantly, it helped them find meaning in a place they had struggled to call home. Through social interaction and the engagement in an immersive narrative, these nursing home residents began to come out of their isolation and battle their symptoms.

Group participation was based upon significant screeners of depression, anxiety, and clinical observation of isolation. Anxiety, depression, and stress clinical screeners such as the PHQ-9 and the DASS-42 were used to gauge severity of clinical symptoms, and all participants had been engaged in months of previous individual psychotherapy. Only one of the five group members had any experience of Dungeons & Dragons, having played the initial edition that came about in the 1970s. Having one semi-experienced player helped the cohesive structure of the group, in that role playing and acting out imaginary scenarios may sometimes feel childish or too whimsical for some adults. The simple modeling of the experienced player in role play appeared to have eased new players into the immersive world.

Many of the group members joined the adventure for various reasons; almost all were experiencing significant levels of social isolation within the rehabilitation and nursing home facility, limiting their communication with peers and often relying on staff to provide them with their social communication needs. Therefore, the primary objective of this group was to assist members in reducing their social isolation, building up their communication skills, and obtaining a general sense of peer support for the medical and mental health symptoms they had been facing. Members were first met in individual sessions with the clinician, establishing individual goals for what they hoped to get from group therapy, as well as building a character that either represented their ideal best self, or a flawed self that would eventually grow in character and skill throughout the adventure.

The party ended up consisting of a Dragonborn Fighter, a Human Monk, a Human Ranger, a Dragonborn Druid, and a High Elf Sorcerer, each character uniquely reflecting the personality traits of their creators. For instance, as mentioned previously a resident who had recently lost their eyesight incorporated this disability into their Monk character as a strength in the perception skill, hearing things from afar and warning the group of oncoming danger. One group member who suffered from significant lymphedema, a medical condition contributed to severe obesity and mobility difficulties, made their Druid character (a magical being that relates to nature) a woodworking artisan, able to craft his own weapons and tools, a skill and self-care activity he missed engaging in outside of the facility. In addition, the Druid's freedom of being able to turn into an animal such as a wolf or a horse and run with additional mobility throughout the game contrasted his frustrated position of being wheelchair bound due to his obesity. The Dragonborn fighter was a resident who felt that they were in a constant battle with unending ruminating anxiety, utilizing the courage and constitution of their character to represent their dominance over psychosomatic symptoms.

As the group progressed, each session was met with excitement about continuing the storyline and getting into more narrative trouble. It began to feel as though playing with a group of older adults was mimicking a bunch of teenagers hitting on barmaids, causing a ruckus in towns, and engaging in the most social interactions they had experienced in over a year. At a baseline minimum, they were having fun in an environment where they had previously believed such a privilege was not possible. Indication of clinical progress no doubt came in the self-reports of looking forward to each group session on a week to week basis, and significantly feeling the loss of a group member if they were out for the week due to medical issues or other responsibilities. It also came in the form of reduced depressed symptoms screened by the PHQ-9 and reduced stress indicators within the DASS-42. There were also clinical observations of residents reaching out and spending time socially to more peers outside of group. While no cognitive skills were measured over the course of the 10 weeks, each member was engaging in recalling information from past sessions and participated in their unique ways when solving puzzles, all contributing to an overall sense of teamwork.

Ending a campaign, let alone a therapy group, can be a difficult and emotional experience for many group members (Benson, 2001). Having the players reflect on their in-game adventure as well as their personal growth and the overall group dynamics was a good way to solidify the important therapeutic challenges many of the members worked through during group. When was said and done, the group members, despite their stage of life, began to realize there was continued room to grow, both in game character levels and enriching social experiences. There is nothing that stands out more than the group reflecting on their individual growth and the support they receive from each other, all within an environment and period of life where uncertainties are just as prominent as ever.

*"Thanks doc, this game is the one thing that got me out of bed all these months..."*
— Sir Gareth, the anxious Dragonborn Fighter

# References

Agronin, M. (2009). Group therapy in older adults. *Current Psychiatry Reports, 11*(1), 27-32.

Andel, R., Hughes, T. F., & Crowe, M. (2005). Strategies to reduce the risk of cognitive decline and dementia. *Aging Health*, 1(1), 107-116. doi:http://dx.doi.org.tcsedsystem.idm.oclc.org/10.2217/1745509X.1.1.107

Beauchamp, M. H., & Anderson, V. (2010). SOCIAL: An integrative framework for the development of social skills. *Psychological Bulletin,* 136(1), 39-64. doi: http://dx.doi.org.tcsedsystem.idm.oclc.org/10.1037/a0017768

Benson, J. (2001). Work at the ending stage of the group: separation issues. In Benson, J. (Ed), *Working More Creatively in Groups*, (145–54), Abingdon, England: Routledge.

Bohlmeijer, E., Prenger, R., Taal, E., & Cuijpers, P. (2010). The effects of mindfulness-based stress reduction therapy on mental health of adults with a chronic medical disease: A meta-analysis. *Journal of Psychosomatic Research, 68, 6, 539-544.*

Carle A. (2007). More than a game: brain training against dementia. *Nursing Homes: Long Term Care Management, 56*(8), 22–61. Retrieved from http://search.ebscohost.com.tcsedsystem.idm.oclc.org/login.aspx?direct=true&db=ccm&AN=106167910&site=ehost-live

Carter, A. (2011). Using Dungeons & Dragons to integrate curricula in an elementary classroom. In M. Ma, A. Oikonomou, & L. Jain (Eds.) *Serious Games and Edutainment Applications* (pp. 329-246). New York, NY: Springer. DOI: 10.1007/978-1-4471-2161-9_17.

Chuang, Y. H., & Kuo, L. M. (2018). Nurses' confidence in providing and managing care for older persons with depressive symptoms or depression in long-term care facilities: A national survey. *International Journal of Mental Health Nursing, 27, 6,* 1767-1775.

Cordell, B. R., Schwalb, R. J., & Wyatt, J. (2014). *Player's Handbook* (5th ed.). Wizards of the Coast. Renton, WA

Crawford, J., Perkins, C., Baker, R. (2019). *Dragon of Icespire Peak: Essentials Kit Rulebook* (5th ed.). Wizards of the Coast. Renton, WA

Herholz, S. C., Herholz, R. S., & Herholz, K. (2013). Non-pharmacological interventions and neuroplasticity in early stage alzheimer's disease. Expert review of Neurotherapeutics, 13(11), 1235-45. doi:http://dx.doi.org.tcsedsystem.idm.oclc.org/10.1586/14737175.2013.845086

Johnson, J. (2017). Appendix N. Kouvola, Finland: Castalia House.

Kelly, K. D. (2014-2015). *Hawk & Moor: The Unofficial History of Dungeons & Dragons*. Middletown, DE: Wonderland Imprints.

Kim, H., Kim, K. M., & Nomura, S. (2016). The effect of group art therapy on older Korean adults with neurocognitive disorders. *The Arts in Psychotherapy, 47,* 48-54. doi:http://dx.doi.org.tcsedsystem.idm.oclc.org/10.1016/j.aip.2015.11.002

Kurniawan I., & Kolopaking M.S.. Management of Irritable Bowel Syndrome in the elderly. *Acta Medica Indonesiana.* 2014;46(2):138-147.

Linehan, M. (2015*). DBT Skills training manual* (2nd ed.). New York, NY: The Guilford Press

Luo, L., & Craik, F. I. M. (2008). Aging and memory: A cognitive approach. *Canadian Journal of Psychiatry, 53*(6), 346-53. Retrieved from https://tcsedsystem.idm.oclc.org/login?url=https://search-proquest-com.tcsedsystem.idm.oclc.org/docview/222797444?accountid=34120

Mearls, M, Crawford, J., Perkins, C., Wyatt, J., Thompson, R., Schwalb, S., Lee, P, Townshend, S., Cordell, B. (2014). *Lost Mines of Phandelver: Starter Set Rulebook* (5th ed.). Wizards of the Coast. Renton, WA.

Norman, R. (2012). Music therapy assessment of older adults in nursing homes. *Music Therapy Perspectives, 30*(1), 8-16. Retrieved from https://tcsedsystem.idm.oclc.org/login?url=https://search-proquest-com.tcsedsystem.idm.oclc.org/docview/1041061474?accountid=34120

Nguyen, L., Murphy, K., & Andrews, G. (2019). Immediate and long-term efficacy of executive functions cognitive training in older adults: A systematic review and meta-analysis. *Psychological Bulletin*, doi: http://dx.doi.org.tcsedsystem.idm.oclc.org/10.1037/bul0000196

Owen, A. M., Hampshire, A., Grahn, J. A., Stenton, R., Dajani, S., Burns, A. S., & Ballard, C. G. (2010). Putting brain training to the test. *Nature, 465*(7299), 775–778. doi:10.1038/nature09042

Papp, K.V., Walsh, S. J., Snyder, P. J. (2009) Immediate and delayed effects of cognitive interventions in healthy elderly: A review of current literature and future directions. *Alzheimer's Dementia. 5,* 50-60.

Rachel, W., & Turkot, A. (2014). Psychotherapy in older adults with major depression in psychogeriatric ward. *Psychoterapia. 171.* 77-87. Doi: 10.12740/PT/30178.

Robertson, I. H. (2013). A noradrenergic theory of cognitive reserve: implications for Alzheimer's disease. *Neurobiology Aging 34,* 298–308.  doi: 10.1016/j.neurobiolaging.2012.05.019

Schmid, W., & Ostermann, T. (2010). Home-based music therapy - a systematic overview of settings and conditions for an innovative service in healthcare. *BMC Health Services Research, 10*, 291. doi:http://dx.doi.org.tcsedsystem.idm.oclc.org/10.1186/1472-6963-10-29

Smyth, J. M., Johnson, J. A., Auer, B. J., Lehman, E., Talamo, G., & Sciamanna, C. N. (2018). Online Positive Affect Journaling in the Improvement of Mental Distress and Well-Being in General Medical Patients With Elevated Anxiety Symptoms: A Preliminary Randomized Controlled Trial. *JMIR Mental Health, 5*(4), e11290. doi:10.2196/11290

Stephenson, R. C. (2013). Promoting well-being and gerotranscendence in an art therapy program for older adults. *Art Therapy, 30*(4), 151-158. Doi:10.1080/07421656.2014.846206

Tse, M. M. Y., Lau, J. L., Kwan, R., Cheung, D., Tang, A. S. K., Ng, S. S. M., … Yeung, S. S. Y. (2018). Effects of play activities program for nursing home residents with dementia on pain and psychological well-being: Cluster randomized controlled trial. *Geriatrics & Gerontology International*, *18*(10), 1485–1490. https://doi-org. tcsedsystem.idm.oclc.org/10.1111/ggi.13509

Wang, X., Cai, L., Qian, J., & Peng, J. (2014). Social support moderates stress effects on depression. *International Journal of Mental Health Systems, 8,* 1.

Williams, K. N., & Kemper, S. (2010). Interventions to reduce cognitive decline in aging. *Journal of Psychosocial Nursing & Mental Health Services, 48*(5), 42-51. doi:http://dx.doi.org.tcsedsystem.idm.oclc. org/10.3928/02793695-20100331-03

# Comic Cons and Fandoms

# Introduction to Comic Conventions, Fandoms, and Cult Followings

# 8

By Shane Tilton, PhD

The building hosting the comic convention acts as a sacred safe space for this celebration of fandom. The space allows those individuals attending to present the various temperaments that fans display in service of sharing and emoting their joy of popular culture (Tilton, 2016). San Diego Comic-Con, the Penny Arcade Expo (PAX), Wondercon, Dragon Con, Origins, and GenCon make up a majority of shared social popular culture experiences.

These comic, gaming, and popular culture conventions allow individuals who enthusiastically enjoy one or more different series from the realm of graphic novels, video games, books, movies, anime, or some other mode of popular culture (i.e., a fan) to celebrate their enjoyment of those titles with others that share their same passions (i.e., a fandom). Some of the more passionate fans within the community share their knowledge about the more nuanced areas of their selected areas of expertise in popular culture.

This expression of knowledge is tied into the sense of social identity for members of this subculture as their connection to the larger community depends on their ability to share their knowledge and expertise toward the lexicon of geek life (McArthur, 2009). These types of fans can recite word for word all of the lines from *Monty Python and the Holy Grail* or could tell others the order of boyfriends that Scott Pilgrim faced in *Scott Pilgrim vs. the World* as easily as someone would sing "Happy Birthday" or say the "Pledge of Allegiance." These choleric individuals are described as "nerds," but a better description would be those fans that want to share what they know with the massive fandom (Matz et al., 2016). Their passions are less in line with caring about how the larger society sees them and more about maintaining their place within the fandom by being the guardians of knowledge related to a specific graphic novel series or some other series in the various modes of mass communication distribution (e.g., film or television show). Those outside of this small in-group can feel that this level of guardianship among the fan community can be tantamount to "gatekeeping" or "nerd-checking." This barrier can prevent those that have not passed the "Litmus Test of Fandom" to become a member of a given community or even interact with members of this community (Lau et al., 2019)

There is another subgroup within the fandom of those individuals that denote a more passionate set of fans that are more extroverted than the previously listed group of individuals. This group feeds on the socialization that events like the San Diego Comic-Con provide. They will proudly show off t-shirts, pins, statues, and posters of the favorite graphic novel series like the way that sports fans will put on the jersey of their favorite player or team while holding a sign supporting their game while attending a game (Robinson, 2018). Both types of fans referred to in the last sentences take pride in their fandom of focus. They can quickly lose themselves to hours of their selected passions and maintain them regardless of how others feel - as long as there are a select few that share those feelings and are willing to perform those rituals of emotion within the group setting (Rothenbuhler, 1998). These sanguine people often wear their geek pride within the immersive social environments that are connected to their passions (Kefir & Corsini, 1974).

Regardless of their quirks, fans generally engage with one or more types of activities to express their fandom to a specific fan community (e.g., fans of the Marvel Cinematic Universe (MCU)) with the larger general public. Engagement with more than one fan base requires a level of cultural literacy and multiple levels of interaction among the members of the fan communities as expression of passion for the fan's chosen media interest.

## Jenkins' Five Levels of Fandom Activity

The famous communication theorist and sociologist Henry Jenkins (1992, p. 277) wrote about these passions in his foundational work, *Textual Poachers: Television Fan & Participatory Culture*. He noted five levels of activity that fandoms traditionally engage in when interacting with core texts essential to their favorite shows, books, movies, or other artifacts of popular culture. Fans of their content will begin their fandom with the reception and consumption of mediated works "with close and undivided attention, with a mixture of emotional proximity and critical distance." Jenkins notes the fans will hyper-analyze every word and action in a film, television episode, or graphic novel with both an emotional connection to the works and the ability to use common tools of media analysis[2].

Steven Braun, information designer and fan of the movie *Big Lebowski*, is the perfect example of Jenkins' quote. His *Visual Guide to the Big Lebowski* (2018) explains how "One can watch the film numerous times without fully grasping how the various plot threads tie together — if they do at all." The fans of the *Big Lebowski*, and by extension fandoms in general, make meaning from the viewing of the fan's given work of passion. Moreover, those fans articulate those meanings by the performance of the lines and actions from the fan's selected graphic novel, film, or other media production.

Secondly, fans learn the community's "critical and interpretive practices"; fans often know how to read a series based on other fans reactions. These readings are based on the fan's media literacy of reading, listening, and watching other series within the same genre (e.g., what is canon to the overall universe of a given comic or series). Members of a fandom even understand how to connect the world presented in their favorite works into the everyday life experience of the fan. For example, there is the *Machete* viewing order to the *Star Wars* films and television series that inform the community of the "preferred way" to view the series; this offers a critical perspective on the value of the different episodes within the series and the perceived issues surrounding one of the movies (Sim, 2018). *The Marvel Cinematic Universe* (MCU) has a similar viewing order

---

[2] Please review any issue of the Journal of Popular Culture or the Journal of Fandom Studies for other examples for applying the common tools of media analysis to these mediated works.

designed to inform the fans the "correct" chronological order to view the movies and television show in order to make sense of the full MCU and see how the different characters from the various Marvel titles interact with one another (Petrakovitz, 2018).

Fans of a given show would create a multi-faceted public memory of the fandom and use the critical and interpretive practices to turn the information associated with fandom into knowledge that can be shared within the community. Jenkins would later argue in "Convergence Culture" (2006) that these two levels of fandom activities would form a "collective intelligence" (Levy, 1997).

The third mode of activities that fans pursue is the ability to organize in service of their favorite works of popular culture. Fandoms typically organize as one collective to present a singular voice expressing the wishes of the fan base. The collective whole shows the studios the power of the fans in a way that a single fan cannot. The most basic form of this activism is to organize rallies in support of a cause.

A prime example of fandom's ability to support causes happened in 2016 when Marvel created a new *Captain America* series entitled *Captain America: Steve Rogers*. It was in this comic series that Captain America took a "heel turn" (Oestriecher, 2018) by proclaiming "Hail Hydra." There was an immediate reaction from the fans in the form of an online, organized protest under the hashtag #HydraCap (Riesman, 2017). The immediate reaction was also in the form of fans of Captain America donating money to the United States Holocaust Museum as a way of fighting Nazis in the spirit of what Captain America originally stood for (Walsh, 2016). It is in this spirit that the fans believe they are performing a type of "social good" to fight an underlying evil in society. Those fans are internalizing in the morality and code of ethics that Captain America would show if Captain America did exist in the real world of those fans.

Fourthly, fans will tend to create works that speak to the aesthetic traditions and practices of the fandom. The popular term for those works would be "fan fiction." These works act as both a type of cultural capital that shows the fans investment in their favorite mediated works and as an artifact that can be gifted to and read by others in the fandom. Consalvo (2003) noted the issues that can come from this level of activity. For example, fans of *Buffy the Vampire Slayer* maintained "Slayer Links," which was a Webring of almost 1,000 stories, fansites, and archives of Buffy fan fiction. 20th Century Fox television issued "cease and desist" orders and threatened the publishers of those pieces of fan fiction lawsuits if they didn't remove their work online. When facing those threats, most of the fandom reverted to the third level of action and organized to protest against attack a central tenet of fandom. Those fans performed "Operation Blackout" in May 2000 to show their disapproval and limit promotion opportunities for 20th Century Fox and WB Channel, which was showing episodes of *Buffy the Vampire Slayer* (Chonin, 2012). The battle over these actions gave fans a feeling of agency over their ability to use characters from the show in creative works and caused intellectual property holders pause with regards to how to interact with fans (Moore, 2002).

This perceived agency is vital from a psychological perspective as it provides an outlet for those fans to have a space to work out issues they may be experiencing by using the heroes and characters from their favorite stories as proxies for themselves and psychological problems they are facing. Jon Cohen (2009) noted this theme in his work on parasocial breakups, as the fans of shows used the parasocial relationship with characters in television shows to essentially supplement their social support systems through pathos-driven expressions about the fan's connection to the characters. Those type of expressions and connections between fans and characters, especially comic book characters, have given professionals an inroad in discussion of key psychological and social issues with patients for transformational growth.

This concept of using comic book characters is not a new style of treatment. Dr. Lawrence Rubin and Dr. Harry Livesay (2006) describe the use of fantasy play therapy as a mode of conflict resolution, tension reduction, and problem solving within childhood and young adult therapeutic sessions and the means to deal with physical/sexual abuse, issues surrounding having a disability, trauma, loss, and grief in the context of adult psychotherapeutic sessions. This ability allows the psychologist to work with the patient on their trauma by using the person's fandom to incorporate a structured set of therapies tied into the patient's favorite character or series (Scarlet, 2017).

The last level of activity that fandom performs is one of community development. Jenkins (1992) makes the argument in this section by stating that this level of activity:

> *"Capture something essential about fandom, its status as a utopian community... the fans' recognition that fandom offers not so much as an escape from reality as an alternative reality whose values may be more humane and democratic than those held by mundane society."* (p. 280)

Fandom exists in a hyperreal state that allows those within the community of fans a sense of closeness with strangers that have similar cultural tastes and maintain strong social ties, even though they may only have interacted with others for just a few hours. The shared social experiences members of fandom have act as the foundation of all interactions among fans.

The world of fandom uses the norms established by comic books and expands those norms to help guide communal interactions. These norms allow for members of the fandom to talk about the personal issues they are facing under the guise of discussing issues associated with their favorite graphic novel (Suskind, 2014). San Diego Comic-Con gives a shared space for fans, content creators, psychological professionals, and researchers to interact with one another in a physical space to connect the issues facing characters in various novels, films, television shows, and games with the issues fans face on a daily basis.

## Conventions as a Natural Outlet to Socialize within Fandoms

Community development is central to the comic convention experience (Rosenberg, 2010). There are promotional materials given out or sold during these events which are highly sought after memorabilia. For example, there are typically limited-edition Funko dolls that are only sold during the San Diego Comic-Con, collector pins which can only be found at certain times, and memorabilia that is crucial for some fans to obtain. Conan O'Brien has made a set of "Ultimate Conan Funkos" designed to celebrate the San Diego Comic-Con community by creating a multi-layered artifact of fandom (e.g., the Funko figure is the collectable currently as it relates to fan culture). Conan incorporates comic book icons like Superman, Hellboy, and Jedi into the design of the Funko by dressing up as those characters for the Funko figure, and they are shared during the shows he tapes during San Diego Comic-Con.

Erving Goffman (2007) essentially argued that these artifacts of fandom act as the means to present one's self as a fan to others in the fandom. Fans collect Funkos and other hard to find items. They attend panels during the Comic-Con. They get an autographs on and a picture with celebrities like John Barrowman, R.L. Stine, or Brian Michael Bendis. These actions allows fans to collect cultural capital (Throsby, 2011) as a means for creating shared social experiences based on the discussions of those artifacts (e.g., "remember that time we stood in line to get Neil Gaiman's signature"), maintaining a person's place in the hierarchy of the fandom (e.g., "I'm the only one that has all 16 *Doctor Who* signatures including John Hurt, Peter Cushing, and Richard E. Grant), or as tokens of private memories that the fan shared with the fandom in the form of autobiographical narratives (Tilton, 2014).

Perhaps the best example of how conventions perform the act of being a natural outlet for fandoms to socialize is the ability of these events to showcase the more obscure elements of popular culture. It is these films, television shows, and other creative works that find their place at conventions, as these events will generally host a critical mass of fans that share the same niche tastes; it is one of the few times that fans that share the same taste can be together in the same room to enjoy them. These groups are best known as cult followings.

*Cult Followings*

The concept of a cult following is based around the idea that a "rabid" group of fans fixate on some form of mediated content that either is:

a.) a cerebral classic like *Blade Runner*,

b.) a surrealist show like *This is Spinal Tap*,

c.) a low-budget laugh fest like *Rocky Horror Picture Show*, *The Room*, or *Clerks*, or d.) a sect of series that never reached a critical mass of success during the time it originally aired like *Firefly*, *Twin Peaks*, or *Mission Hill* (Olson, 2018).

The definition of what makes a cult film or cult television series is relatively fluid. Therefore, the definition of a cult following is also fluid. One reasonable interpretation for this term is a cult following is made up of fans that self-identify as enjoying a cerebral classic, surrealist show, low-budget laugh fest, or sect of series listed above.

It also means that these fans will be more likely to "hyper-perform" the Jenkins' Five Levels of Fandom Activities. Cult followings typically have more restrictions when compared to other fan focuses (e.g., not many public outlets might show *The Room*, or getting copies of the posters for *Clerks* might be difficult). Therefore, fans of cult classics will become more emotional in a convention space, as their object of affection is on display and potentially enjoyed by others.

Conventions represent one of the few times that fans of these cult classics can display the artifacts of their favorite programming (e.g., wearing a Browncoat is important to fans of *Firefly / Serenity*) or performing the meaningful rituals of fandom (e.g., all of the audience participation associated with attending a viewing the *Rocky Horror Picture Show*). These artifacts and rituals associated with cult programming and cult followings makes up the "voluntary performances" (Rothenbuhler, 1998, p. 27). These performances that fans take part in show their connection to the fandom. In addition, those fans can recite the entire movie and invoke key pieces of dialogue to express their emotions (e.g., saying "Oh, hi Mark" communicates a level of absurdity that is understood by fans of *The Room*).

## Conclusion

Conventions can provide a framework for understanding ideal representations of fandom and the actions that occur among fans of popular culture. The visual depictions of fandom shown through the convention center when those centers host these expressions of popular culture are also home to fans and their passions. These passions can be a joyous presentation of love for the imaginary and can also be a malevolent environment to those that break the norms of geek culture. It is fair to note the potential harms within this environment as a gentle warning that any human interaction can be psychologically damaging when those people involved do not observe Wheaton's Law of "Don't be a dick."

These events should be on the radar of anybody that interacts with geek culture regularly. They often act as the epicenter of fan culture and fan studies. Fans can define part of their identity based on their ability to attend these conventions year after year. Others develop parasocial relationships with celebrities that show up at these events. Still more may come to these gatherings as a means to feel like they are an insider who knows what is happening. Finally, there is a select group of fans that attends for the same reason they would attend a family reunion: they feel like they are part of a bigger whole than themselves. Further interest in conventions and the power they provide for therapy clients is clearly a must for the clinical realm of psychology as the power held is more than meets the eye.

# References

Braun, M. (2018, September). A Visual Guide to The Big Lebowski. Retrieved February 18, 2019, from https://web.archive.org/web/20190219143721/https://www.stevengbraun.com/page.php?p=item&type=datavis&id=2018_the-big-lebowski

Chonin, N. (2012, August 06). 'BUFFY'-HEADS FIGHT BACK / Fansites organize to force Fox TV out of copyright Dark Ages. Retrieved February 19, 2019, from https://web.archive.org/web/20190219152115/https://www.sfgate.com/entertainment/article/BUFFY-HEADS-FIGHT-BACK-Fansites-organize-to-2789418.php

Cohen, J. (2009). Parasocial interaction and identification. In Mary B. Oliver & Robin Nabi, eds., Thousand Oaks, CA: *The Sage Handbook of Media Processes and Effects,* Sage, 223-236.

Consalvo, M. (2003). Cyber-slaying media fans: Code, digital poaching, and corporate control of the internet. *Journal of Communication Inquiry, 27*(1), 67-86. doi:10.1177/0196859902238641

Goffman, E. (2007). *The presentation of self in everyday life.* London: Penguin Books.

Jenkins, H. (1992). *Textual poachers: Television fans and participatory culture.* New York: Routledge.

Jenkins, H. (2006). *Convergence culture: Where old and new media collide.* New York: New York University Press.

Kefir, N., & Corsini, R. J. (1974). Dispositional sets: A contribution to typology. *Journal of Individual Psychology, 30* (2), 163.

Lau, J. C., Gbinigie, A., DePass, T., Boccamazzo, R. & Thompson, C. (2019). *Gaming while other: Accessibility, Diversity Representation.* Presented September 30, 2019 at PAX West 2019 in Seattle, WA.

Lévy, P. (1997). *Collective Intelligence: Mankinds Emerging World in Cyberspace.* Cambridge, Mass: Perseus Books.

Matz, S., Chan, Y.W.F., & Kosinski, M. (2016). Models of personality. In Tkalčič, M., De Carolis, B., de Gemmis, M., Odić, A., & Košir, A. (eds) *Emotions and Personality in Personalized Services.* Springer, Cham, Switzerland. 35-54.

McArthur, J. A. (2009). Digital subculture: A geek meaning of style. *Journal of Communication Inquiry, 33*(1), 58–70. https://doi.org/10.1177/0196859908325676

Moore, J. C. (2002). Comment: Copyright protection or fan loyalty-must entertainment companies choose? Alternate solutions for addressing internet fan sites. *North Carolina Journal of Law & Technology, 3*(2), 273-304. Retrieved February 19, 2019, from http://ncjolt.org/wp-content/uploads/2016/09/18_3NC-JLTech2732001-2002.pdf

Oestriecher, B. (2018, December 02). 5 Huge Heel Turns WWE Must Pull Off ASAP. Retrieved February 19, 2019, from https://web.archive.org/web/20181203213509/https://www.forbes.com/sites/blakeoestriecher/2018/12/02/5-huge-heel-turns-wwe-must-pull-off-asap/

Olson, C. J. (2018). *100 Greatest Cult Films*. Lanham, MA: Rowman & Littlefield.

Petrakovitz, C. (2018, November 19). Watch every Marvel movie *and* show in the perfect order. Retrieved February 18, 2019, from https://web.archive.org/web/20190212132219/https://www.cnet.com/how-to/marvel-cinematic-universe-timeline-order-avengers-4/

Riesman, A. (2017, June 27). First Captain America Became Evil, Then the Comics World Erupted. Retrieved February 19, 2019, from https://web.archive.org/web/20181202044414/https://www.vulture.com/2017/06/marvel-hydra-captain-america-nick-spencer.html

Robinson, M. (2018, October 05). Why Wearing Your Team's Jersey is the Only Socially Acceptable Cosplay. Retrieved February 17, 2019, from https://web.archive.org/web/20190217172454/https://melmagazine.com/en-us/story/why-wearing-your-teams-jersey-is-the-only-socially-acceptable-cosplay

Rosenberg, R. S. (2010, August 6). Comic-Con: Nerd and Geek Community. Retrieved June 6, 2019, from https://www.psychologytoday.com/us/blog/the-superheroes/201008/comic-con-nerd-and-geek-community

Rothenbuhler, E. W. (1998). *Ritual Communication: From Everyday Conversation to Mediated Ceremony*. Thousand Oaks, CA: Sage.

Rubin, L., & Livesay, H. (2006). Look, up in the sky! Using superheroes in play therapy. *International Journal of Play Therapy, 15*(1), 117-133. doi:10.1037/h0088911

Scarlett, J. (2017, May 11). Superhero Therapy-Healing through fiction. Retrieved March 3, 2019, from https://www.psychologytoday.com/us/blog/the-real-superheroes/201705/superhero-therapy-healing-through-fiction

Sim, J. (2018, February 20). Where Does 'Rogue One' Fit Into the Machete Order? Retrieved February 18, 2019, from https://web.archive.org/web/20190218181607/https://futurism.media/where-does-rogue-one-fit-into-the-machete-order

Suskind, A. (2014, February 17). The Rise of Superhero Therapy: Comic Books as Psychological Treatment. Retrieved February 19, 2019, from https://web.archive.org/web/20181229220637/https://www.thedailybeast.com/the-rise-of-superhero-therapy-comic-books-as-psychological-treatment

Throsby, D. (2011). Cultural capital. *A Handbook of Cultural Economics,* 142-146. doi:10.4337/9781781008003.00025

Tilton, S. (2014). Mobile public memory: The (digital/physical) (artifacts/souvenirs) of the (archiver/tourist). *SAGE Open, 4*(3), 1-11. doi:10.1177/2158244014547324

Tilton, S. (2016, June). The Four Temperaments of Fandom. Retrieved February 17, 2019, from https://www.academia.edu/26449531/The_Four_Temperaments_of_Fandom

Walsh, D. (2016, May). Fans Protest The 'Captain America' Controversy Through Positivity. Retrieved February 19, 2019, from https://web.archive.org/web/20170317145443/http://uproxx.com/gammasquad/captain-america-fans-holocaust-museum/

# When Heroes Become Villains: Developing Parasocial Relationships with Characters and the Expectancy Violation of Meeting the Actors

# 9

Emory S. Daniel Jr., PhD

In 2013 at a Tampa Bay Comic Con, three actors from the television series *Game of Thrones* hosted a panel concerning the show. Rory McCann (Sandor "The Hound" Clegane), Jason Mamoa (Khal Drogo), and Masie Williams (Arya Stark) participated in this panel, sharing their experience in the show and answering questions from the audience. One of the most emotional moments came from Masie Williams concerning one of her colleagues and friends. One of the attendees asked a question to the panelists about what it was like working with Jack Gleeson. Gleeson played the character "Joffrey Baratheon" in the series, and the character is generally hated amongst fans due to his cruel and vile nature towards people and animals, while cowering in fear during any real danger. When the question came up, Rory responded by sarcastically saying:

*"Jack? Well it's no problem really, because he, in real life, he's a little shit. So, there's no acting required, and it's pretty easy, really."*

Masie had a much more honest and sympathetic response towards the question:

*"Rory's lying, Jack is really nice. Fantastic actor, obviously because you guys all hate him. But um, yeah, but he's lovely, and he's really nice, and he gets a load of hate in the street, and that's really sad. 'Cause... He's lovely, and he doesn't even want to be an actor that's how... He's fantastic, and doesn't even want to act. He's a good guy. Stop hating on Jack. Hate Joffrey, not Jack.*

Clear from the differing viewpoints of the actors from the series itself, there are many different ways of viewing playable characters within media series that impact how they are seen off screen. The viewpoints held by all individuals help to demarcate what and how people feel about them, their acting, and perceptions of who they are as a person outside of their acting career as well.

## The Fallacy of Fanbases

There are many actors that experience the same hostility for different reasons. Robert Pattinson who plays Edward Cullen in the famous movie series *Twilight*. While he did not enjoy his character in the film and thought he was written as "too perfect," he noted that fans screaming at him felt *"like the sound you hear at the gates of hell."* Jake Lloyd who played young Anakin Skywalker for the *Star Wars* prequels expressed how other children were mean to him after his role in the film.

Many actors have trouble with life after the roles they played in popular media. Actors often find themselves not liking the character they played or the film they starred in, or even the fans they interact with frequently. Interestingly, the role the actor plays can create fan bases that actors were not expecting.

However, most actors have an expectation about who their character is, and how they should act. Actors have stated that they hate playing the protagonist. They could experience hostility from fans when their real-life self does not mirror their character on screen. William Shatner, who played Captain Kirk on the hit sci-fi show *Star Trek*, has expressed his anger with fans who constantly walk up to him to ask for an autograph in public. This demeanor has not gone unnoticed by *Star Trek* fans, who have called him "Captain Jerk." It has also spurred many online articles and forum posts on Quora and Reddit, sharing negative stories about their interactions with Shatner at conventions. While generally being unkind to fan bases would turn any loyal fan in the wrong direction, it is an interesting question to determine how much do an actor's and their character personality match. Perhaps more importantly, the actors are supposed to behave their on-screen character according to their fans? However, it raises the question: why do fans feel this way? Why do people have expectations concerning how a celebrity interacts with their fan base? Why are the connections so important to fans, knowing that they've never met their favorite characters? And how can scholars and therapists apply this research into application with their clients? It is important to first understand what connections we have with characters and the actors that play them.

## Parasocial Interaction

A viewer's one-way experience with a spokesperson is known as a parasocial interaction (PSI). Although the spokespeople typically do not feel them on screen, viewers still perceive realness in the communication. Cohen (2009) refers to these interactions as the emotions and behaviors an audience member experiences while viewing the person in the media. The feelings are often consistent with the emotions that the character is experiencing or trying to convey (Klimmt et al., 2006). The parasocial interaction is central to the relationship between two individuals as it has the potential to influence advertising a product based on the interaction a person has with the celebrity. Horton and Wohl (1956) further explain that PSI is a "seeming face to face relationship between spectator and performer," (p.215) and that a character can become a greater part of a social network through factors like commitment and identification (Eyal & Dailey, 2012). With greater identification and engagement, audience members can experience a near real world social relationship, even though the actual relationship is one-sided (Horton & Wohl, 1956). Moreover, Giles (2002) suggests that these one-sided interactions can become a usual social activity for the viewer. Although viewers do not consider these interactions to be comparable to actual social relationships, they often act similarly to how they would in typical social relationships. Similar emotions can occur that parallel social interaction, which makes them comparable in some ways (Daniel & Westerman, 2017).

Social interactions and PSI often share some similar traits with each other. One such commonality is from Giles (2002), who offers many different levels to PSI and how they compare and contrast with social interactions. For instance, Giles exemplifies two main factors for PSI that shares similarities with social interaction: companionship and personal identity. Companionship refers to the idea that viewers would remind them of other friends that they knew and thus would be able to increase or decrease the value of PSI. Additionally, personal identity refers to viewers using character situations and behaviors as a way of understanding their lives. Self-reflexive elements help create a strong bond with the viewer, and in some cases, PSI is valued more than actual social friendships (Gleich, 1996). Through companionship and personal identity, there are some similarities on how PSI can parallel and even supersede social relationships.

With PSI, there is also variance in the strength of interactions within the relationship itself (Gleich, 1996). First, viewers have to feel the need for companionship through their experience of the actor, which is gratifying a need for social interaction. Next, people might be so attached to a character and that they would enjoy seeing them in other programs or commercials, which is known as person-program interaction. This may even lead to empathetic interaction, which refers to some degree of affective, behavioral response from the observer to the actor on the screen (Gleich, 1996). For example, a viewer might verbally address a character, or feel empathy if the character makes a mistake. Within entertainment media and advertising, PSI can be a very sophisticated experience for an audience member. For instance, John Snow from the show *Game of Thrones* never addresses the audience, however when stabbed several times by his peers in the show, fans took to social media and expressed their sadness, anger, denial, bargaining, and acceptance towards his supposed fate (Daniel et al., 2018; Daniel & Westerman, 2017). It is because of the continued exposure that we feel like there is legitimate interaction and thus form an emotional bond with the character that enriches each subsequent interaction.

## Parasocial Relationships

While PSI focuses on the singular interaction that the viewer has with the character, the idea of PSR focuses more on recurring interactions. Horton and Wohl (1956) coined the term parasocial relationship by the way audience members develop a one-sided relationship described as a perceived real experience. Parasocial relationships (PSR) are relationships between viewers and characters they watch, and can potentially involve emotions and reactions towards the characters after the interaction has ceased (Horton & Wohl, 1956). The viewer, in this case, feels like they are having an interaction long after the program has concluded (Cohen, 2009). Some of the original research on PSR and interactions stems from the relationships that people develop towards television news anchors, which in part is due to the illusion of connection that the anchor makes while he/she was staring at the camera (Levy, 1979). People create an illusion of presence by watching and feeling as if the anchor was talking directly to them, where a news anchor feels as if they are present with the viewer watching them in the living room; even though they cannot physically see them (Noble, 1975).

Rosaen and Dibble (2008) stated that people typically know PSRs are not real, but other research has indicated that the experiences felt by these states of being are similar to interpersonal relationships (Horton & Strauss, 1957). The perceived similarity of relationships occurs because they have similar cognitive and emotional effects on the viewer (Schramm & Hartmann, 2008). Development of the relationship also shares similarities with other social relationships. Both types of relationships contained components such as proximity, attraction, similar attitudes or values, and frequency. As time progresses, and if a viewer watches this character for long enough, then comfort, closeness, perceived friendship, and self-disclosure increases creating a sense of closeness (Eyal & Dailey, 2012). However, the main difference between a PSR and a social relationship is the reciprocity of the relationship (Horton & Wohl, 1956). Compared to an actual friendship, there is little or no real interaction that occurs between the viewer and the character. Therefore, some individuals may prefer PSR to actual relationships because of vicarious social experiences (Vorderer et al., 2004) without many demands, obligations, and responsibilities that real relationships may require.

While PSI is not perceived as having the same interaction standards compared to face-to-face social interaction, for the viewer, PSI feels like a genuine attachment with social interactions between the viewer and the character.

## Fandom

Being a fan is an experience within the area of popular culture. Whether an individual is captivated by comics, fantasy, sci-fi, games, anime, etc., people watching have an attachment to the phenomena that they are experiencing. Cavicchi (2014) argued that fandom is "an extraordinary form of audience that includes everything from emotional attachment to performers of obsessive collecting" (p. 52). Typically, fandom is perceived as a mediated action, as the individual is not actually engaging interpersonally with the celebrity on a regular interpersonal basis. While a fan can parasocially interact with John Snow, it is far less likely to communicate with Kit Harrington interpersonally face-to-face or through social media. In turn, this is why many of the interactions with celebrities are so treasured at Cons, because they are very special to the fan. While individuals feel distant from the object or person that they are viewing, it is important to them that they establish a relationship despite the distance (McCutcheon et al., 2002). Fans go to comic cons in order to feel accepted and closer to their fandoms. If they know that a celebrity or several cast members will be at a con, this increases the want and need to be a part of the culture. For instance, in 2008, the first *Twilight* movie was announced to be released, and a special trailer and panel would be offered at the San

Diego Comic-Con. Fans swarmed to the convention and it became the first time that San Diego Comic-Con completely sold out. However, fandom has only increased, as comic-con regularly sells out, and shows like *Game of Thrones* have yearly panels with extensive attendance. All that said, fandom is important to people because it contributes to personal identity, is emphasized within communities with shared social identity, and adds a social interaction to their fandom towards the character.

Fiske (1992) established a model that included three main elements to fandom. First, discrimination and distinction was a category in the model; second fandoms create culture and original work (e.g. jargon, dress, theories, art), and third fans also establish cultural capital that emphasizes areas like knowledge or collections. Discrimination and distinction establishes boundaries within fandom groups. Much like the premises within social identity, things like: time, money, collections, participation all establish levels of fandom. The boundaries (which vary in fan groups), weed out the "true fans" from people that are considered "casuals" or someone who is not as dedicated as those who fall under the true fandom category. Waiting an entire Con to watch a panel of *Star Wars* characters would be perceived as a stronger level of fandom. Culture applies here as well, as fans show off their Funko Pop! figures from their favorite series, signed by their favorite actors. Other fans of the series recognize this and want to engage in conversation including jargon, fan theories, and rumors about upcoming games. Third, video games are another example of social hierarchy through potentially how many times they have been to a Con to see their favorite show. This creates group boundaries and separates groups by creating social capital amongst those most interested (Loporcaro et al., 2014).

All these variables determine the strength of the interaction and/ or connection that is perceived between a viewer and a character/actor in a series. Talking with a celebrity or getting their autograph might be a momentous occasion, particularly if the viewer is a fan of the product the character/actor that they are featured. However, the problem links back to the beginning of this chapter: when fans see a visual or verbal inconsistency with their perceived view of a character/actor's demeanor.

## Expectancy Violation

As a whole, through interpersonal relationships, individuals have a shared schema on how the people in each relationship should respond to one another (Planalp & Honeycutt, 1985). Over time, as relationships develop, individuals observe their friends in different contexts, thus being able to predict future responses to encounters (Burgoon & Hale, 1988). While fans typically expect celebrities to not remember certain gestures or interactions, a fan would feel that a celebrity would be excited to meet someone who admires their work. However, as people experience more frequent interactions, there is an opportunity for behavior that deviates from the perceived norm. These deviations act as any behavior that fails to live up to an idea of expected behavior (Davis & Todd, 1985).

Divergences from anticipated behavior fall within the category of a recognizable theory in communication research called Expectancy Violation Theory (EVT). At the core, EVT explains how fans and celebrities alike will fail to meet expectations in their interactions, though this can be a positive or negative violation of the norm. For example, celebrities might play a villain and fans might perceive them as a villain. However, in reality, the actor is perceivably a genuinely kind person. In turn, this is a positive violation from the perceived norm. However, the opposite could be true, too, which would lead to a negative violation.

Cohen (2010) argues there is a differentiation between EVT in the context of social and otherwise mediated relationships. Traditional social interactions would experience EVT because of direct communication between both parties. However, audiences do not have a reason to develop expectations involving interaction or expressions of relationship commitment from a media figure. Mainly because, unless the audience is yelling at the television, there is no social interaction, and the characters will not communicate in return. That said, Cohen (2010) found that expectancy violations occur in mass media messages through parasocial relationships. This process happens in three different ways with both social and parasocial relationships (see Table 9.1).

| Relational Expectancy Violation (REV) | |
|---|---|
| Defined | Examples of REV |
| First, relationships suffer when a partner deviated from moral relationship norms. Things like abusive nature, drug abuse, and sexual harassment could all be examples within EVT existing with moral norms | For example, Johnny Depp has been a beloved actor from his roles in the *Pirates of the Caribbean* movies, has had a streak of violent behavior, leading to moral violations with fans, thus creating a strain for subsequent roles with *Fantastic Beasts*. |
| Second, trust violations can occur when someone breaks a promise, or even acting in an inauthentic manner to impress others (Jones & Burdette, 1994). | In an ABC News morning segment, broadcasters interviewed Harvii Kindlon, a young man who tried to give Megan Fox a yellow rose at a *Transformers* movie premiere, which she snubbed him. While Kindlon went on record to say he was not upset or felt ill feelings towards Fox, he did mention that he felt rejected and disappointed with the encounter. |
| Third, social violations occur when an individual expects their friends to adhere to a code of social decency. | Being rude or making others feel small are considered breaking rules within this social conduct of universal rules (Argyle & Henderson, 1985) |

Table 9.1 Relational Expectancy Violations.

However, all three instances can be turned into a positive violation. JK Rowling wrote a young girl named Natalie into her book *Harry Potter and the Goblet of Fire*, while donating millions of pounds to various charitable organizations. David Harbour, an actor from the show *Stranger Things*, fulfilled a promise to officiate a wedding in Illinois, and Tom Hanks took selfies with a newly married couple in New York's Central Park. These are all examples of positive violations.

Obviously, when violations occur, there can be a plethora of different reactions that will subsequently occur. However, violations are not created equal. We might expect a celebrity to act a certain way based on their character. If it's a villain, and the actor is nice, then that is a positive violation, and vice versa. Arousal occurs as an outcome to the previously mentioned positive or negative violation. The psychological attention of the fan is aroused from the message(s) delivered by the celebrity (Burgoon & Hale, 1988). The message itself may not be that negative, as in William Shatner not wanting to sign an autograph while he's at dinner, but the negative arousal towards Shatner might be much worse than the action. Burgoon & Hale, 1988 (1978) categorized our violations into different levels of tolerance towards those committing the violations. People typically have either low or high levels of tolerance. So even if a celebrity is rude, and the fan does not expect it, they still might not feel that threatened by the deviation. However, there are cases where expectations are actually understood and they match what actually occurs. For example, if a fan heard about how kind Tom Hanks is in real life, and upon meeting him, experiences the same positive interaction, there would be no violation.

## Expectations Versus the Myth

Perhaps the most difficult component of the conversation concerning interactions between fans and celebrities is the client's point of view. What happens when a client meets their fandom hero and the expectations were not what they anticipated? How does one work with this difficulty when the real world doesn't match their fandom expectations? One likely scenario would be the creation of a problem to the client's psyche, self-object, and warp their sense of reality. When this occurs, clients require adequate support to help them through the process of rectifying their self-concept and personal fandom feelings, but there are additional aspects of care that can be used as proactive clinical management.

First, it's important to understand that many actors and streamers are not aware of the viewers communicating with them via different areas of media. Fans can have meaningful, genuine interactions when viewing their favorite fandom, and the actor likely is unaware of the other person due to the anonymity of being on screen. Therefore, the actor might not be having the same experience as the fan, which also increases the fan's expectancy violation towards the celebrity. This often generates scenarios similar to William Shatner's mentioned above and creates a discord between the fan and the actor. Clinicians can help prevent this from becoming overwhelming when they communicate about what their client's expectations of the meeting may or may not be, with an effort to keep them within a rational boundary of reality.

Second, there are fans that like to remain anonymous and prefer that the celebrity is not aware of them out of personal shyness or because of privacy concerns relating to voyeurism. Nabi et al. (2003) argues there is a role within voyeurism with reality-based television and other media based applications. This becomes not only a privacy concern for celebrities, but also a stalking concern as fans might pursue the celebrity physically (in rare cases) or through transmedia bordering upon obsession. Ultimately many actors have expressed concerns that their lives are their business, and the fan needs to respect that privacy. Having conversations about healthy boundaries and what they consist of can help with these concerns within the clinical realm. Enforcement may be difficult in some cases, but creating a list of what is reality based, what the character may represent, and consistent reminders that an individual being viewed is an actor playing a role who likely does not represent those same characteristics in real life is superbly helpful.

Lastly, it is important to understand the dynamics between character and the celebrity. While expectations can be based in and out of reality that the actors do not match the fictional character, it should always be understood that the character is not a real representation of the actor themselves. Perhaps even more importantly, even if the actor is not necessarily playing a fictional character, they might put on an alternate version of themselves to keep viewership and appearance. The idea of being "on" all the time is difficult in streaming and acting, and it should be respected by all parties. By discussing these different viewpoints in the therapy room, the client can express themselves accurately, but also the clinician can help with bringing the fantasy back into a reality based intervention.

These suggestions may not change the way fans perceive celebrities or their favorite show, movie, or game, but it is important to lessen the violation whenever possible to ensure the client's meeting celebrities does not impact them negatively. Regardless of whether the valence of the interaction is positive or negative, transparency between the celebrity and their fans are important to positive interaction and self-identity. Celebrities hold a great deal of power through their mass-mediated microphones, and if they can communicate a level of respect with their fan base, this will only increase the joy of fan and celebrity interactions. Fans feel a connection to their fandoms and the messages from them, and the impact upon their self-identity makes these instances important to not just negotiate interpersonally, but also intrapsychically. By having these conversations ahead of the meeting, many personal difficulties can be avoided and proactively circumvented.

# References

Burgoon, J. K., & Hale, J. L. (1988). Nonverbal expectancy violations: Model elaboration and application to immediacy behaviors. Communication Monographs, 55, 58–79.

Cavicchi, D. (2014). Fandom before" fan": Shaping the history of enthusiastic audiences. Reception: Texts, Readers, Audiences, History, 6(1), 52-72. https://doi.org/10.5325/reception.6.1.0052

Cohen, E. (2010). Expectancy violations in relationships with friends and media figures. *Communication Research Reports 27*(2), 97-111

Cohen, J. (2009). Parasocial interaction and identification. In Mary B. Oliver & Robin Nabi, eds., Thousand Oaks, CA: *The Sage Handbook of Media Processes and Effects,* Sage, 223-236.

Daniel, E. S., Crawford, E., & Westerman, D. (2018). Understanding the influence of Social Media Influencers: Using the Lens of Taylor's Strategy Wheel and Parasocial Interaction to Understand Online Vaping Communities. *The Journal of Interactive Advertising* https://doi.org/10.1080/15252019.2018.1488637

Daniel E. S. & Westerman, D. (2017). Valar Morghulis (All parasocial men must die): Having nonfictional responses to a fictional character. *Communication Research Reports.*

Davis, K. E., & Todd, M. J. (1985). Assessing friendship prototypes. Paradigm cases and relationship description. In S. W. Duck & D. Perlman (Eds.), Understanding personal relationships: An interdisciplinary approach (pp. 17–38). Beverly Hills, CA: Sage.

Eyal, K., & Dailey, R. (2012). Examining relationship maintenance in parasocial relationships. *Mass Communication and Society, 15,* 758-781.

Fiske, J. (1992). The cultural economy of fandom. In L. A. Lewis (Ed.), The adoring audience: Fan culture and popular media, 30-49. New York; London: Routledge. https://doi:10.4324/9780203181539

Giles, D. (2002). Parasocial interaction: A review of the literature and a model for future Research. *Media Psychology, 4,* 279–305.

Gleich, U. (1996), Sind Fernsehpersonen die "Freunde" des Zuschauers? Ein Vergleich zwischen parasozialen und realen sozialen Beziehungen [Are TV personalities/characters "friends" of the viewers? A comparison between parasocial and real social relationships], in Fernsehen als "Beziehingskiste": Parasoziale beziehungen und interaktionen mit TV-personen [TV as "relationship crate": Parasocial rela- tionships and interactions with TV personalities/characters], P. Vorderer, ed., Opladen, Germany: Westdeutscher Verlag, 113–44.

Horton, D. & Strauss, A. (1957). Interaction in audience-participation shows. *American Journal of Sociology, 62,* 579–587.

Horton, D. & Wohl, R. (1956). Mass communication and para-social interaction. *Psychiatry, 19,* 215–229.

Klimmt, C., Hartmann, T. & Schramm, H. (2006). Parasocial interactions and relationships. In J, Bryant & Vorderer, P. eds., Mahwah, NJ: *Psychology of entertainment*, Lawrence Erlbaum Associates, 291-313.

Levy, M. (1979), Watching TV news as para-social interaction. *Journal of Broadcasting, 23,* 69–80.

Loporcaro, J. A., Ortega, C. R., & Egnoto, M. J. (2014). The hardcore scorecard: Defining, quantifying and understanding "hardcore" video game culture. Proceedings of the New York State Communication Association, (2013)7, 1-15.

McCutcheon, L., Lange, R., Houran, J. (2002). Conceptualization and measure of celebrity worship. *British Journal of Psychology, 93,* 67-87.

Nabi, R., Biely, E. N., Morgan, S. J., & Stitt, C. R. (2003). Reality-based television programming and the psychology of its appeal. *Media Psychology, 5*(4), 303–330

Noble, G. (1975). *Children in Front of the Small Screen.* Beverly Hills, Calif.: Sage.

Planalp, S., & Honeycutt, J. (1985). Events that increase uncertainty in personal relationships. *Human Communication Research, 11,* 593–604.

Rosaen, S. & Dibble, J. (2008). Investigating the relationships among child's age, parasocial interaction, and the social realism of favorite television characters, *Communication Research Reports, 25*(2), 145-154.

Schramm, H. and Hartmann, T. (2008). The PSI-process scales: A new measure to assess the intensity and breadth of parasocial processes. *Communications: The European Journal of Communication Research, 33*(4), 385-401.

Vorderer, P., Klimmt, C. & Ritterfeld, U. (2004). Enjoyment: At the heart of media entertainment. *Communication Theory, 14*(4), 388-408.

# No Girls Allowed: The Gendered Attendance of Conventions

# 10

Sarah A. Hays, PsyD

## A Note to the Reader

It would be prudent to point out a couple of things prior to your reading this chapter. Firstly, that the term "geek convention(s)" is purposed only for this writing – rarely does anyone actually uses this terminology. This is used to refer to the general genre of geek-related interests that pertain to convention events (such as anime conventions, gaming conventions, and the like). The typical terminology used to describe conventions would be either by their actual name, or perhaps even as short as the proper noun use of "con."

Secondly, this chapter will be an overview of the way geek conventions have evolved over time, particularly relating to gender and Social Identity Theory. Though it would be ideal to address all gender identities rather than the duality between male and female, very little has been written about the experience of those outside the male-female dyad in this context.

There is much written and worthy of discussion beyond the topic of gender, and it is encouraged that the reader seek further information on the experience of any minority (in gender, age, disability, race, heritage, and beyond) in convention spaces. It is entirely possible (and this author argues probable) that those who do not fit the White, cisgender, straight male category of "traditional geeks" have experienced some sort of discrimination in their lived experience of the geek identity and its communal spaces. This is a chapter based on the context of its time and the available data – with the hope that in coming years, there will be more to report regarding gender and its greater spectrum relating to conventions.

## A Review of Social Identity Theory

Social Identity Theory was created to describe how social interactivity and grouping occurs (Tajfel & Turner, 1979). Overall, this theory states that individuals we develop social identity through understanding "those aspects of an individual's self-image that derive from the social categories to which he perceives himself as belonging" (p. 40). Per Tajfel and Turner (1979), people like to have *positive* social identities, which relates to the relative quality of personal self-esteem. To create good self-esteem with social identity, people compare their affiliated social groups (in-groups) with other groups (out-groups) in hopes that their affiliations are superior to the others. If they do not find their in-groups to be satisfactory or positive, they will often either try to improve their in-groups or leave for the more preferable out-groups. Tajfel and Turner (1979) suggest people compare themselves through personal and individual attributes or qualities (e.g. race, language, unique descriptors). A common and unfortunate side-effect of comparing in-group to out-group is often a negative interpretation of the out-group, in order to compensate and view the in-group as positive. For the active comparison below, the "in-group" will be considered male con attendees and the "out-group" will be considered female con attendees.

In an article on the exploration of the psychology behind geek cultural engagement, McCain et al. (2015) described belongingness as a crucial element of social identity - where geeks tend to find belongingness through common connections. Given that the common connections in geek communities vary, the simplest way to consider these are through an anthropological lens, such as cultural artifacts and consumer goods (McCain et al., 2015). Connecting around artifacts and goods revolves primarily around sharing and deepening of knowledge, particularly through fandoms, and is used as social currency in interactions (McCain et al., 2015). Belongingness and its role in group cohesion is an important aspect of conventions, attendees, and social comparison groups for those within geek culture.

## Conventions: A Brief Demographic History

When considering *who* attended early conventions, there is little description given in the available literature and history; this is typical of past documentation of fandoms (Fuller-Seeley, 2017). Most early records on convention statistics are from those attending the convention rather than from the convention staff. Current convention companies (such as ReedPOP, who have put on many conventions including PAX and New York Comic Con) sporadically release press statements on general attendee data. These, at most, include a gender binary on attendees; more typically, the general headcount is all that is shared. Furthermore, this data is difficult to obtain beyond news articles about conventions and is nearly impossible to find on the website of any given convention itself.

From the data that does exist and is available, modern gender split of attendance for New York and San Diego's Comic Cons are about half women and half men (SDCC; Eventbrite, 2014; Holloway, 2018). This is a far cry from SDCC's origin, attended by exactly one woman in its inaugural event of 300 total attendees (Mayer, 2019). Though the data is difficult to find in consistent hard numbers, there is repeatedly a discussion of the balancing of gendered attendance – citing, in particular, the release of the movie *Twilight* and its debut in the con space in 2009 (Holloway, 2018; Scott, 2019). This resulted in significant backlash with several attendees toting signs stating *Twilight has ruined comic-con*; though unspoken, the underlying issue was directed at the increase in female fans (Holloway, 2018).

A survey of self-identified female geeks revealed that as of 2014, 70.5 percent were in attendance of "nerd events" (Robinson, 2014; see Table 10.1). Nearly 60 percent of participants indicated participation in geek interests multiple times a day, and over 90 percent participated on a weekly basis or more (Robinson, 2014). A breakdown of the reported interests and engagement in sectors of geek culture showed a diverse range of responses. Many of the identified subcultural categories are present in the convention space.

| Respondent Subcultural Interests | |
| --- | --- |
| Subcultural Interest | Respondent Participation (%) |
| Cosplay | 30.1 |
| Anime-Based Media | 33.2 |
| Collectibles | 43.5 |
| Table-Top Gaming | 50.3 |
| Cartoon-Based Media | 54.4 |
| Comics | 60.1 |
| STEM | 66.8 |
| "Nerd Events" | 70.5 |
| Video Games | 73.1 |
| Fantasy/Scifi | 78.2 |
| Internet Culture | 90.2 |

Table 10.1. Respondent Subcultural Interests, Adapted from Robinson (2014).

## The Media Mirror: Assumed Fandom and the Male Story

The lukewarm welcome given to *Twilight* fans is nothing new for girls and women hoping to enjoy fandom in convention spaces. There is a long-standing history of the message that geeks and fans, creators of the content, and interested future consumers are overwhelmingly male (Cicci, 2017; Scott, 2013, 2019; Waldman, 2014). For example, the characters contained in comic books visually portray the cultural combat between the male in-group and female out-group. Characters early in comics included female roles as companions, highly sexualized and emotionally weak heroes, and typically tertiary or secondary roles to the dominant male-marketed hero story (Scott, 2013). Though comics are only one example, this theme is echoed throughout other forms of media. In a survey of geek women, 94 percent reported that the portrayal of nerds in mainstream culture was depicted as males... yet 60 percent of respondents said "no" when asked whether their personal experiences in geek spaces were in a "primarily male" population (Robinson, 2014). Pruitt's (2018) qualitative study of geek women also revealed that nearly all participants felt geek culture is overwhelmingly geared towards males.

Those who attempt to diversify content often receive significant pushback against their integration of the perceived in- (male) and out-groups (female) – or expectation of respect between them (Salter & Blodgett, 2012). In the case of Kelly Marie Tran, an actress from the most recent Star Wars trilogy films, pushback from fan outrage led her to take down her social media accounts and question her value as a person (Tran, 2018). *Star Wars* fans took to social media following the debut of the eighth movie in 2017, harassing Tran with racist and sexist comments through the summer of 2018 (Arnold, 2018). Tran (2018) shared the thoughts she experienced during the backlash in an op-ed piece for the *New York Times*:

> *Their words seemed to confirm what growing up as a woman and a person of color already taught me: that I belonged in margins and spaces, valid only as a minor character in their lives and stories... Because the same society that taught some people they were heroes, saviors, inheritors of the Manifest Destiny ideal, taught me I existed only in the background of their stories, doing their nails, diagnosing their illnesses, supporting their love interests — and perhaps the most damaging — waiting for them to rescue me... I believed those words, those stories, carefully crafted by a society that was built to uphold the power of one type of person - one sex, one skin tone, one existence.*

Worsening the divide, a viral meme called the "fake geek girl" was created to justify the belief that attractive women would only attend conventions to lure unsuspecting nerds into dating them (Welsh, 2013). This meme was used to imply that female fans did not actually know the references they used, thus trivializing their fandom. Scott (2019) reflected the futile experience for women most directly:

> *The "fake geek girl" presents a zero-sum game for female fans, not only because "fakeness" is predicated on the notion that fan affect is quantifiable and must be authenticated but also because within this paradigm, only male fans (or those who align themselves with*

*an affirmational notion of "authentic" fan culture) are empowered
to define and delimit what constitutes a "real" fan. Accusations of
"fakeness" can always be applied without grounds, and "proving
oneself" becomes an ongoing challenge, and one that is ultimately
impossible to achieve* (p. 99).

Knowledge of geek content is often used as social currency, social
identity, and sense of belongingness (McCain et al., 2015). The label of
"fake geek girl" directly stands to hinder the out-group's ability to spend
any of the social currency they may have in an effort to be accepted by
the in-group. This pushes the out-group away from active belongingness
to geek cultural identity and groups them with the general populous as
less aware and less intelligent (McCain et al., 2015). The way that many
women feel is reflective of this rejection; in a survey of geek-identifying
women, only nine percent of respondents reported feeling that women
are consistently welcome in the nerd community (Robinson, 2014). In
the same survey, only one third of respondents felt consistently comfortable in the community (Robinson, 2014). Pruitt (2018) interviewed female
geeks and discovered a small measure of within-group exclusion against
women who chose to dress in sexy costumes. Pruitt (2018) noted that the
women in sexy costumes were assumed to be trying to attract male nerds
- even among other geek-identified women. Regardless of intent, nearly
all respondents in Pruitt's (2018) study reported feeling the need to prove
themselves as nerds.

Another way that the male in-group of geek culture creates the
gender divide is through the pervasive belief that women will ruin their
enjoyment of their fandoms (Woo, 2018). If not seeking dates, they are
expected to be wives, girlfriends, or sisters dragged to conventions by male
fans (Woo, 2018). These attached out-group members are seen as threats
to unbridled enjoyment of fandoms, or as women intending to sabotage
and police male engagement in their geeky passions (Woo, 2018). The
oft-spoken stereotype is that women or girls do not like their boyfriends
and husbands to play video games or read comics – women only want
men to put away childish toys for more serious or adult pleasures. With
the notion of ulterior motives, women are seen as a general challenge to
"true" fandom and inauthentic in their knowledge of the culture to which

they strive to belong. This creates an active challenge toward out-group members of the geek community at in-person community events, leading to what can sometimes be difficult experiences.

The idea that women and girls belong to the out-group is even delivered through the language used when describing the differences between genders in the academic analysis of geek content. Scott (2013) puts it plainly, stating in her analysis of female comic characters how

> *"the issue is not simply that popular and academic literature generally renders female comic book readers invisible; it is also that the moments in which they are visible, they are too frequently compartmentalized and contained"* (p.4).

A repeated – yet false – theme is how females are just now realizing their fandom with pop culture and media (Cicci, 2017; Holloway, 2018; Woo, 2012). In a study on geek experiences in geek-related community spaces, many respondents reported believing that women and girls are "new participants in the scene"; notably, the entirety of the sample for this particular study was male (Woo, 2012). The oft expected response, particularly culturally, is that females who are interested in joining the in-group must compromise their female identity to do so – thus becoming "one of the boys" (Scott, 2013; 2019). Pruitt (2018) reported every participant in her study described the performance of gender explicitly:

> *The gender performance of women is often, knowingly or unknowingly, negotiated carefully. Displays of too much femininity can have women treated as an "other," someone "less than" in the nerd community, while displaying too much masculinity can have women seen as "just one of the guys."* (p. 74)

## Cosplay and Consent

As mentioned in the introduction to conventions, a unique cultural element to geek conventions is cosplay (originating from the Japanese term Kosupure, or costume play; University of Montana Library, 2019). Cosplay is where individuals or groups will dress up in representative fashion to appear like a favorite character from media. This often includes makeup, custom-made outfits and accessories, and even acting like or quoting the character when in-costume. Not all attendees cosplay, but it is relatively common. Of course, women are among those who cosplay.

As women began to speak up about their experiences in convention spaces, there became a clear pattern of harassment of the out-group surrounding their cosplay. Attendees reported several instances of non-consensual contact: photos taken of women's backsides or breasts, lewd questions in interviews or passing, touching or grabbing of women's bodies or cosplay accessories (Geeks are Sexy, 2013; Donnelly, 2019). The ever-present argumentative response, when these actions are declared unwarranted and unwanted, is that the woman dressed in a sexy way so she was clearly "asking for it" (Geeks are Sexy, 2013). The unfortunate cycle of out-group exclusion, in this circumstance, is that many female characters included in stories or media are frequently sexualized; female cosplayers who want to cosplay as female characters often face the decision of presenting in costume that is sexualized in nature, thus the characters featured in the male-dominated narrative cater to an explanation the in-group uses to exclude women.

Another article described the harrowing experience of one convention attendee, who was a female cosplayer dressed as Valkyrie. She reflected how she was cornered for photos, then was held in the center of a circle of unmoving men – bumping into her and only let free once another female fan convinced two tall men to create a gap in the circle (Moore, 2017). This led to the cosplayer refusing to attend SDCC – a convention reputed for its struggle to create clear guidelines around harassment (Moore, 2017; Waldman, 2014). Among relevant studies, one revealed that all participants had heard about or experienced sexual harassment in geek community spaces (Pruitt, 2018).

## Out-Group Cohesion

Tajfel and Turner (1979) theorized that in-group cohesion plays a primary role in building self-acceptance and self-esteem. Within the out-group, togetherness can create a sense of positive belonging on its own; this can lead to the desire from the in-group for integration (Tajfel & Turner, 1979). Amidst the harassment at geek conventions, women have created communities together to combat the negativity. One response from the out-group was the formation of the 16-Bit Sirens, a group that created CONsent – a movement that declared how costumes do not equate with consent (Cosplay is not Consent, 2013). At Emerald City Comic Con, (ECCC, Seattle's annual show) the organizers have made efforts to be more inclusive in the content offered and the culture it provides. Women outnumber men in attendance of ECCC, and this is largely attributed to the inclusive approach to panels, policies, and staff behaviors (Talbott, 2019). Comparatively, SDCC only had 29% female panelists over the past 10 years of events (Holloway, 2018). This too is changing as more female panelists presented in recent years than in the earlier decade (Talbott, 2019).

An annual uprising has become tradition, specifically surrounding a *Star Wars* character, Rose Tico (played by Kelly Marie Tran). There is a cosplay parade that occurs annually outside of SDCC where fans dress up like Rose and rally to support Kelly. The rally was started to create a sense of belonging after Kelly faced immense shaming and bullying from male *Star Wars* fans (Donnelly, 2019). This rally has shifted the narrative of conventions from a classically fandom-engaging space to one of togetherness and acceptance, especially for those who have felt rejected by the traditionally male-centric culture.

## Considerations for the Geek's Therapist

Conventions are exciting gatherings and may seem awfully dismal for women after reading the above content. It is worth noting that this comparison has dissected the cultural experience of female fans in convention spaces, particularly through the lens of what articles and discourse exist at present. There are many who do not experience any discrimination in their time at conventions, and many others who do – this analysis stands as an effort to bring light to the uncomfortable facets of gendered experiences. It is vital to consider how clients anticipate, experience, and walk away from geek conventions; how their social identity is formed and transformed through their time at geek community events. By building a plan detailing safety measures and boundary expectations, clients will be able to enter convention spaces with more confidence. If clients express interest in cosplay, clinicians can explore with clients how they embody the heroes and dynamic narratives of their favorite characters. Utilizing empowerment and positive psychological strategies can help clinicians reinforce self-esteem for clients, thus allowing clients to consider their in- and out-groups at play in the geek cultural community.

Conversations about expectations and safety at conventions should always be considered in order to prepare the individual for entrance into this busy domain. By creating expectancies, boundaries, and self-governing rules, the individual can feel safer when they enter the realm of conventions. Truly they are a wonderful place to feel safe, merge with fellow geeks, and enjoy cultural artifacts together.

# References

Arnold, B. (2018, June). Rian Johnson slams Star Wars trolls after Kelly Marie Tran Quits Social Media. *Yahoo! Movies*. Retrieved from https://uk.movies.yahoo.com/rian-johnson-slams-star-wars-trolls-kelly-marie-tran-quits-social-media-112051795.html.

Cicci, M. (2017). The invasion of Loki's army? Comic culture's increasing awareness of female fans. In Click, M.A., and Scott, S. (Eds.) *The Routledge Companion to Media Fandom* (193-201). London, United Kingdom: Routledge

Donnelly, M. (2019). Women creators, fans at Comic-Con rise up against culture of misogyny. *Variety*. Retrieved from variety.com/2019/film/features/women-at-comic-con-fan-culture-1203276161/

Eventbrite (2014). Cons: Behind the mask. Retrieved from www.eventbrite.com/cons

Fuller-Seeley. (2017). Archaeologies of fandom. In Click, M.A., and Scott, S. (Eds.) *The Routledge Companion to Media Fandom* (193-201). London, United Kingdom: Routledge.

Geeks are Sexy. (2013, April). Costumes are not consent: Combating cosplayer harassment *Geeks are Sexy*. Retrieved from geeksaresexy.net/2013/04/04/costumes-are-not-consent-combatting-cosplayer-harassment/.

Holloway, D. (2018, July). Comic-Con: Why is Hall H still lacking in female panelists? *Variety*. Retrieved from variety.com/2018/film/features/comic-con-hall-h-women-sexism-gender-gap-1202874821/

Mayer, P. (2019, June). San Diego Comic-Con is turning 50: Here's its origin story. *National Public Radio*. Retrieved from npr.org/2019/07/19/743341846/san-diego-comic-con-is-turning-50-heres-its-origin-story

McCain, J., Gentile, B., and Campbell, K. (2015). A psychological exploration of engagement in geek culture. *PLoS ONE, 10*(11), 1-38. doi: 10.1371/journal.pone.0142200

Moore, R. (2017). Comic-Con can still be intimidating for female fans. *San Diego City Beat*. Retrieved from sdcitybeat.com/culture/features/comic-con-can-still-be-intimidating-for-female-fans/

Pruitt, S. (2018). Pwning it: Voices of nerd women in a male-dominated subculture (Master's Thesis). Retrieved from ProQuest. (10636588)

Robinson, S. (2014). Fake geek girl: The gender conflict in nerd culture (Master's Thesis). Retrieved from ProQuest. (1566724)

Salter, A., and Blodgett, B. (2012). Hypermasculinity & dickwolves (sic): The contentious role of women in the new gaming public. *Journal of Broadcasting & Electronic Media, 56*(3), 401-416. doi: 10.1080/08838151.2012.705199

Scott, S. (2013). Fangirls in refrigerators: The politics of (in)visibility in comic book culture. *Transformative Works and Cultures, 13*. doi: 10.3983/twc.2013.0460

Scott, S. (2019). *Fake Geek girls: Fandom, gender, and the Convergence Culture Industry*. New York, New York: New York University Press.

Tajfel, H., and Turner, J. (1979). An integrative theory of intergroup conflict. In Austin, W.G., and Worchel, S. (Eds.) *The Social Psychology of Intergroup Relations* (33-47). Monterey, CA: Brooks/ Cole Pub. Group

Talbott, C. (2019, March). Bam! Pow! Women rule at Emerald City Comic Con. *Seattle Times*. Retrieved from seattletimes.com/entertainment/events/ bam-pow-women-rule-at-emerald-city-comic-con/

Tran, K.M. (2018, August). Kelly Marie Tran: I won't be marginalized by online harassment. *The New York Times*. Retrieved from https:// www.nytimes.com/2018/08/21/movies/kelly-marie-tran.html

University of Montana Library. (2019). Cosplay resources at the Mansfield Library: What is cosplay and where did it originate? Retrieved from https://libguides.lib.umt.edu/cosplay

Waldman, K. (2014, June). Comic-Con International has no interest in taking on sexual harassment. *Slate*. Retrieved from slate.com/ human-interest/2014/06/sexual-harassment-at-comic-con-san-di- ego-convention-says-no-to-a-more-comprehensive-policy.html

Welsh, K. (2013, August). Does misogyny lie at the heart of "fake geek girl" accusations  Or is it self-loathing? *New Statesman*. Retrieved from newstatesman.com/culture/2013/08/does-misogyny-lie-heart- fake-geek-girl-accusations-or-is-it-self-loathing/

Woo, B. (2012). Alpha nerds: Cultural intermediaries in a subcultural scene. *European Journal of Cultural Studies, 15*(5), 659-676. doi: 10.1177/1367549412445758

Woo, B. (2018). *Getting a Life: The Social Worlds of Geek Culture.* Québec, Canada: McGill-Queen's University Press.

Comics, Superheroes, and Anime

# Introduction to Comic Book Characters

# 11

Aaron C. Cross, PhD

As "geek culture" continues to grow in leaps and bounds, people are exposed to characters and experiences that are superhuman in nature. This is not just because of the superheroes themselves, but because of the connection between the reader and the storyline. Consumers of comic book movies and readers of the books forge real and personal connections with characters that go beyond simply "this character looks cool" and that even allow them to understand parts of themselves when paired with psychological theories. These connections, then, can help readers figure out who they are, what they feel, and that they are not alone with whatever they are personally experiencing.

## A Brief History

While characters such as Buck Rogers, Flash Gordon, Dick Tracy, and The Phantom existed in the 1920s and early-to-mid-1930s as newspaper comics, the world of comic book characters truly began April 15th, 1938 with *Action Comics #1* (Klock, 2002). This was the debut of Superman and perhaps the most famous issue of comics ever. Less than a year later, the darker counterpart to Superman – Batman – began with his introduction in *Detective Comics #27*. With these two characters leading the way, comics grew and began to flourish until the 1940s. It was at this point the market exploded and hundreds of characters were created. These characters, usually outfitted with a clear sense of good versus evil, let readers feel a sense of contributing to making the world a place where good prevailed (Vollum & Adkinson, 2003).

However, with the onset of World War II, there was a tremendous surge of characters with a patriotic bent, such as Captain Freedom, American Crusader, U.S. Jones, Yank and Doodle, Star-Spangled Kid, Fighting Yank, and American Eagle, with the only nationalistic toned character to currently remain to this day being Captain America. The year 1941 also marked the creation of Wonder Woman, one of the – if not the - most long-lasting and memorable female characters in comic book history. The stories and tone of these comics were and are thematically polarizing, with the common enemy for many of the characters being Nazis and unfortunately-exaggerated caricatures of Japanese soldiers (Hirsch, 2014; Scott, 2011). For example, the cover of *Captain America Comics* #1, the debut of Captain America, was even illustrated with Steve Rogers punching Adolf Hitler in the face.

However, it was not until the 1960s that Stan Lee, Jack Kirby, and Steve Ditko expanded the realm of comic books with some of the most iconic characters. Between 1961 and 1967, these three men combined to create, among others, the Fantastic Four, Ant-Man, The Hulk, Spider-Man, Thor, Iron Man, Doctor Strange, the X-Men, and the Avengers. The introduction of so many new characters also allowed writers and creators to experiment more with different stories and heroic themes. These new tools also allowed them to dive into deeper issues. Characters such as the X-Men have been explained as illustrating bigotry in several forms – from racism to anti-semitism to homophobia – and the loneliness, isolation, and pain inflicted by those actions (Baron, 2003; Fawaz, 2011; Shyminsky, 2006). The Hulk, in contrast, was designed to illustrate the common fear of nuclear war, while also tapping into a sense of frustration and rage surrounding the uncertainty of the climate of the world (Poole, 2011).

Flash forward to the 1980s and 1990s, where the tonal shift of comics began to evolve to a darker, grittier style to match consumer desires. As a result, the characters created and released in those decades were significantly darker than in years past. Individuals such as Lobo, Cable, and Deadpool eschewed the standard superhero style of unabashedly "good" in favor of more morally gray or anti-hero attitudes. Stories shifted focus from good versus evil to those with more nuanced and thought-provoking plots spurring readers to philosophically connect to the character ideals. The Punisher, after Vietnam, finds himself unable to cope with the normal world, illustrating to a violent degree how PTSD can irreparably damage people (Earle, 2018). Characters from Watchmen showed a wide range of experiences, outlooks, and damages, many of which fit potential readers' belief systems (Hughes, 2006). Even Batman took a darker path, with Frank Miller's reimagining of the character touching on aging and how the world continues to change no matter what someone does (Klock, 2008).

The 2010s brought even more change, and the idea of what makes a superhero has evolved to culturally represent more of the world. Characters such as Miles Morales and Amadeus Cho provide different stories for timeless characters, while brand-new creations such as Kamala Khan and Spider-Gwen offer a way for a more diverse consumer population to see themselves as the heroes from the outset. Of course, one would be remiss to not mention the effect that the comic book movie universes have had on characters and consumers as well. With the Marvel Cinematic Universe, characters such as Black Panther and Captain Marvel represent a different type of comic book fan through new stories and compelling character work that illustrate cultures, not just characters. In terms of the DC Extended Universe, Wonder Woman, through the work of Gal Gadot, has also become another empowering icon for women and girls of a new generation. Through these stories in this format, a wider range of consumers can identify with what they see and celebrate who they are. More importantly, the viewers that, up to this point, may not have seen superheroes like them, are now able to feel connected to the characters they see. Beyond that, they are also provided the chance to connect with a wider audience of comic book readers and movie viewers they may not have previously had.

## Real Life Importance

With such a long and expansive history, it stands to reason that comic book characters have and continue to influence those who read about or watch them on the cinematic screen. The reader is able to accompany the character as they go through adventures and experiences in their own lives thus allowing a point of reflection after the story has ended. It seems unlikely that someone will watch Thor wield Stormbreaker and truly believe that they could fight back an army. However, watching that same character deal with PTSD, self-loathing, and depression is a story that many more patrons can connect with on a personal level. When these characters who seem all-powerful reveal that they are, in fact, flawed and human, they are providing a way for people to relate to them in more meaningful ways.

Take, for instance, one of the most famous stories in Iron Man history – the "Demon in a Bottle" storyline. Rather than fighting against Fin Fang Foom or the Mandarin, Tony Stark finds himself fighting against his own nature and his addiction to alcohol. Instead of super-powered foes, Stark is battling a common – and more importantly real – problem that readers may actually face. People may not put on a literal suit of armor in their day to day lives, but they very well may be experiencing a deep need to drink that they feel is getting out of control. For them, that character becomes someone they understand and relate to because they are going through the same experience formulating a kinship between the reader and the character.

Similarly, one can consider how grief is presented through characters such as Batman and Spider-Man. Even though consumers are not likely to be bitten by radioactive spiders or be billionaires who turn to crime fighting, they could still be experiencing the loss of father figures or other loved ones. In those moments, seeing that characters grieve and mourn and go through that self-same loss could provide them with a sense of knowing they are not alone (Clyman, 2012). Those consumers can understand that they do not have to experience Batman's trauma of seeing his parents gunned down to still be undergoing that sense of confusion, sadness, anger, and loss of direction that the characters feel. They can see themselves and, perhaps, that can help them more properly grieve.

Beyond grief and addiction, the presence of characters can also help readers and consumers to simply feel as if they are seen and acknowledged (Neve, 2004). This is exemplified in the experience that many viewers had with *Black Panther*. With the representation of a culture outside of the typical white experience, African-American viewers were able to see themselves shown on the big screen in a way that was not frequently represented (Allen, 2018; D'Agostino, 2019). T'Challa is noble and strong and clearly the lead, while the country of Wakanda has a culture uniquely – and proudly – its own. For many, "Wakanda Forever" was not just a movie line. It was a symbol that allowed them to feel as if they were now fully invested in and accepted as a vital part of the broader comic book community.

Similarly, with *Wonder Woman* and *Captain Marvel* coming out in a movie form over the last few years, women and girls have also seen themselves represented on-screen in ways that they may not have experienced before. While characters such as Black Widow, Gamora, and Valkyrie are interesting characters, the amount of agency they experience tends to be limited, with all of them serving mostly as ancillary characters that help to enhance the growth of other people. Wonder Woman and Captain Marvel, though, put the female characters front and center and behaving with courage, strength, and femininity. In short, they show that women can carry – and more importantly, lead – their own heroic stories.

## Emboldened Future

What, then, does the future hold? Right now, the comic book world is undergoing some growing pains as it tries to figure out what exactly the role is that it plays in culture today, be it escapism, political commentary, a mix of both, or something utterly new (Begg, 2019; Proctor & Kies, 2018). In the era of Stan Lee, comic books tended to couch messaging in their stories rather than make things explicit (Lee & Mair, 2002). Now, however, what people believe comics can and should mean drives them forward into building new stories. Some creators are eschewing traditional publishing (e.g. DC or Marvel) and are utilizing crowdfunding to create comics they feel are not driven by larger political forces. Others are foregrounding their political beliefs front and center in the work they create. In both cases, this has translated into the representation of all different kinds of communities, religions, sexualities, and genders. As this process continues, particularly regarding who comics are for and who has ownership of what as fans, there has been and will be anger and frustration and arguments. There will be and is, however, room for creativity in new ways with new creators and new characters.

In all the change occurring in comics, one critical component does remain: the desire to make characters and stories that will connect with readers and make them feel something. For instance, Scott Snyder's work on *Batman* through the storyline of "Death of the Family" taps into a type of worry and fear not commonly felt in many comic books. The arcs (the narratives which are driven via the storylines) by Gerry Duggan in *Deadpool* that touch on ideas such as loss and marriage create a new sense of depth for a character that is often written off as purely comedic rather than someone with complicated emotions. This extends beyond the comic books as well. Thor in *Thor: Ragnarok* can show that self-doubt can happen, even to those who are powerful, while the final snap of Thanos's fingers in *Avengers: Infinity War* is a reminder that, in fact, good does not always win. Sometimes, despite their best efforts, people will lose.

Perhaps these stories illustrate best what comic book characters can be for people. Whether they can fight, turn invisible, heal quickly, shoot webs, or simply just afford to put on body armor and scare criminals, these characters retain deep, abiding feelings about what it means to be human - a connection that the readers experience themselves. They provide a way for people to be seen in their stories and try to figure out who they are on their own. From Captain America punching Hitler in the face back in the 1940s to the movie *Logan* illustrating in painful, heart-breaking detail what it is like to deal with ailing, aging family and the complications and emotions behind loss, comic book characters have shown that readers, viewers, and consumers are ultimately not alone in this world. We have these characters and they have us.

# References

Allen, M. D. (2018). If you can see it, you can be it: Black Panther's black woman magic. *Journal of Pan African Studies, 11*(9), 20-23.

Baron, L. (2003). X-Men as J Men: The Jewish subtext of a comic book movie. *Shofar: An Interdisciplinary Journal of Jewish Studies, 22*(1), 44-52.

Begg, M. (2019). Drawing the line. *Institute of Public Affairs Review: A Quarterly Review of Politics and Public Affairs, 71*(1), 16.

Clyman, J. (2012). The Amazing Spider-Man: Growth Over grief. *Psyccritiques, 57*(36).

D'Agostino, A. M. (2019). "Who are you?" Representation, identification, and self-definition in Black Panther. *Safundi, 20*(1), 1-4.

Earle, H. (2018). Conflict then; trauma now: Reading Vietnam across the decades in American comics. *European Journal of American Culture, 37*(2), 159-172.

Fawaz, R. (2011). "Where no X-Man has gone before!" Mutant superheroes and the cultural politics of popular fantasy in postwar America. *American Literature, 83*(2), 355-388.

Hirsch, P. (2014). "This is our enemy": The writers' war board and representations of race in comic books, 1942–1945. *Pacific Historical Review, 83*(3), 448-486.

Hughes, J. A. (2006). "Who watches the watchmen?" Ideology and "real world" superheroes. *The Journal of Popular Culture, 39*(4), 546-557.

Klock, G. (2002). *How to read superhero comics and why.* A&C Black.

Klock, G. (2008). Frank Miller's new Batman and the grotesque. *Batman Unauthorized: Vigilantes, Jokers, and Heroes in Gotham City,* 35-46.

Lee, S., & Mair, G. (2002). *Excelsior!: The Amazing Life of Stan Lee.* Simon and Schuster.

Neve, B. (2004). *Film and politics in America: A Social Tradition.* Routledge.

Poole, W. S. (2011). *Monsters in America: Our Historical Obsession with the Hideous and the Haunting.* Baylor University Press.

Proctor, W., & Kies, B. (2018). On toxic fan practices and the new culture wars. *Participations, 15(1), 127-142.*

Scott, C. A. (2011). *Comics and Conflict: War and Patriotically Themed Comics in American Cultural History From World War Ii Through the Iraq War.* Loyola eCommons.

Shyminsky, N. (2006). Mutant readers, reading mutants: Appropriation, assimilation, and the X-Men. *International Journal of Comic Art, 8(2), 387-405.*

Vollum, S., & Adkinson, C. D. (2003). The portrayal of crime and justice in the comic book superhero mythos. *Journal of Criminal Justice and Popular Culture, 10(2), 96-108.*

# From the Hulk to Captain America – How Values and Emotions Influence Our Approach

**12**

Matthew J. Fellows, MA

Everyone's lives are deeply complex and seemingly full of unwritten social rules and constant struggles to balance personal needs and wants against the needs and wants of others in life. Everyday living is so often defined by the problems at hand in any given moment, and so rarely defined by personal successes or accomplishments. In addition to this push-and-pull dynamic everyone is constantly living in, leisure time is increasingly devoted to observing others within our social circle; people who, more often than not, put forward their best face and hide their own struggles. We, as clinicians, see this day in and day out in the people we work with, people who unconsciously train themselves to compare personal failures to others' successes, while everyone else silently does the same. It would be tough to design a more efficient method of fostering self-doubt, anger, isolation, and anxiety if one tried.

Thus it is often of little surprise to see clients that would prefer to spend their time engaged in fictional worlds. From Hogwarts to Hoth, Westeros to Wakanda, and every space between, the illustrious lore of other worlds with other beings offer a solace from the misery of social media and interpersonal critique. One who works in the field of counseling and therapy may see clients utilize this to manage their stress, anxiety, depression, and even symptoms of more serious psychological disorders.

## Avenging Emotional Inadequacy

Taking a respite from daily life into a world where one understands the rules, on a universal level, is to step into a place where one cannot be truly hurt - even the greatest trials present as fascinating story developments instead of anxiety-producing or traumatic events. This inherent barrier between the reader and the world they choose to engage with lies at the core of using stories to address the real-life struggles of our clients. Readers use these worlds, in this case the Marvel Cinematic Universe (MCU), to bridge the gap between their own passions and self-reflection (Berkowitz, 2012).

As with most therapy sessions, a client isn't going to get very far very fast if the therapist and the client aren't able to correctly identify emotions, at least in retrospect, and preferably in the moment (Lieberman & Eisenberger, 2007). This can be very difficult for some who are new to therapy, especially if the client was raised in or acclimated to an environment that actively pushed them to suppress or not express certain emotions (Flynn et al., 2010).

A good example of this emotional suppression can be seen in the development of young men, who are often told that experiencing emotions such as fear, sadness, and embarrassment is unacceptable, and that anger or rage are more appropriate responses to feelings of vulnerability (Butler et al., 2007). In this case, it is not difficult to see the similarities between the client described here and The Hulk, whose defining characteristic (until *Avengers: Endgame* (2019), more on that later) is his inability to control himself when he gets angry, and the damage and hurt that loss of control can result in. Learning to label emotions can take time and there are many different avenues a therapist can take to help guide their client to a place of self-reflection. Yet, when one has an established universe full of complex and relatable characters that the client is already familiar with, such as the MCU, an effective way to do this can be through identifying emotions of the characters and then drawing parallels to the client's life.

Seemingly insignificant parallels could help a therapist and their client connect behavioral or emotional struggles between themselves and those of the members of The Avengers. In fact, all of the Avengers have their own personal battles that clients can relate to outside of their super-hero persona (i.e. alcoholism, narcissism, abandonment issues, etc.). Yet, it is important to keep in mind, one could not possibly address all the members of the MCU's Avengers and the issues they face in one therapy session, let alone an entire lifetime.

Although clients can likely relate to many of the personal struggles, narratives, and relationships throughout the films, it is likely that there is at least one character they feel connected to most. For example, the therapeutic application of The Hulk's character journey to a client who struggles with controlling their anger can lead to further discussions and methods of coping strategies used within the film that may translate to such a client's life. However, there are many more examples within the MCU that could be used to draw parallels between a client and the char-acters in The Avengers.

## Starting From Ground Zero

Tony Stark, (AKA Iron Man), is the first character that viewers are intro-duced to in the Marvel Cinematic Universe, and one that shows some of the most poignant examples of personal growth throughout the series. For example, in the movie Iron Man 3 (2013), we see what is arguably one of his darkest moments: Tony Stark's battle with post-traumatic stress disorder (PTSD).

Viewers of this film find that Tony Stark has begun to show the telltale signs of PTSD, including flashbacks, panic attacks, nightmares, and hypervigilance. He carries with him the terror of having nearly died and the guilt of the people who perished in the attack despite the best efforts of The Avengers. Initially, to Tony, these symptoms appear unre-lated, and even he is surprised when the artificial intelligence within his suit, J.A.R.V.I.S., identifies a panic attack that he experiences when asked by a child about the details of the invasion. A client experiencing similar trauma responses may find this example useful in helping them tie together symptoms to form a narrative that can help begin the healing process. By watching Stark's acceptance and transformation of these symptoms, the narrative itself helps to provide the basis of change, acceptance, and transcendence, but also a perfect launching point to discuss the symptoms in a realistic atmosphere.

Tony Stark is also uniquely positioned to show a distinct and drastic personality growth throughout his story arc, with the viewer's first introduction to the character in *Iron Man* (2008) showing a narcissistic, self-centered man who is only invested in his own self-interests, even at the expense of the loss of others' lives. Throughout the MCU, viewers watch Tony Stark develop not only empathy and compassion for others, but eventually a sense of selflessness and self-sacrifice, which culminates in him laying down his life for the preservation of the universe. This is obviously an extreme example of a personality change, but one that is methodically laid out throughout his films within the MCU, showcasing a separation of Ego from the self. A therapist working with a client who struggles to show empathy for others could use this to show the overall improvement in the quality of Tony Stark's life and those around him, without the expectation that the client sacrifice themselves for the survival of the known universe.

## Grieving for Others

Natasha Romanoff, (AKA The Black Widow), is a former soviet spy turned S.H.I.E.L.D. agent and later a member of The Avengers, and is one of the most skilled and intelligent members of the team. She is presented initially in the MCU as a calculating, emotionally-distant, and pragmatic person who is able to manipulate even the most cunning adversaries into revealing secrets. While her character undergoes considerable personal development throughout the next films, her most prominent changes happen following "the snap" in Avengers: Infinity War (2018), where the film ends with half the life in the universe being extinguished due to Thanos using the Infinity Gauntlet.

The next film, which takes place five years in the future, following the snap, shows us that Natasha has entirely devoted herself to her work, ignoring her self-care, and even making hostile statements towards friends who she thinks may ask her to "look on the bright side." In these scenes, one sees that she is barely eating or sleeping, and is crying in private, something we have not seen before, indicating a break in the quiet confidence seen in previous films. This presentation and change of the character is a good example of what can happen to someone who undergoes a major loss in their life or experiences a tragedy that takes something important from them.

Viewers will notice Natasha continually searching for answers, displaying irritability, sadness, and hopelessness, and demonstrating an uncharacteristic lack of self-care. These are all things a client dealing with a major loss may experience or do. Within a therapeutic setting, a client and therapist could use Natasha's journey into grief and loss to identify themes within the client's own life, and work to create individualized coping strategies before destructive thought patterns and behaviors become the norm.

## Persevering Through Life

When it comes to helping clients draw parallels between the experiences of The Avengers and their own experiences, one would be hard-pressed to find a character who has been through more than Thor. Thor Odinson has, since he was first introduced to the MCU, been exiled from his home by his own father, been betrayed by his own brother multiple times, gone through a major breakup, lost his mother and father in separate but traumatizing ways, learned of a sister his family had hid from him, watched his homeworld be destroyed (by said sister and an apocalyptic demon), had his hammer shattered, lost an eye, became king of the remaining Asgardians following the destruction of his world, watched the remaining Asgardians (including his brother and best friend) and their culture be wiped out by Thanos, and then failed to kill Thanos when he had the chance, resulting in the death of half of all living beings in the universe.

Within all these tragedies, it is not hard to pick out themes of trauma, personal failure, and significant loss of pretty much everything that could

be important to someone. From these events, we come to see more character development in Thor than arguably any other member of The Avengers.
Most notably, we see Thor, who has become used to victory and success
for at least the past 1,000 years, suddenly come to terms with what it is
like to experience a series of failures. Later in this chapter, we discuss
the impact of these failures and losses on Thor's psyche and how to tie
them into a meaningful discussion with a client in a therapeutic setting.

Of course, this is not a comprehensive breakdown of all the members
of the MCU that could be used in therapy. Other characters that could
just as easily be used in therapy include Scott Lang, AKA Ant-Man, and
the family dynamics he deals with during a divorce and the relationship
he has with his daughter during this time, Valkyrie, who uses alcohol to
combat her PTSD and depression she experiences for being the only sur-
viving member of the Asgardian Valkyrie force, or T'Challa, AKA Black
Panther, who is forced to decide whether to forfeit the secrecy and security
of his home nation in order to share their advanced technology to help a
world that previously exploited them.

## The Staging of the Clinical Room

Identifying themes of personal challenges and growth are only the first
part of using the MCU in a therapeutic context. The next step is often
the most enjoyable; bridging the gap between characters and clientele by
watching the movies. When a therapist working within this framework
encourages a client to watch the movies, it serves three important clinical
purposes. Firstly, it lays out and highlights the issues the client may be
dealing with in an engaging and narrative-driven way. Second, it forces
the client to focus on how the issue is resolved in the context of the story,
which could provide them with ideas on how they might effectively handle
their own problems moving forward. Third and finally, it provides them the
opportunity and an excuse to take time for themselves and watch a movie
they'll likely enjoy. As always, self-care and engaging in enjoyable activities are an important part of mental wellness and recovery, and clinicians
using these characters in a therapeutic setting should be careful not to
over-analyze these characters and take the joy out of them for the client.

While it is important that the client enjoys their time watching these movies, a structured goal should be in place to help guide the client and focus their attention on the relevant issues that are addressed in the film. This will be a highly individualized goal based on the client, the therapeutic approach used in sessions, the client's identified issue, the movies the client watches, and where in their recovery process they are. This is where the homework comes in. While giving clients homework may not be a standard practice for every therapist, it may prove difficult to address parallels between clients and the characters without first having a client re-watch the relevant films through the lens of mental health. When possible, merging previously established homework practices or techniques with the MCU characters may help clients focus on the most important patterns of behavior. The following is a quick example of how this might work:

The clinician is working with a client who shows features of Borderline Personality Disorder, if not an outright diagnosis. In this particular case, they have a history of unhealthy and unstable relationships in which they have suffered significant emotional abuse and have lost respect for themselves. Very often in a situation like this, a practitioner may look to dialectical behavior therapy (DBT) skills as a means of addressing this (Swales et al., 2009). When integrating the themes of the MCU, a therapist gets to add a new layer of understanding. Not only can the therapist in this case teach the client about the DBT skills that help address their lack of self-worth, but they can provide an example of an MCU character that reflects those values. In the example here, one may choose to teach the client the "FAST" skill, as introduced in Marsha M. Linehan's book, *Skills Training Manual for Treating Borderline Personality Disorder* (1993). This skill is used to serve as a way to help clients remember how to maintain respect for themselves in relationships, reminding them to be **F**air to themselves and others, give no unjustified **A**pologies, **S**tick to their own values, and be **T**ruthful. For someone familiar with the MCU, Captain America is a clear representation of these values, and serves as a wonderful example of someone who shows respect to himself and others. At this point, the therapist would request that the client watch films that show Captain America displaying these values and ask them to identify not only moments where the skills of FAST are demonstrated, but how people around Captain America react to him using these skills. Through the films, it is shown that not everyone appreciates when Captain America stands by his values, which could help the hypothetical client prepare for possible negative reactions to newly-found boundaries and self-respect in their life.

## Coping with the Emotional Core

With the core basics laid out of how to draw parallels between the MCU characters and a client, one can move to incorporate the next step in therapeutic healing by addressing another important feature of many of the characters within the MCU: emotional regulation and coping strategies. The MCU is so jam-packed with the emotional reactivity of the characters and the coping strategies they use to deal with the problems that they face (and each other), that it would be nearly impossible not to find some examples in these films that one could easily connect to a client. The best part of this is that the emotional regulation and coping strategies of the MCU characters run the gamut from inspiring and effective to downright self-destructive, but nearly all the characters eventually exhibit some form of positive growth.

As was mentioned above, The Hulk (Bruce Banner) is a clear-cut example of coping strategies and self-reflection being utilized in a positive manner throughout the films. When the viewers first meet Bruce Banner, he is a timid, intelligent, quiet man who becomes The Hulk when he gets angry. While in his Hulk form, he causes large-scale destruction and chaos everywhere he goes and assaults friends just as easily as enemies. By the time the movies progress to *Avengers: Age of Ultron* (2015), we see that Bruce/Hulk has developed a calming mantra ("sun's getting real low") that can help him regulate his emotions and leave his Hulk state more voluntarily than he could before. As the films continue, the viewer eventually sees that Bruce Banner and his alter-ego Hulk are at odds with one another and that the Hulk will not appear, even to help Bruce when he needs it most, leading Bruce to say *"We've got a lot to figure out, pal."* Finally, in *Avengers: Endgame*, the viewer finds that in the years that have passed since "the snap," Bruce Banner has been able to integrate the best parts of himself with the best parts of The Hulk, resulting in "Professor Hulk," who is able to stay as logical, friendly, and intelligent as Bruce Banner, but maintain the physical strength and resiliency of The Hulk. The viewer sees that he has accepted his anger for what it is without letting it control him, and as a result, he has become "the best of both worlds." A client struggling with emotional regulation may find Banner's journey to be a helpful blueprint for what people can do to respect and acknowledge their emotions for what they are, without being controlled by them. Mindfulness practices could easily be worked into sessions at this point, including breath counting, progressive muscle relaxation, guided imagery, and meditation.

But what about the characters who don't cope so well, what can be drawn from their experiences? When Thor Odinson is first introduced, he is arrogant, powerful, resilient, and seemingly invincible, but over the films, he undergoes more tragedy and hardship than likely any other Avenger, as was noted earlier. In *Avengers: Endgame*, five years after the snap, the viewer finds Thor as he has never appeared before: depressed. He reveals that he has lost everything that was important to him, and in turn has isolated himself, taken to heavy drinking, stopped maintaining personal hygiene, and views the future as hopeless.

Throughout *Avengers: Endgame*, Thor works through these barriers to offer help to the Avengers and eventually finds himself in the past in Asgard, where, on a hunch, he tries and is able to call his old hammer, "Mjolnir" back to him. This moment is important for a couple of reasons, but they all revolve around one key piece of information: Mjolnir can only be called or lifted by someone who is worthy of it. When Thor calls Mjolnir, the viewer sees that Thor's depression does not make him any less worthy of wielding his hammer, which drives home the ever-important message that people struggling with depression so often forget: even at the lowest moments, when one feels more hopeless than ever before, people are *still worthy* of happiness, love, affection, support, and respect.

In addition to Thor's worthiness, a message is conveyed that failure in one's life does not reflect on who an individual is at their core, nor diminish what they are capable of in the future. In all of this, it is worth noticing that Thor's depression doesn't go away after he retrieves Mjolnir. He still has those same feelings, and he doesn't magically lose weight or get a haircut, but he does find the motivation to keep fighting for himself and those he cares about.

## Endgame

As one works with clients and utilize geek culture to connect with them, it is important to remember that there are many other resources at one's disposal. The MCU is a wonderful entry point, as the characters are wide-ly-known, and their stories are presented on film in a beautiful and engag-ing way, but there are hundreds of characters and thousands of story arcs in comic books and television series that can be used in the same way. A therapist who identifies a client with an affinity for the MCU should not be afraid to venture into the X-Men comics or movies to find themes of feeling outcast or rejected by society. Similarly, DC's Batman comics have been beautifully addressing themes of loss, trauma, and developing personal values for 80 years.

Whether or not using popular geek culture like Marvel's MCU is right in one's personal practice or therapy style, it is important to keep in mind that these resources should be used in conjunction with evidence-based therapeutic practices, and not as a replacement for them. The ultimate goal in this practice is to utilize aspects of geek culture that one's client identifies with, and link themes within the stories and characters to the problems or barriers a therapist's client is facing in their own life.

# References

Berkowitz, D. E. (2012). Framing the future of fanfiction: How The New York Times' portrayal of a youth media subculture influences beliefs about media literacy education. *Journal of Media Literacy Education, 4(3)*, 198–212.

Butler, E. A., Lee, T. L., & Gross, J. J. (2007). Emotion regulation and culture: are the social consequences of emotion suppression culture-specific? *Emotion, 7*(1), 30–48.

Flynn, J. J., Hollenstein, T., & Mackey, A. (2010). The effect of suppressing and not accepting emotions on depressive symptoms: Is suppression different for men and women? *Personality and Individual Differences, 49*(6), 582–586.

Lieberman, M. D., & Eisenberger, N. I. (2007). Putting Feelings Into Words. *Psychological Science, 18*(5), 421–428.

Linehan, M. M. (1993). *Skills training manual for treating borderline personality disorder*. New York, NY, etc.: The Guilford Press.

Swales, M., Heard, H. L., & Williams, M. G. (2009). Linehan's Dialectical Behaviour Therapy (DBT) for borderline personality disorder: Overview and adaptation. *Journal of Mental Health, 9*(1), 7–23.

# Positive Psychology and (Super) Heroes

# 13

Ryan M. Kelly, PhD & Jason M. Bird, PhD

The original concept of the superhero has been around for over 80 years with the earliest known superheroes being the Clock in 1936 and DC Comics' Superman in 1938. These early superheroes served as a working prototype for the thousands of future superheroes that followed them. In the early 1940s, a massive eruption of new comic-book superheroes entered onto the scene including the Flash, Green Lantern, Aquaman, Captain Marvel, and Wonder Woman. At the same time that America saw the growing emergence of superheroes, psychology was quickly evolving in the mid-20th century. Almost instinctively, superheroes began to serve as a meaningful representation of our human condition and real-life experiences. As we start to witness from a very young age, we as human beings are able to identify with and relate to the superhero narrative. At the most basic level of comparison, we realize that all superheroes have both superpowers, or personal strengths, and weaknesses, or vulnerabilities. With this basis of understanding, a new era of psychology and psychotherapy has now evolved with the inclusion of superheroes and their experiences as a model for enhancing positive mental health and overall well-being. This has led to many different models of working therapeutically with superheroes in the clinical setting (Scarlett, 2017).

## Overview of Positive Psychology and Positive Psychotherapy

Over the past two decades of psychological research, scientists and practitioners have been striving to find a healthy balance between *disease*, or *deficit-focused*, models of mental health and *strengths-based, positive well-being* models. Acknowledging that traditional deficit-focused models of mental health do not effectively promote optimal human functioning, the field of *positive psychology* has begun to challenge conventional treatment methods for improving one's mental health. Leading researchers have defined positive psychology as the scientific study of how human beings function at their best, which is often associated with people's positive emotions, character strengths, and life circumstances that contribute to their overall happiness (e.g., subjective well-being) or the "good life" (Seligman & Csikszentmihalyi, 2000; Seligman et al., 2005). As a whole, positive psychology research has identified the need to study critical areas of development associated with optimal functioning and happiness (Proctor et al., 2009). In combination with one another, positive psychotherapy and superhero therapy provide a harmonious relationship for mental health providers to be able to integrate more engaging and strengths-based therapeutic approaches.

Positive psychology researchers have posed several theoretical models of well-being and happiness that complement and may further enhance the use of superhero therapy. One theory of positive psychology outlines well-being as a collection of multiple emotional responses across time (Kahneman, 1999; as cited in Kim-Prieto et al., 2005). By utilizing this theory to explain the development of SWB, Durayappah (2011) proposed an elaborated model known as the *3P Model of Subjective Well-Being*. The 3P Model hypothesizes that the development of well-being is a product of a person's cognitive and emotional responses to past, present, and prospective (future) experiences. Durayappah (2011) suggested that present experiences are the strongest determinants of well-being because they are often the most salient to one's life. Previous research indicates that individuals who are presently experiencing positive emotions and high social self-efficacy are also more likely to report greater levels of well-being or happiness (Bird & Markle, 2012; Lyubomirsky, King et al., 2005). Likewise, our past experiences also contribute to present levels of well-being. For example, previous studies have indicated that reminiscing, experiencing gratitude, and finding meaning in previous life events can positively influence a person's level of well-being (Emmons & McCullough, 2003; Froh et al., 2008). Finally, research demonstrates that prospective experiences (i.e., anticipated events in the future) can also contribute to a person's happiness. Previous studies have found that focusing on positive prospective experiences can increase one's sense of hope (Snyder et al., 2005), optimism (King, 2001) and purpose in life (Sheldon et al., 2002).

Another burgeoning topic complementary to positive psychology is the research on human resilience. For our purposes, resilience can be defined as a developmental process or dynamic capacity to successfully adapt to adversity or disturbances that may threaten an individual's or system's overall functioning (Yates et al., 2014). Simply stated, resiliency is the characteristics or factors of a person that allows them to overcome adversity and continue to thrive in their daily lives.

Appropriately, the field of positive psychology has developed a number of intervention strategies that have demonstrated strong efficacy for providing a catalyst for improving well-being, resilience, and changing human behavior. Examples of these evidence-based, positive interventions have included keeping a gratitude journal (Emmons and McCullough, 2003), writing a letter of gratitude (Seligman et al., 2005), practicing forgiveness of other people in our lives (McCullough et al., 2000), counting one's blessings regularly (Lyubomirsky, Sheldon et al., 2005), participating in goal setting (MacLeod et al., 2008), and engaging in acts of kindness (Lyubomirsky, Sheldon et al., 2005). These strengths-based, positive psychology interventions have been rigorously tested, and outcomes of these research studies have shown significant increases in individuals' life satisfaction (Froh et al., 2008), school satisfaction (Suldo et al., 2010), problem-solving self-efficacy (Ayres and Malouff, 2007), as well as significant decreases in participants' self-reported negative affect (Froh et al., 2008) and overall depressive symptoms (Seligman et al., 2005). As described in Durayappah's (2011) *3P Model of Subjective Well-Being*, focusing on past, present, and prospective experiences of one's life may all contribute to the development of well-being.

## Comparing Superheroes to the 3P Model of SWB

The superhero's journey to success or well-being shares several similarities to our own human experience and development. In context, both humans and superheroes evolve from influences of their past, present, and future experiences. The narrative of superheroes is a caricaturized, yet still relatable, depiction of the real human experience, providing mental health professionals with a very useful means of conceptualizing and intervening with their clients. To elaborate on this point, let's consider an instance of each temporal experience as it relates to Batman (past), Deadpool (present) and Dr. Strange (future).

*Batman's Past (Post-Traumatic Growth)*

Bruce Wayne's greatest trauma and tragedy was the death of his parents, Thomas and Martha Wayne. They were murdered for the first time by Joe Chill in Detective Comics #33, November 1939, and have since died over 100 times in varying depictions across comics, cartoons, movies, and video games. As sadistic as this may seem, it is by design, for it is the death of Bruce's parents that gives Batman life; specifically, the meaningful evaluation of his parents' gruesome murder that transforms his trauma into focus. This may also be referred to as "post-traumatic growth."

Post traumatic growth is defined as the "experience of individuals whose development, at least in some areas, has surpassed what was present before the struggle with crises occurred. The individual has not only survived, but has experienced changes that are viewed as important, and that go beyond the status quo" (Tedeschi & Calhoun, 2004). Bruce goes through something terrible, which for many would remain as a haunting past that affects present and future functioning, but instead of withering away, he becomes a prolific hero. How? Perhaps the social support from Alfred? Or the financial means to meet his other psychological needs? Yes and yes, but more importantly, Bruce found meaning in his suffering. Instead of being held prisoner by the flashbacks of his parents' demise, perseverating on the pain and senselessness of it all, he lets himself observe them, proactively evaluating his trauma in attempt to prescribe meaning to it. Evaluating his past, he determines that this suffering through his parents' death was a result of a systematic problem with his hometown, Gotham City, and that by overcoming his traumatic bereavement, he could pursue a purposeful future. He becomes Batman—a knight in matte, black armor—who saves those who would otherwise experience the same injustice and misery he faced. This in turn allows him to experience gratitude for his remaining loved ones.

*Deadpool's Present (Sense of Humor)*

One might be surprised by the remarkably tragic history of Deadpool, aka Wade Wilson, at a glance. He is usually very positive and humorous and lives in the moment, as if devoid of pain or worry; however, he has one of the most tragic backgrounds of any comic book superhero. Among other things, Wade Wilson lost his mother to cancer when he was six years old, was abandoned by his father (in some comic variants, was tricked into killing his family), suffered physical and emotional child abuse, struggles with schizophrenia and depression, lives in a perpetual state of progressive brain cancer, loses everyone he loves tragically, and has experienced an incomparable amount of combat-related physical trauma. Furthermore, regarding his prospective future, he is essentially immortal and destined to watch everyone die as he experiences the ebbs and flows of humanity as a hollow spectator, becoming increasingly distant from humanity. So why is he always joking? What's there to joke about?

The same question was asked of Dr. Victor Frankl—a tragic holocaust survivor and innovative psychiatrist and neurologist— about his time at the concentration camps. He addresses this in his book *Man's Search for Meaning* (2006):

> *"Humor was another of the soul's weapons in the fight for self-preservation. It is well known that humor, more than anything else in the human make-up, can afford an aloofness and an ability to rise about any situation, even if only for a few seconds... Everything can be taken from a man but one thing: the last of the human freedoms – to choose one's attitude in any given set of circumstances, to choose one's own way"* (p. 63; p. 116).

Deadpool would certainly agree, especially with the notion that perception is affected by choice. There is something to be said about the self-determinism of someone who can set aside unhelpful past and future evaluations – defy thinking or acting upon the negative emotions of reactive (e.g., bereavement) or nonreactive (e.g., clinical depression) neurochemistry – and just experience a mindful, positive moment. In fact, research has found that experienced affect from a bad or good event can account for more variance in subjective well-being than external factors like the circumstance itself (Campbell et al., 1976).

In spite of everything, humans have the ability to smile and laugh – to reframe a "threat" into a "challenge" or "joke" – effectively distracting or augmenting feelings of anger, stress, or fear. Laughing and smiling (even fake smiling) have been shown to decrease cortisol (i.e., stress) and increase endorphins (i.e., pleasure) and T-cell efficiency (i.e., physical immunity; see Scott, 2015 for a review). Deadpool provides a running, caricaturized way of doing this in even the darkest of moments. In his words:

*"When you're confronted with a horrible situation, there are only two reactions that make sense: laughter and tears. And laughter, after all, is nature's anesthesia. Tears hurt too much."*

– Deadpool, *Xmen Origins, Deadpool*

*Doctor Strange's Prospective Future (Intrinsic Aspirations and Purpose)*

Similar to the comics, in the movie depiction of Doctor Strange, Dr. Stephen Strange is the world's leading neurosurgeon. He is renowned for his surgical skills, as well as for his exceptional arrogance and hubris. His genius intelligence, skill, and achievement at the top of his field have given him a superiority complex and, to some degree, a god complex. That is, until he experiences a serious car crash, resulting in catastrophic injuries to his hands that leave him unable to perform surgery. This sends him spiraling into panic, anger, resentment and depression. Ultimately, in a desperate attempt to regain control over the future he destined himself with, he begrudgingly subscribes to non-scientific doctrine of mystic arts, where he incidentally finds a sense of purpose and well-being that he realized was missing all along. But how is that possible? How could such a confident man with such exceptional skill and achievements be so deficient in well-being or purpose?

This is actually not that uncommon – we see that it depends largely on the type of aspirations one may have, and the way they look towards the future. Dr. Strange began with extrinsic aspirations— he aimed for wealth, fame and image— and his achievements reflected that; however, intrinsically, he was bankrupt. He did not have a sense of meaning or purpose beyond these superficialities, and he was unaware of what he wanted when it came to aspirations like affiliation, personal growth, or community. Research indicates that extrinsic aspirations relate negatively to well-being indicators, and that attainment of such aspirations provides little psychological benefit (Kasser and Ryan, 1993, 1996). The opposite is true of intrinsic aspirations – in fact, they've been found to increase the commitment and confidence one has towards their own goals and allow for more purposeful, hopeful pursuits and meaningful achievement. As a note, both the pursuit and achievement of such a meaningful, purpose-drive prospect have been found to increase one's SWB, self-actualization, self-agency, and lifespan (see Durayappah, 2010 for review).

## A Balance of Temporal States

The reality is, there is a unique benefit to each temporal state in assessing and intervening in one's life, as well as a unique cost. Like most things, what matters most is balance – in this case, a temporal balance through which one may simultaneously perceive their past, present, and future positively. Batman finds meaning in his past, which allows for the development of a purpose-driven future; however, he rarely appreciates the positive emotions of the present. He worries that by doing so, he will accidentally interfere with his past evaluations and future expectations (he's not wrong) and is fearful that such personal changes for Bruce Wayne would absolve the "necessary" existence of the Batman (it would). Deadpool is able to live happily in the present, using humor to reframe strife as a challenge and avoid his painful past, but also seems to wander purposelessly, unable to accumulate meaning (especially towards the future). Dr. Strange finds meaning in his past, positivity in his present, and purpose in his future, but also dwells (literally) in a multitude of prospective futures through the time stone (a fortune-telling cosmic gem). Much like "what if" questions for people with clinical anxiety, this becomes all too encompassing, and interferes with his well-being. So, with this in mind, what would a good temporal balance look like? Consider the following Figure 13.1:

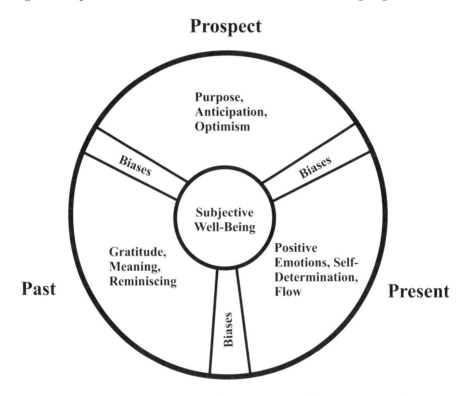

Figure 13.1 The 3P Model of the Components of Subjective Well-Being.

As indicated, SWB under our temporal states is not confined neatly into the past, present, and prospect (future) – instead, judgments of SWB between temporal states are notably discrepant. This is because they all affect each other through cognitive biases or "channels," and while the list of psychological rules and cognitive distortions is ever growing, there are a few basic examples to consider. Specifically, the biased interplays between the present and past, past and (prospect) future, and future and present. These examples will draw from relevant comic book narratives.

In 1985, Strack and colleagues (1985) demonstrated that people use recent events to help evaluate their current lives (e.g., "how am I doing lately?"), but as recent events begin to be seen more as distant memories (five years or older), those events begin to be used as a *standard of comparison* for life satisfaction (e.g., "is my life as good or meaningful as it used to be?"). We see this frequently in superhero comics in the form of the "James Dean Effect" (Diener et al., 2001) — many heroes often prefer to die abruptly at the peak of their crime-fighting career rather than dying comfortably some years later. A good tongue-in-cheek example of this is through *The Watchmen's* Hollis Mason, the retired Nite Owl vigilante, who became stuck in the "good ol' days," only to be ironically beaten to death by the trophy given to him by the city during his prime. Such preoccupying reminiscence has been shown to decrease one's ability to find satisfaction in the present (Bryant, 2003).

Regarding biases that exist between the past and future, one example is that we tend to overestimate the generality and magnitude of feelings (positive or negative) originally experienced during a given moment when predicting our future (Brickman et al., 1978). Such an overestimation of the effect of a past event on our well-being is often referred to as retrospective impact bias, and has been shown to cause poor future planning and negatively affect impact bias – the overestimation of the affective impact of future events (Wilson et al., 2003). Consider an example from the *Star Wars* comic book *Doctor Aphra*. She is essentially an interstellar archeologist repeatedly risking her life for the next big artifact to find and sell. Over and over, she anticipates that finding the item will be amazing and life-changing (impact bias), but is then disappointed or endangered when she finally does obtain it. Once out of danger, she (defensively) belittles or dismisses the misfortunes of the event, later falsely recalls that the event went well (or at least, not that bad), and then plans to essentially make the same mistake despite rejections from her less biased crew (retrospective impact bias). These types of temporal biases are among the primary reasons why some people (like Aphra) do not learn from their mistakes (Wirtz et al., 2003).

Lastly, there are the biases that exist between the prospect and the past. A common example is counterfactual thinking, the concept that humans tend to imagine alternative outcomes to a life event that has already occurred—essentially, wishing something had gone better or appreciating that something could've been worse based upon how real the alternative feels. A good example of this is that Olympic medalists who win bronze medals tend to be more appreciative than those who win silver medals. This is because the bronze winners can easily imagine having lost entirely (and thus are grateful), while the silver winners can easily imagine winning gold (and thus may feel disappointed) (Medvec et al., 1995). Comics are notorious for creating alternative timelines and universes to explore such counterfactual thinking, both by the author and the characters (e.g., Bishop and Cable from *Uncanny X-Men*, The Flash, Superman, Spiderman, and Hal Jordan as the Green Lantern).

The key to finding balance despite these biases is to experience temporal states in a clockwise direction; that is, experiencing prospective future, then the present, then the past, and back to the future. Consider the direction of Hollis Mason (*The Watchmen*'s Nite Owl), as well as an amended direction based on the clockwise model:

> **Hollis Mason:** Past ("life used to be so meaningful") → Present ("I wish life was as meaningful as it used to be") → Prospect ("I'm looking forward to Saturday to talk to Daniel about my past") → Past ("those were the days")

> <u>**Amended**</u>: **Hollis Mason**: Prospect ("I'm going to find a new, purposeful way to be heroic") → Present ("I'm enjoying brainstorming ideas and feeling empowered!") → Past ("my past bravery made me the heroic man I am today, and I'm grateful!") → Prospect ("I'm anticipating success!")

While the old model was imbalanced towards a temporal preference of the past, in the amended model, Hollis finds a renewed sense of purpose, which then allows him to engage and enjoy the present, giving greater meaning to his past with greater utility of his memories, increasing the likelihood of having thoughts and actions that improve life satisfaction and positive emotions. Here is another way to view it:

> Optimism and Purpose → Positive Emotions and Self-Determinism → Gratitude and Learned Meaning → Anticipation/Achievement of Goals

Contrary to the traditional model of mental health, positive psychology demands attention by both researchers and clinicians to focus on what makes something work, in addition to addressing what impairs functioning. A particularly useful model found within the field of positive psychology is the 3P Model, which considers how humans' SWB is affected by their experience within different temporal states (past, present and future), as well as how these states affect one another. Superheroes and their narratives can serve as a helpful way for clinicians and clients to better understand the power of positive psychology, providing caricaturized depictions of the real human experience with a focus on strengths over weakness, resilience over frailty, meaning over trauma, purpose over hedonism, and mindfulness over fear. Clinicians should pursue more education and training on how to apply this increasingly popular medium (superhero comics, movies, shows, video games) to help connect with their clients and improve their well-being.

# References

Ayres, J., & Malouff, J. M. (2007). Problem-solving training to help workers increase positive affect, job satisfaction, and life satisfaction. *European Journal of Work and Organizational Psychology, 16*, 279-294.

Bird, J. M. & Markle, R. S. (2012). Subjective well-being in school environments: Promoting positive youth development through evidence-based assessment and intervention. *American Journal of Orthopsychiatry, 82*, (1), 61-66.

Brickman, P., Coates, D., & Janoff-Bulman, R. (1978). Lottery winners and accident victims: Is happiness relative? *Journal of Personality and Social Psychology, 37*, 917–927.

Bryant, F. B. (2003). Savoring beliefs inventory (SBI): A scale for measuring beliefs about savoring. *Journal of Mental Health, 12*, 175–196.

Campbell, A., Converse, P. E., & Rodgers, W. (1976). *The Quality of American Life.* New York, NY: Russell Sage. Carver, C. S., L

Diener, E., Wirtz, D., & Oishi, S. (2001). End effects of rated life quality: The James Dean Effect. *Psychological Science, 12*, 124–128.

Durayappah, A. (2011). The 3P Model: A general theory of subjective well-being. *Journal of Happiness Studies, 12*, 681-716.

Emmons, R. A. & McCullough, M. E. (2003). Counting blessings versus burdens: An experimental investigation of gratitude and subjective well-being in daily life. *Journal of Personality and Social Psychology, 84*, (2), 377-389

Frankl, V. E. (2006). *Man's Search for Meaning.* Boston: Beacon Press.

Froh, J. J., Sefick, W. J., & Emmons, R. A. (2008). Counting blessings in early adolescents: An experimental study of gratitude and subjective well-being. *Journal of School Psychology, 46*, 213-233.

Kasser, T., & Ryan, R. M. (1993). A dark side of the American dream: Correlates of financial success as a life aspiration. *Journal of Personality and Social Psychology, 65*, 410–422.

Kasser, T., & Ryan, R. M. (1996). Further examining the American dream: Differential correlates of intrinsic and extrinsic goals. *Personality and Social Psychology Bulletin, 22,* 80–87.

Kim-Prieto, Diener, E., Tamir, M., Scollon, C., & Diener, M. (2005). Integrating the diverse definitions of happiness: A time-sequential framework of subjective well-being. *Journal of Happiness Studies, 6, 261*-300.

King. L. A. (2001). The health benefits of writing about life goals. *Personality and Social Psychology Bulletin, 27,* 798-807.

Lyubomirsky, S., King, L., & Diener, E. (2005). The benefits of frequent positive affect: Does happiness lead to success? *Psychological Bulletin, 131* (6), 803-855.

Lyubomirsky, S., Sheldon, K. M, & Schkade, D. (2005). Pursuing happiness: The architecture of sustainable change. *Review of General Psychology, 9*(2), 111-131. Retrieved from https://escholarship.org/uc/item/4v03h9gv

MacLeod, A. K., Coates, E., & Hetherton, J. (2008). Increasing well-being through teaching goal-setting and planning skills: Results of a brief intervention. *Journal of Happiness Studies, 9,* 18-196.

McCullough, M. E., Pargament, K. I., & Thoresen, C. E. (2000). The psychology of forgiveness: History, conceptual issues, and overview. In M. E. McCullough, K. I. Pargament, & C. E. Thoresen (Eds.), *Forgiveness: Theory, Research, and Practice* (p. 1–14). Guilford Press.

Medvec, V. H., Madey, S. F., & Gilovich, T. (1995). When less is more: Counterfactual thinking and satisfaction among Olympic medalists. *Journal of Personality and Social Psychology, 69,* 603–610.

Proctor, C. L., Linley, P. A., & Maltby, J. (2009). Youth life satisfaction: A review of the literature. *Journal of Happiness Studies, 10,* 583-630.

Scarlett, J. (2017). *Superhero Therapy: Mindfulness Skills to Help Teens and Young Adults Deal with Anxiety, Depression, and Trauma.* Oakland, CA: New Harbinger Publications.

Scott, E. (2015). The Stress Management and Health Benefits of Laughter. http://stress.about.com/od/stresshealth/a/laughter.htm

Seligman, M. E. P., & Csikszentmihalyi, M. (2000). Positive psychology introduction. *American Psychologist, 55,* 5-14.

Seligman, M. E. P., Steen, T. A., Park, N., & Peterson, C. (2005). Positive Psychology Progress: *Empirical validation of interventions. American Psychologist, 60,* (5), 410-421.

Sheldon, K. M., Kasser, T., Smith, K., & Share, T. (2002). Personal goals and psychological growth: Testing an intervention to enhance goal attainment and personality integration. *Journal of Personality, 70,* 5-31.

Snyder, C. R., Rand, K. L., & Sigmon, D. R. (2005). Hope theory: A member of the positive psychology family. In C. R. Snyder & S. J. Lopez (Eds.), *Handbook of Positive Psychology* (pp. 257-276). New York: Oxford University Press, Inc.

Strack, F., Schwarz, N., & Gschneidinger, E. (1985). Happiness and reminiscing: The role of time perspective, affect, and mode of thinking. *Journal of Personality and Social Psychology, 49,* 1460–1469.

Suldo, S. M., Huebner, E. S., Savage, J., & Thalji, A. (2010). Promoting subjective well-being. In M. A. Bray, T. J. Kehle, & P.E. Nathan (Eds.), *The Oxford Handbook of School Psychology* (pp. 504-522). Oxford University Press: New York.

Tedeschi, R. G., & Calhoun, L. G. (2004). Target Article: "Posttraumatic Growth: Conceptual Foundations and Empirical Evidence". *Psychological Inquiry, 15*(1), 1–18

Wilson, T. D., Meyers, J., & Gilbert, D. T. (2003). "How happy was I, anyway?" A retrospective impact bias. *Social Cognition, 21,* 421–446.

Wirtz, D., Kruger, J., Scollon, C. N., & Diener, E. (2004). What to do on spring break? Predicting future choice from online versus recalled affect. *Psychological Science, 14,* 520–524.

Yates, T.M., Tyrell, F., & Masten, A.S. (2014). Resilience theory and the practice of positive psychology from individuals to societies. In S. Joseph (Eds.), *Positive Psychology in Practice: Promoting Human Flourishing in Work, Health, Education, and Everyday Life* (pp. 773-788). Retrieved from https://doi.org/10.1002/9781118996874.ch44

# The Psychology of Anime: Belongingness, Resilience, and Hope

# 14

Ryan M. Kelly, PhD

Whether one is aware of it or not, the global impact of Japanese visual culture is omnipresent and ever-flowing, imbued with the relatively modern, influential power of "manga" (i.e., Japanese comics) and "anime" (i.e., Japanese animation). Through paint and paper, the spirit of Japan successfully reached the entirety of the colonized world by the early 20th century (Macwilliams, 2008). Then, in 2019, thanks to the unbelievable pilgrimage of a man named Logic Watanabe, anime reached the uninhabitable continent of Antarctica. Mr. Watanabe wanted to pursue an ambition inspired by the narrative storyline of his favorite anime *A Place Further Than the Universe* (K, 2019). But why? What is so remarkable about manga and anime that makes it so expansive? Why would it inspire a fan to go to such great lengths? Consider Mr. Watanabe's triumph:

For but one warm moment on the cold shores of a harsh tundra, a young man stood alone, proudly holding a flag of four anime characters who, like him, had traveled painstakingly to Antarctica in search of something lost. In the story, the characters traveled together to find their mother who was lost on an expedition. Not so dissimilarly, Mr. Watanabe went to "overcome a profound sense of loss," and to purposefully explore the

212 THE PSYCHOLOGY OF ANIME: BELONGINGNESS, RESILIENCE, AND HOPE

gleam of meaning he had gained from connecting with the characters and narrative of the anime (K, 2019). Both the characters and Mr. Watanabe faced great obstacles and fears, and overcame them through resilience and social support, ultimately finding their own sense of achievement.

Pain, resilience, meaningful connections, and victory. These are the essential components of anime and manga narratives and contribute greatly to the breadth and depth of the influence on its fans and our world culture. They provide the stories that people want to hear — the one's that validate who they are now and help them discover who they want to be. They are the stories that humans deeply relate to. Mr. Watanabe, through the inspiration of an otherwise "trivial" TV show, became the protagonist of a similarly inspirational story and discovered a profound sense of purpose and achievement.

Humans vicariously learn from creative narratives and story characters. They help us better understand ourselves, the nature of the world and our place in it, and provide powerful imagery (real and imagined) that can elicit significant emotional inspiration. Together, anime and manga represent a world-wide phenomenon, and even compared to other forms of visual story-telling, have a remarkable influence on our collective culture and psychosocial development. That being said, it's clear that clinicians must deeply consider the stories being told, how they affect clients, and how therapists might utilize the psychological power of Japan's visual culture in a therapeutic context.

## Origin of Manga

Although some equate manga in Japan to comic books in the United States, that would be inaccurate. While comic book and graphic novel sales in the US and Canada totaled around one billion dollars in 2018 (Griepp & Miller, 2018), manga sales in Japan total 10 billion dollars annually, accounting for roughly 40% of all books and magazines sold (Hayes, 2013). To further emphasize its popularity, reportedly, more paper is used in Japan to make manga than toilet paper (Lee & Burunova, 2019).

The first use of the word "manga" (translated to "random drawings") appeared in 1814, Japan; specifically, appearing as *Hokusai's Manga,* which included 12 volumes of simplified drawings of things like famous beauties, sumo wrestlers, samurai, landscapes, and urban merchants. Essentially, Katsushika Hokusai painted and sketched a visual summary of traditional life in Japan. Hokusai provided an alternative outlet — volumes of pictures that caricaturized and criticized social conditions that readers were experiencing and could relate to — including starvation, oppression, desperation, neglect, and fear. More than that, they felt a catharsis and release reading these works that validated their difficult experience, and in some ways eluded to a more hopeful outcome.

In 1853, at the behest of Matthew Perry, the American Commodore, Japan opened their ports to the US, resulting in a massive exchange of visual culture resources between the two countries. Western themes began to appear in manga, and Eastern themes became more prevalent in US visual culture. Manga was further brought to the West at the World Expo in Paris (1867), once again increasing its influence over the West, and vice versa. More than ever, Western cultures were able to experience a unique way of connecting with narratives and characters in positive, meaningful ways (Macwilliams, 2008).

## Origin of Anime

Although there is much anime that stands on its own, a majority of works are actually based on of existing manga. For instance, *Sazae San*, the longest running animated TV series in the world (1969 – present), is based off the manga first published in 1946. For 50 years (73 years including the manga), the people of Japan have relied on *Sazae San* to help cope with the trials and tribulations of common Japanese life, so much so that some viewers even experience "Sazae San Syndrome" – a temporary depression that occurs when the credits roll at the end of the show (Macwilliams, 2008).

"Animated manga" was largely inspired by the technicolor innovations of Walt Disney, as suggested by the current chairman of Toei Animation (first anime publisher), Kozo, in the documentary *Enter the Anime* (Lee & Burunova, 2019).

*"Japanese animation, that is, Toei Animation, started right after Japan lost the war. It was based on Disney. It was a brand new industry. It was a way to give kids hope after losing the war. That's how Toei Animation began… That's why Toei Animation's target audience is always kids. That's why they make anime that makes them happy. And that's something they shouldn't stray from. I really love the phrase "Friendship, Effort, Victory." How to teach that to kids is where the love in anime is."*

Although Toei Animation is largely meant for children, the theme of "friendship, effort, and victory" is a running one within most anime to this day. Specifically, if that were to be expanded upon, it would include friendship (meaningful connections, belongingness, acknowledgement), effort (resilience, persistence, integrity, strength) and victory (achievement, external validation, self-acceptance). Although other animated shows may focus on these as well, anime provides an unparalleled, concentrated form that could only be derived from the hopelessness of traumatic desolation and, from that, an achievement of actualized hope. In other words, anime is the visual projection of a people who suffered an unprecedented nuclear devastation and, instead of withering away, raged against that hopeless blight to become a thriving, technological superpower.

Anime first arrived in the States after WWII with shows like *Astroboy and Gigantor*, prompting the "boy and his powerful companion" theme. In the 80s, classics like *Akira, Speed Racer, Dragon Ball*, and *Voltron* appeared along with the rise of Studio Ghibli (e.g., *Totoro),* further demonstrating the genre's diversity and potential to succeed in western culture. Then, in the 1990s, the presence of anime skyrocketed. A mainstream population of young viewers became enthralled with shows like *Pokémon, Sailor Moon, Dragon Ball Z, Evangelion, Cowboy Bebop, and feature films like Princess Mononoke, Ghost in the Shell,* and *Ninja Scrolls*. Cartoon Network even launched "Toonami," a nightly program that played back-to-back anime that appealed to girls and boys of all ages. The fact is, Americans were relating to these shows, and discovering that they wanted something more than their current culture and lifestyle. They were finding something that was missing all along.

## The Allure of Japanese Visual Culture

As far west as one might go, the presence of these mediums is unavoidable. Go to your local bookstore and you will find manga books like *Naruto*. Watch TV on Amazon and Netflix and you'll scroll past "original" anime titles like *Blade of the Immortal* or *Seven Deadly Sins*. Shop at a Walmart in rural North Dakota and you will see *Pokémon* cards at the front and *Dragon Ball Super* toys at the back. Manga and anime imagery, as well as the Japanese culture embedded within them, have a massive presence within our collective human visual culture.

The reality is, Eastern and Western cultures are both fundamentally different and complimentary; such is the case with their primary cultural perspective. Western cultures tend to be individualistic, meaning that society prioritizes being of an independent mentality rather than a group one. Conversely, Eastern cultures (including Japan) are often collectivistic, meaning they emphasize the needs and goals of the group over the individual. As can be observed in anime, they often promote ideas like honor, respect, and (family) duty. Yet, both cultures appear to have an appreciation for their differences. For many in the West, the ideals and principles or a collectivistic culture are alluring, in that it appears that people belong to and become something more than themselves. At the same time, the East has historically demonstrated an interest in the cavalier, worry-free wanderer that embodies the Western priority.

In addition to differences in cultural perspectives, the East and West differ in communication style, especially as it relates to "context." In the West, people are more willingly to adopt a "low context" form of communication, where thoughts and feelings are explicitly stated, reducing the demand for "reading between the lines," environmental context, or non-verbal communication. In Eastern cultures, it's the opposite – verbal messages are often indirect, and the context of non-verbal communication and relationship dynamics become much more significant. Interestingly, anime meets the needs of both of groups. While the characters often interact within a high-context style, much of the dialogue is internal – to the consumer, an outward expression of the thoughts and feelings of the characters. Furthermore, everyone seems to be able to use high-context communication incredibly well, in that they *truly* know what the other person is thinking or feeling without them needing to express it. Even in low-context communication, people can feel misunderstood. For both types of consumers, it's incredibly alluring to see people interact such that they're able to express themselves accurately and have others fully understand (and validate) their experience.

Overall, the general allure of anime and manga is that it allows us to both connect and escape. For the prior, it offers a window into the Japanese culture – their aspirations, fears, fetishes, and dreams – that offers a unique reflection into who we are and who we want to be. Through its characters, it provides exaggerated archetypes that we may easily relate to. As a whole, anime and manga contain "extraordinary powers to determine people's demands on reality" and are themselves "coveted substitutions for firsthand experience" (Macwilliams, 2008). Regarding escape, the director of Aggretsuko, Rarecho, states it eloquently — especially for those who feel abnormal or constrained, it can "liberate people bound by the mundane," where the mundane may be forced upon them by their environment or the world they create for themselves (Lee & Burunova, 2019).

## Fanship and Fandom

Regarding the sense of belongingness and connection that manga and anime provide, there is no better representation than within the powerful world of fanship and fandom. Fanship refers to a great connection to an interest, both emotionally and as it relates to one's own personal identity (e.g., "being an anime/manga fan is a part of me"). In addition to watching a varying plethora of animes and/or reading multitudinous volumes of manga, anime and manga fans high in fanship may write their own stories or fan fiction, fan dub (i.e., narrate over existing anime), draw anime themselves, or cosplay their favorite characters. Fandom, on the other hand, refers to connecting to and identifying with a fan group with the same fanship (e.g., "I see myself as a member of the anime community"). Examples might include attending anime conventions or anime clubs. When discussing the therapeutic benefits of manga and anime, both fanship and fandom will be referenced, as they are equally essential as the narratives and characters themselves.

## Therapeutic Benefits: Cathartic Expression

As previously mentioned, Eastern culture can be emotionally repressed, due in large part to a high-context communication style and a collectivistic culture. Individual needs can fall to the wayside and expressive outlets can be scarce. Manga and anime provide the perfect medium to address this. To this point, manga expert Frederick Schodt discusses the power of anime and manga in expressing people's feelings:

> *"(Manga) are mediascapes of dreamscapes where stressed out modern urbanites daily work out their neurosis and frustrations. Viewed in their totality, the phenomenal number of stories produced is like the constant chatter of the collective unconscious – an articulation of a dream world"* (Schodt, 1996, p. 31).

The overt expression of emotions in anime is deeply embedded within the animation style. For instance, Hiroyuki Seshita, supervising director of the anime Levius, talks about the importance of matching the colors of a fight scene with the emotions of the fighters (Lee & Burunova, 2019). Initiatives such as these allow for the visual language to match, and be a magnified projection of, the viewers' mood and energy level as it relates to the characters, the narrative, and the extreme emotions they feel in life.

The creators of *Max Gamer,* the first comic book about an autistic superhero, took special note of this, as their primary demographic included individuals on the spectrum who struggled greatly understanding emotional context and theory of mind (Gaskill & Kelly, 2011). They specifically incorporated a manga style to allow aspies to fully understand and vicariously express intense feelings of loneliness, fear, anxiety, anger and love by matching emotional scenes to befitting backgrounds (e.g., red background for anger, floating hearts for love) and commonly used manga symbols (e.g., cross-mark for frustration, tear-drop for stress, speed lines for excitement). Per the aspie readers' reports, the once hard to discern, implicit information became explicitly expressed and comprehendible through the environment context, character narration and emotional symbols. Furthermore, for young learners, the high-emotional expression found within the art style and narrative has been found to provide "a visual vocabulary of sorts for scaffolding writing techniques, particularly dialogue, tone and mood" (Frey & Fisher, 2004).

In addition to allowing individuals to understand and express their own individual emotions, manga and anime have also been used to express communal feelings of oppression and provide a means of rebellion against those oppressive forces. As examples, "Chibi" anime (i.e., cute, childish animation style) was a large part of Kawaii culture in Japan in the 1960s (i.e., "cuteness" culture) that rejected the traditional demands of adulthood, while female viewers have historically watched anime to escape the sense of oppression, gender discrimination, and the romantic status quo (Chen, 2004). Regarding the latter, although some stories continue to depict women as submissive characters at the disposal of the male protagonist (e.g., Elizabeth Liones, *Seven Deadly Sins*), more and more are portraying them as (1) remarkably strong fighters who grow to simultaneously accept their feminine nature (e.g., Casca, *Berserk*) or (2) fierce, androgynous women who the males look up to (e.g., Masaaki Yanagisawa, *Natsuki Crisis*).

## Therapeutic Benefits: Family, Friendship, and Belongingness

According to Maslow's Hierarchy of Needs, a sense of love and belongingness is an essential human psychological need, preceded only by food, water, and safety. Unsurprisingly, this is something many manga and anime consumers seek, whether vicariously through the stories or directly through fandom. In fact, in one study, a primary predictor of individuals pursuing anime (and fandom) was self-reports of gaining a sense of belongingness (for women) and uncertainty reduction (for men) by watching anime (Ray et al., 2017). Simply put, these mediums make viewers feel like they are a part of something bigger than themselves – a large community of misfits, connected by a visual culture made by misfits — that offers the reassuring warmth of acceptance. Examples of fandom resources that might directly address these needs include anime/manga conventions, clubs at school (very common), and online communities (e.g., forums). Furthermore, consumers become acculturated to the relational values and principles embedded within these mediums, gaining a sense of friendship, family, and romance.

Within anime and manga, friendship is seen as the "strong supporting foundation from where the hero launches into other pursuits, whether it is revenge against wrongdoers or rampaging aliens, or fight against inner demons and weaknesses" (Reynor, 2017). It is an essential component of anime. It stands as a reminder that we need to share our beliefs and passions with others, and that resilience can be found through teamwork. There are two Japanese terms that refer to general categories of "friends." The first is "Tomodachi," which is basically a reliable friend found within a good friend group (e.g., Edward Elrich and Louis Armstrong, *Fullmetal Alchemist*), and the second is "Nakama," which refers to a deeply loyal, sensitive, and potentially contentious friendship bound by mutual goals, beliefs, and values (e.g., Kai Ichinose and Shūhei Amamiya, *Forest of Piano*). It submits that everyone has a group they belong to, and that all individuals are capable and deserving of intimate, meaningful connections. Furthermore, the stories inspire a pursuit for a system of peer support while providing a vicarious escape from feelings of loneliness, especially for those who are often withdrawn.

When it comes to family, manga and anime strongly promote values of respect, love, forgiveness, and acceptance. This is often done through an initial "sacrifice." Often times, the protagonist of the story has experienced a great loss, such as the death of a parent or devastating isolation from a community. This device was largely influenced by the massive influx of orphaned children from the bombing of Hiroshima and Nagasaki, exemplified by mangas such as *Fruit Basket* and animes like *Clannad X Wolf Children*. The beginning of these stories include agonizing themes of alienation and a deep longing for family – a desire to have the opportunity to be loved and become a part of a collective good. Through a formulaic narrative, the protagonist often finds acceptance from others and a family (of sorts) thanks to goal-oriented actions, resilience, and self-discovery. Regarding the latter, it's important to consider the well-established theory that positive self-identity is dependent upon interactions with friends and family, and vice versa, referred to as social identity theory.

## Therapeutic Benefits: Positive Self-Identity

Social identity theory (Tajfel et al., 1979) maintains that individuals belong to groups to maintain positive and distinct social identities as part of a broader need for positive self-evaluation. The word "distinct social identity" should be noted, as it is believed that standing out meaningfully from others is a separate psychological need, as proposed within Brewer's (1991) optimal distinctiveness theory. Consequently, men and women who watch anime and participate in fanship and/or fandom do so because they report gaining a sense of personal distinctiveness, purpose and positive self-esteem from these novels and shows (Ray et al., 2017). In general, having a positive social identity has been shown to foster a sense of efficacy, meaning, continuity (i.e., connection between the past, present and future), belongingness, interpersonal distinctiveness (Vignoles et al., 2006), uncertainty reduction (Hogg, 2000), friendship (Wann, 2006), social support, and formation of a world view (Haslam et al., 2009). It would seem crucial, then, to capitalize on this widely available medium that has been shown to contribute towards this – one that promotes a wealth of positive values (e.g., honesty, loyalty, persistence) and principles (e.g., fairness, self-worth, honor) for individuals to adopt, and does so in an engaging, meaningful way. So with that being said, how might one apply it?

## A Therapeutic Application: Positive Conceptualization of Diagnoses

The therapeutic applications of anime are limitless – even a multi-chapter book on therapeutic anime would struggle to provide a comprehensive review – but for the sake of exemplification, consider the conceptualization of one's diagnosis. Many anime characters embody mental illness and victimization, and it's really no surprise; many anime writers themselves have struggled with mental illness and social ridicule. For example, the creator of *Neon Genesis Evangelion,* Hideaki Anno, suffered from depression and psychosis. Another good example is the author of *Attack on Titan,* Hajime Isayama. Reportedly, he was frequently bullied as a child, and claims that those experiences are what originally lead him to anime and continue to shape his works.

In every anime, you can find at least one main character that could easily be diagnosed with a mental illness, such as Attention Deficit Hyperactive Disorder (ADHD), a mood or anxiety disorder, or Asperger's Syndrome (AS). In this light, this section will review a handful of characters from popular anime series that fall into common mental health categories, along with a few examples of how they meet the criterion, and will follow up with a discussion on why this is so significant. These strengths are important to note because they are often what make these individuals exceptional and allow them to develop extraordinary resiliency.

## ADHD

ADHD is one the most common childhood brain disorders, and generally refers to marked impairments in regulating attention and energy. People with ADHD often have poor executive skills (e.g., disorganized) and difficulty with self-inhibition and regulation. However, they have also been shown to demonstrate notable strengths, such as greater athletic ability, creativity, sense of humor, social engagement, and empathy. A popular example of an anime character with ADHD is Naruto Uzumaki from *Naruto* and *Naruto: Shippudden.*

Naruto is a young boy studying to be a ninja, and he easily fits the bill. Because of his inattention, he hates studying, bombs his tests, gets in trouble for not listening, and often forgets instructions. He is notoriously disorganized and messy, is usually running late, and is often losing things. Because of his hyperactivity, he impulsively says or does things that he immediately regrets, gets in trouble for being rambunctious, finds himself in dangerous situations, and is usually bothersome to those around him. However, Naruto never gives up. He excels at things that require trial and error learning, and has more energy and stamina then his peers. Because of this, he excels in hands-on tasks, can practice harder and longer, and can push himself past normal limits. Although he is not good at traditional problem-solving, he is often thinking outside of the box and being creative. Furthermore, although he tends to lack social grace, he is extremely outgoing and has unlimited empathy for even the worst of enemies.

*Mood and Anxiety Disorders*

Not including lifetime prevalence, roughly 5-12% of children and adolescents are diagnosed with a mood and/or anxiety disorder. Although these disorders are distinct, they are usually "comorbid" with one-another (i.e., co-occurring). People with these disorders generally engage in irrational, negative thinking, perseverate on worrisome or depressing life events, isolate themselves, and have greater difficulty adjusting to their environment. They also may somaticize (i.e., express psychological distress physically), especially young children, or have irregular eating and sleeping habits. However, they have also been shown to demonstrate notable strengths, such as exceptional creative abilities (e.g., music, art) and greater self-awareness. Furthermore, when managed, those with anxiety are often more motivated to succeed. Two examples of anime characters who struggle with mood and anxiety problems include Tatsuhiro Satou (*Welcome to the NHK)* and Shinji Ikari (*Evangelion).*

Satou is a 22-year-old "hikikomori," which is essentially the Japanese word for agoraphobic. As a note, the term hikikomori often implies a "failure to launch" or "quarter-life crisis." His anxiety confines him to his room, where he frets about every little thing and struggles with some paranoia. His condition is bleak, and because of this, he is very depressed and engages in suicidal ideation. However, despite his hopelessness, his story is about breaking the confines of his condition and pursuing social engagement. This is especially relevant today, as both anxiety and failure-to-launch rates have increased in the US. For instance, in 2016, 15% of Millenials ages 25-35 reported that they were living with their parents, compared to the 10% of Generation Xers in 2000 (Fry, 2017). Satou's story offers an inspiring example of overcoming these states. As a note, this anime can either be therapeutic or contribute to negative thinking, but in any case, it is a fair depiction of what it is to be clinically anxious, depressed, or generally stagnant.

Shinji is a young boy who has been called upon his distant father to pilot a "mecha suit" – a weaponized robotic suit – despite suffering from clinical depression and anxiety. Sometimes he is isolating himself and ruminating on his loss of the will to live, while other times he is proud of being an exceptional pilot and having skills that others do not possess. He is often seeking approval from his father and peers, seemingly as a way to make up for his sense of self-worthlessness. Shinji's character offers a good reflection to individuals with strained parent-child relationships and provides a relatable sense of intermittent self-doubt and internalizing symptoms paired with a victorious overcoming. As a note, what makes this anime great is that it's been directly tied as a projection of the author's own mental state.

*Asperger's Syndrome*

Though technically no longer a separate diagnosis, AS is a high-functioning form of autism that generally refers to marked impairments in social interaction and communication, as well as repetitive behaviors, pervasive interests and/or sensory issues. People with AS, or "aspies," often have difficulty understanding and interacting with those around them, grasping conceptual ideas like emotions, and adjusting to their environment. However, they have also been shown to demonstrate very notable strengths. Some of these strengths include greater cognitive abilities, extraordinary breadth and depth of knowledge and experience in their "special interest area" (e.g., art, history, computers), and unique splinter skills (e.g., art, composing music), and they are generally some of the coolest kids you'll ever have the pleasure to know. A great example of an anime aspie anime character is "L" from *Deathnote*.

"L" is a world-renowned detective who takes on investigating a supernatural serial killer. For the vast majority of his life, and for a large part of the anime, he is painfully isolated. Like many aspies, this appears to be because his chronic failures to form relationships have disheartened him to even try. In addition to difficulties similar to Sai, "L" has very odd and seemingly uncoordinated movements, as well as very particular eating habits. He also appears to suffer from a serious sleep disorder, which is not uncommon among aspies. But "L" is a genius. His ability to think logically is off the charts, which is what makes him such a great detective. Furthermore, like many aspies, he bravely decides once again to attempt to form relationships, despite a lifetime of failures.

## Conclusion

Above all else, anime and manga provide inspiring, emotionally expressive stories of friendship and resilience in the face of crippling adversity. They suggest that no matter how hopeless, weak, and rejected one may feel, there is something special within them – a powerful potential to be achieved– that will help them succeed and flourish. They suggest that no matter how daunting an obstacle may be (whether it be dealing with a bully or defeating a god) or how much others doubt you, if you believe in yourself, remain strong and work hard, you can overcome it and find acceptance. Ultimately, they encourage them to have hope and to belong to something greater.

Everyone wants to be happy, and to garner love, respect, and power (e.g., control). This is especially true for those who are unhappy, or who feel like their psychological needs are not being met. Young children rely primarily on family for such approval and self-worth; however, an essential part of adolescence is becoming less dependent on family and more dependent on peers. This can also be observed in the formulaic narrative found in anime. The family is often killed off, thrusting the protagonist to look towards their peers to meet their psychological needs; however, because the protagonist is so different and their peers are prejudicial, the protagonist must again look elsewhere. They must look inside themselves to find self-dependence, a sense of self-worth, and the ability to adapt to their environment.

As this happens, they begin to be acknowledged by their peers, and also tend to adopt a family of sorts. They form meaningful connections, which consumers experience vicariously, and through their interest and social identity within the anime community, obtain a sense of belongingness and achievement, as well. Because of this, anime and manga have a lot to offer, especially therapeutically. Mental health professionals can easily use this medium to enhance and enrich their practices by having an interest in anime, growing curious as to the draws, and becoming familiar with how the narratives can impact their clients positively and negatively.

# References

Brewer, M. B. (1991). The social self: On being the same and different at the same time. *Personality and Social Psychology Bulletin, 17*(5), 475–482.

Chen, J. S. (2004). Mediating on the voiceless words of the invisible other: Young female anime fan artists - narratives of gender images. *Social Theory in Art Education, 24*(1), 213-233.

Frey, N. & Fisher, D. (2004). Using graphic novels, anime, and the internet in an urban High school. *The English Journal, 93*(3), 19-25.

Fry, R. (2017, May) It's becoming more common for young adults to live at home – and for longer stretches. Pew Research Center, Washington, D.C. (2016) https://www.pewresearch.org/fact-tank/2017/05/05/its-becoming-more-common-for-young-adults-to-live-at-home-and-for-longer-stretches/

Gaskill, F. & Kelly, R. (2011). *Max Gamer: I am a Superhero*. Charlotte, NC. Hero House Publishing

Griepp, M. & Miller, J.J. (2018, July). Comics and graphic novel sales hit new high in 2018. Retrieved July 27th, 2019, from http://comichron.com

Haslam, S. A., Jetten, J., Postmes, T., & Haslam, C. (2009). Social Identity, health and well-being: An emerging agenda for applied psychology. *Applied Psychology-An International Review-Psychologie Appliquee-Revue Internationale, 58*(1), 1-23.

Hayes, J. (2013, July). Manga industry in Japan: Artist, schools and amateur manga. Retrieved July 27th, 2019, from http://factsanddetails.com

Hogg, M. (2000). Subjective Uncertainty Reduction through self-categorization: A motivational theory of Social Identity Processes. *European Review of Social Psychology, 11*(1).

K, B. (2019, February). Anime fan is now reporting from Antarctica, furthest anime pilgrimage site on Earth. Retrieved July 26th, 2019, from http://grapee.jp

Lee, E. & Burunova, A. (2019). *Enter the anime*. United States: Netflix

Macwilliams, M. W. (2008). *Japanese Visual culture: Explorations in the World of Manga and Anime.* Armonk, N.Y: M.E. Sharpe.

Ray, A., Plante, C. N., Reysen, S., Roberts, S. E., & Gerbasi, K. C. (2017). Psychological needs predict *The Phoenix Papers, 4*(1), August 2018, 37, Fanship and Fandom in anime fans. *The Phoenix Papers, 3,* 56-68.

Reynor, F. (2017, February). Four ways in which anime impacts culture and influences male fans [Blog Post]. Retrieved from: https://good-menproject.com/guy-talk/4-ways-in-which-anime-impacts-culture-and-influences-male-fans-wcz/

Schodt, F. L. (1996). *Dreamland Japan: Writings on Modern Manga.* New York: Stone Bridge Press.

Tajfel, H., Turner, J. C., Austin, W. G., & Worchel, S. (1979). An integrative theory of intergroup conflict. *Organizational identity: A Reader,* 56-65.

Vignoles, V. L., Regalia, C., Manzi, C., Golledge, J., & Scabini, E. (2006). Beyond self-esteem: Influence of multiple motives on identity construction. *Journal of Personality and Social Psychology, 90,* 308-333. doi:10.1037/0022-3514.90.2.308

Wann, D. L. (2006). Understanding the positive social psychological benefits of sport team identification: The Team Identification--Social Psychological Health Model. *Group Dynamics: Theory, Research, and Practice, 10,* 272-296.

# Finding Identities: Why Being a Geek Is Socially Powerful

# 15

Kelli Dunlap, PsyD & Chrisha Anderson, PhD

Mental illness pertains to the presence of a mental health condition or disorder that has a significant negative impact on a person's mood, thoughts, and behavior. Mental wellness, however, is more than just the absence of mental illness; as defined by the World Health Organization (2013) as, "a state of well-being in which the individual realizes his or her abilities, can cope with normal stresses of life, can work productively and fruitfully, and is able to make a contribution to his or her community" (World Health Organization, 2007).

Exploring how identifying as a geek can benefit persons experiencing a mental illness, support individuals seeking to improve their mental wellness, and bolster overall mental health is becoming a movement within psychology (McArthur, 2009). Specific ways geeks actively engage in their own mental health, both in managing mental illness and advancing mental wellness through specific lenses of geek culture, is vastly important to explore and understand. Areas of geek fandom have the potential to be problematic and harmful if used incorrectly by the untrained clinician. Examples of and recommendations for how mental health providers can leverage the positive and supportive aspects of geek culture and promote a geek-culture identity to achieve therapeutic ends will be explored here.

## What Does Geek Fandom Have to Do with Mental Health and Wellness?

In its present form, the word "geek" can be traced back to 1876 where it was used as a synonym for "fool" or "a person uncultivated" (Perlman, 2019). In the early 1900s, the term was used to describe circus performers who bit the heads off of snakes, but by the 1950s, the meaning shifted to refer to overly diligent and unsociable students or a person obsessed with a certain activity or cause. The concept of "geek" as a negative continued strongly into the 1980s and 1990s where nearly all 700 citations of the term were used to describe undesirable people or traits (*ibid*). Today, the Webster's New World College Dictionary (2014) defines geek as, "a person regarded as being especially enthusiastic, knowledgeable, and skillful, esp. in technical matters." For people who consider themselves to be geeks, the term is an identity marker that conveys a passion and connection to a specific piece of culture (or cultures) and, at its core, is about the desire to connect with others around a shared interest or idea.

Humans are a social species and tend toward wanting to feel accepted, valued, and have a sense of belonging. In Maslow's hierarchy, love and belonging are the most important needs we have after our basic needs for survival (Maslow, 1943). For geeks, the desire for social connection can be complicated due to the stigma those within this community often face. Many individuals identifying as geeks feel judged or stereotyped due to their interests, which can lead to challenges in getting social needs met and feeling safe enough to be genuine in relationships. Despite these difficulties, geeks have found a variety of ways in which to connect over the years. In the past, finding and maintaining these activities was often tricky, leading to feelings of isolation and purposeful exclusion (Jenkins, 1992). With the rise of the Internet, however, geeks found and invented new and creative ways in which to connect and form relationships with others of similar interests.

Social media platforms such as Facebook and Twitter have seen an explosion of fandom and geek-related activity (Booth & Kelly, 2013; Jacobs, 2018). On Facebook, easily searchable pages and groups provide a digital space through which like-minded people can connect to discuss these shared interests. Hashtags for specific topics, such as television shows, movies, games, and technology make it easy for users on Twitter to find others to connect with, as well as providing an open environment through which to chat with any public Twitter user. This ease of connection over common geeky interests and activities can and has helped geeks not only with fulfilling social needs, but also providing normalization and validation of interests and identity (Anderson, 2019). The globalization of geek culture and the Internet also means that no geek is ever truly alone, as there are always other people available to talk to through social media.

Of course, not everything is kittens and rainbows; geekdom is not immune to the same problems that plague larger socio-cultural interactions. Sexism, racism, and misogyny continue to be problematic in many geek spaces. Perhaps the most prominent example of this was Gamergate, an organized harassment campaign centered on issues of sexism and progressivism in video game culture (Gray & Leonard, 2018). Another famous example was in 2017 when the television show *Doctor Who* announced that for the first time a woman would play the lead role of the Doctor and faced vitriol from a small group of misogynistic fans. The organized social media harassment against *Star Wars'* Kelly Marie Tran, which forced her off of social media, is yet another example of the misogyny that plagues geek culture to this day at times.

Geek spaces also have a problem with gate-keeping. Gate-keeping in geek spaces refers to a person or community takes it upon themselves to decide who can and cannot belong within a specific group. Gate-keeping has traditionally mostly been focused on the exclusion of women, leading to stereotypes like the "fake geek girl," which posits that the only reasons a woman is involved in a geek community is for attention. Issues of race are also prevalent across the spectrum, from lack of representation and stereotyped portrayal in media to racial attacks when a cosplayer of color cosplays outside their race.

Again, it's important to emphasize that these problems do not stem from geek culture but rather the larger socio-cultural environment in which the members of geek culture were raised. Ending on a positive note, however, is the push of geeky spaces to embrace inclusion and diversity. Progress, like all social change, is slow but cultural items like the latest edition of Dungeons & Dragons including gender-inclusive language

(McGrane, 2018), the latest *Star Trek* series featuring a woman of color in a lead role, and the omnipresent conversations at conventions and across the internet around diversity and inclusion in geek spaces is reason for hope.

Now that an understanding of geek culture has been established, it is important to examine a few specific ways in which geek culture functions as an asset to mental health and wellness. While each domain of geekdom has its own norms and culture, common therapeutic factors are found throughout the different geek-o-spheres and provide opportunities for healing, growth, and connection.

## Fanfiction

Fanfiction is a type of story that is written by fans and based on established characters and/or universes. This type of writing can be used to expand or fill in the blanks of an existing story, be a "fix it" for storylines or endings the fans didn't appreciate, or develop romantic (often queer) pairings between characters that may or may not be romantically involved in the original content. These stories are written and consumed primarily by women, creating a tight-knit community of participatory fandom culture. Fanfiction also provides authors and readers alike the freedom to utilize their favorite media as a sandbox to engage in characters and storylines that mirror issues they may be facing in their own lives (Anderson, 2019; Jenkins, 1992).

### How it Helps

Within the context of mental health, fanfiction can and does serve several positive, therapeutic purposes. As these works are created by fans without the confines of what is deemed acceptable (rather than obscene, indecent, or profane) within mainstream media, society, or Federal Communications Commission (FCC) regulation. Fan writers have the power to put well-known characters into scenarios that are not seen in canon text (e.g. material considered official), such as changing of sexual orientation or gender expression, analysis and processing of character's emotional trauma, setting of characters in an alternate universe different from their canon placement, and exploration of sexual fantasies. Fanfiction authors often put their own emotional difficulties or challenges onto the characters they are writing, helping their characters – and ultimately themselves — work through those issues. This type of writing has been seen by authors as a type of therapeutic journaling, which is widely seen as an effective mental health intervention unto itself (Costa & Abreu, 2018), as well as a component of other expressive therapy modalities, such as narrative therapy. For example, fanfiction could easily be used to help clients envision stories of how they would like to live their lives, applying exaggerated traits seen in characters like Captain Marvel or Frodo Baggins to their own struggles.

For some, reading fanfiction can be a welcome escape or distraction from the stress in their day-to-day lives, just as any other book or work of fiction can be, helping with emotional regulation or allowing for a joyful boost during a challenging day. However, fanfiction is freely available on the Internet, making it far more accessible than other forms of entertainment. The fanfiction sharing site Archive of Our Own (AO3) is home to over 2 million users, 4.8 million fan works, and more than one billion hits per month. It was nominated for a Hugo Award in 2019 for "Best Related Work," giving a new and frequently desired sense of validity to this type of literature. The format through which these works are disseminated allows and even encourages feedback from readers, including commenting, leaving "kudos," and even making requests for further stories. Themed fanfiction community events and charity drives also encourage collaboration between authors to co-write stories, and the ability to add images to fan stories also encourages collaboration between fan authors and fan artists. This leads to additional possibilities for the formation of relationships and community among those in fandom, as well as creating a rich, layered platform for creative expression and exploration of deep, emotional themes.

## Social Contributions

A common and consistent theme within geek culture is helping others. Video games are typically aimed at solving problems or saving the world. Superheroes defeat supervillains, Harry Potter battles the Dark Lord

Voldemort, and the Winchesters fight against literally anyone or anything that threatens humanity. It's therefore no surprise that the people who identify as being geeky are also interested in being heroes.

Avenues through which geeks can give back to their communities are plentiful, as the communities have not only embraced the idea of helping others, but formed its own highly successful charitable foundations. For example, within the science fiction community, multiple charitable organizations aimed at improving mental health and wellness have formed, led by both actors and fans. *Supernatural* (SPN) actor Jared Padalecki, after openly discussing his own battles with mental illness, launched a t-shirt campaign entitled *Always Keep Fighting*, which raised money for multiple organizations who work with mental illness. Its massive success led to the *You Are Not Alone* campaign by fellow Supernatural actors Jensen Ackles and Misha Collins, which helped fund an online crisis support network to provide immediate intervention to individuals who are in crisis from mental health related issues or cyberbullying. Misha Collins has also founded Random Acts, which is a charitable organization whose mission is "to conquer the world one random act of kindness at a time," and has helped with disaster relief in Haiti, and to build a school in Nicaragua. SPN Survivors and Attitudes in Reverse are two fan-founded organizations, both of which are aimed at raising awareness for mental illness and suicide, and both of which were inspired in part by the Supernatural fandom.

While *Supernatural* is perhaps the fandom most associated with mental health and charitable work, it is not the only fandom within the science fiction community to promote altruism. The Harry Potter Alliance has been in operation since 2005 and has encouraged fans to engage in activism in a variety of social justice topics, including racism, gender equity, and LGBTQ rights. Other organizations such as Stands work with celebrities to make fandom merchandise where part of the proceeds for the sale go to benefit charitable organizations of the celebrity's choice, allowing fans to have merchandise that highlights their favorite artists while also helping others.

Gaming, a genre of geek that frequently is in the news for all the wrong reasons, also serves up serious philanthropy. For example, Games Done Quick (GDQ) is a series of video game marathons that have raised over 19 million dollars for charities such as Doctors Without Borders over the last nine years; Able Gamers is the world's largest charity for gamers with disabilities; Child's Play is a charity that donates toys and games to children's hospitals; Gamers Outreach equips nurses and child life specialists with the means to make activities and technology accessible to hospitalized kids and teens. Clearly there is a serious need for promoting the identity of being a geek that has vast potential mental health benefits.

## How it Helps

Research consistently highlights the benefits of altruism on mental health and mood (Post, 2005). Helping others helps us, which is likely what draws so many people to these organizations. Often people want to help others and improve their communities, but aren't sure how to get involved. Organizations founded and promoted by celebrity favorites can make philanthropic engagement easier to get involved with, but also becomes tied to social identity and community. Becoming involved in charities that are geeky in nature means that participants aren't only reaping the emotional benefits of helping others, but are also becoming more entrenched in their geek community, sharing the experience of helping with other like-minded individuals, as well as feeling closer to and supportive of their favorite celebrities.

Within the geek community there is a solid connection between philanthropy and mental health. Several charitable endeavors focus specifically on mental illness and have had an impact that is deeply personal to those who choose to involve themselves. The *Always Keep Fighting* campaign has had a direct impact on the mental wellness of those in the *Supernatural* fandom, as it encouraged fans to talk about their own emotional struggles, and connected fans through the #AKF hashtag on social media who were in need of support or encouragement. The *You Are Not Alone* campaign similarly connected others needing support through the #YANA hashtag, but also directly led to funding a network of trained volunteers providing crisis support to the fandom. Both of these programs also led to ongoing open conversations between the cast and the fans on the topic of mental health, decreasing stigma attached to mental illness, and encouraging ongoing discussion and education. These are just a few examples demonstrating the passion and determination geeks can leverage within themselves and mobilize en masse to achieve goals important to them. Charity events like this, due to their public nature, work to destigmatize mental illness and promote psychological wellness in the geek space. For clinicians, these kinds of events can be used as examples of the power of community to make a difference, as well as potential activities that may help clients connect with a community that shares their experiences or values.

## Conventions

While social media has become a staple of communication among geeks, in-person events such as conventions are of massive importance to geek culture. Conventions can have a wide variety of themes, including comics, specific television shows or films (e.g. *Star Trek* or *Doctor Who*), gaming (e.g. video or role-playing games), or even technology (e.g. hacker conventions). The purpose of any convention is to get together with other like-minded individuals, as well as getting to meet or listen to leaders and celebrities within those genres.

Having an event at which to meet with other people in the geek community serves a critical function in the social lives and identities of its attendees, as it provides a physical space, date, and time for people to come together around their shared interests. For those brief hours or days, individuals are able to be amongst others who also identify as geeks, providing a primarily safe and non-judgmental environment with which to engage fully in fan fiction interests and activities without fear of stigma (Anderson, 2019).

### How it Helps

While many geek interests are becoming more mainstream with the recent popularity of franchises such as Harry Potter and the Avengers, being a geek continues to be associated with stigma in a way other fandoms are not (Cohen et al., 2017). This can contribute to people tamping down their enthusiasm for things that bring them joy and not being open about these interests with people around them. This can lead to feelings of isolation and othering, which attendance at geek-themed conventions surrounded by individuals of similar interests can work to improve or heal.

Additionally, while the stereotype of a geek as an individual who is socially awkward is not always accurate, there are individuals within the community that suffer from social anxiety or other types of mental illness which can make connecting with others and forming relationships difficult. Conventions can not only provide a common interest to help break the ice when meeting new people, it can also provide a non-judgmental and comfortable environment for people to let their geek-flag fly proudly. Social media can facilitate these relationships going far beyond the convention floor, leading to long-term friendships, and meeting people in person that are already known from social media can lead to similar relationship formation.

It is also worthy of note that many organizations that are associated with mental health and philanthropy have booths at these conventions, giving resources, mental health, and more to individuals that may need them. National organizations like Random Acts, as well as local groups (such as body positive cosplay, geek themed non-profits, and mental wellness organizations) attend all types of conventions and can serve as a first-contact point for mental health education and support. For example, Take This is the first mental health organization created to cater to a gaming audience, both players and developers, and is best known for providing quiet, low stimulus spaces at gaming conventions known as AFK Rooms. AFK rooms are staffed by trained mental health professionals and volunteers and offer everything from a place to rest and charge your phone to mental health resources to crisis intervention. Furthermore, academic-fan led panels exploring psychological themes of geek-related fiction and activities are also becoming more frequent, adding additional ways attendees can use conventions as a way to improve and better understand their own mental wellness.

Access to celebrities is also a way in which conventions can contribute to mental wellness for attendees. Fans of science fiction and fantasy genres are not only interested in this genre as a hobby, but look at participation in this community as more of a lifestyle and identity (Chadborn et al., 2018). Works of fiction provide characters and stories which people can gain inspiration from, and access to the actors and authors who portray them can be very meaningful. However, social media and conventions now also give a new way for artists and audiences to have direct communication and insight into the lives of these celebrities, allowing fans to gain inspiration from the creators and performers themselves. Being able to share these experiences with artists has also been shown to help individuals who are managing mental health related issues such as depression, addiction, and even suicidality. Finding connections and forming relationships with celebrities – even if those interactions are very brief – can be extremely validating and improve mental wellness (Zubernis, 2017).

## Cosplay

A portmanteau of the words "costume" and "play," cosplay involves creating costumes and/or dressing up as a specific person, character, or aspect of a fandom. Persons who participate in cosplay are referred to as cosplayers. Costumes can range from relatively simple to extremely elaborate and can be bought, hand-made, or a combination of the two. Many conventions offer cosplay contests where cosplayers get to show off their creations.

Cosplay transcends a wide variety of geek cultures including gaming (pictured left), anime, science fiction, and fantasy. Costuming and performance date back thousands of years, but the notion of creating a costume specifically for geeky interests has its origins in the 1930s. The first record of wearing costumes to a convention was World Con in 1939 (Pettinger, 2014). Attendees Forest J. Ackerman and Myrtle Douglas wore "futuristic costumes" - futuristic jumpsuits and capes created by Myrtle - to the convention, becoming the first cosplayers (Pettinger, 2014). The term cosplay itself, however, wouldn't be invented until 1983 when it first appeared in an issue of My Anime by Nobuyuki Takahashi (Plunkett, 2014).

*How it Helps*

Cosplay almost inherently embodies core attributes of several different kinds of expressive therapies, such as expressive arts therapy, drama therapy, and role play. For creators, cosplay is an active, tactile activity that requires problem solving, critical thinking, creativity, imagination, patience, and persistence. Some cosplayers have reported that crafting cosplay helped them cope with depression and anxiety by giving them a task to focus on, connecting them to a large community of fellow cosplayers, developing new skills, and gaining a sense of achievement (McGeehon, 2018).

> *"As a generally not 'popular' person, being able to be someone else for a day is fun. Building my armor is a great way to take my focus off of my depression and wearing it to a con makes me almost forget that I even have depression. Bringing smiles to kids' faces, having full grown adults go crazy when they see you, and feeling like a celebrity with people taking pictures of you is a totally awesome feeling. When I'm in my armor, I'm not afraid to be myself. I'll be silly, dance around, and talk with people I usually wouldn't have the bravery to talk to normally. For me it is a huge self-esteem booster and a great way to enjoy my life without worries, even if it is just temporarily."* – Cosplayer "Magikarp" (K. Dunlap, personal communication, 2019.)

Cosplayers who dress as characters or objects from their favorite fandom may also benefit from performative or role playing actions. Role play is widely utilized in therapeutic settings as an intervention tool, from therapeutic D&D social skills groups (Connell & Boccamazzo, 2019) to job readiness training. This kind of role play can be equivalent to creating an avatar, allowing someone to project an idealized self into the world or to hide behind a mask which makes social situations easier for those with social anxiety. "Crossplay" is another common kind of role play where a person cosplays as a gender other than their own. Because crossplay is normalized, cosplay spaces can foster safe places to explore or experiment with gender identity.

Geek fandoms are a culture unto themselves and, like all cultures, can provide context through which mental health professionals can better understand a person. Recognizing the importance of geek culture for those who identify themselves as geeks is a form of cultural competence. The simple act of practicing genuineness and positive regard for geek clients around their geeky passions is a critical first step. Utilizing a client's interests and strengths is a core component to any kind of good therapy and this remains true even when those interests include going to a convention with 40,000 of your fandom friends dressed as Tetris block.

# References

Anderson, C. (2019). *Women in Online Science Fiction Fandoms: Perceived Impact on Psychological Well-Being.* (Doctoral Dissertation). Available from ProQuest Dissertations and Theses database.

Booth, P., & Kelly, P. (2013). The changing faces of Doctor Who fandom: New fans, new        technologies, old practices? *Journal of Audience & Reception Studies, 10*(1), 56–72. http://doi.org/10.1177/1367549413476011

Chadborn, D., Edwards, P., & Reysen, S. (2018). Reexamining differences between fandom and local sense of community. *Psychology of Popular Media Culture, 7*(3), 241-249. http://doi.org/10.1037/ppm0000125

Cohen, E. L., Seate, A. A., Anderson, S. M., & Tindage, M. F. (2017). Sport fans and sci-fi fanatics: The social stigma of popular media fandom. *Psychology of Popular Media Culture, 6*(3), 193–207. http://doi.org/10.1037/ppm0000095

Connell, M. & Boccamazzo, R. (2019). Dungeons, Dragons, and Psychology: Applied Theory of Tabletop Role Playing Games in Mental Health. In-person training. Retrieved from: https://www.antioch.edu/seattle/event/dungeons-Dragons-psychology-applied-theory-tabletop-role-playing-games-mental-health-2/

Costa, A. C. & Abreu, M. V. (2018). Expressive and creative writing in the therapeutic context: From the different concepts to the development of writing therapy programs. In Rui P. (Ed), *Psychologica, 61,* 69-86. Coimbra University Press.

Dunlap, K. (2019, June 11). Personal Twitter communication with @ Lvl25Magikarp.

Gray, K. L., & Leonard, D. (2018). *Woke Gaming: Digital Challenges to Oppression and Aocial Injustice.* Seattle: University of Washington Press.

Jacobs, N. (2018). Live streaming as participation: A case study of conflict in the digital/physical spaces of Supernatural conventions. *Transformative Works and Cultures, 28.* https://doi.org/10.3983/twc.2018.1393

Jenkins, H. (1992). *Textual poachers: Television fans & participatory culture.* New York: Routledge.

Maslow, A. H. (1943). A theory of human motivation. *Psychological Review, 50*(4), 370-396.http://dx.doi.org/10.1037/h0054346

McArthur, J. A. (2009). Digital Subculture: A Geek Meaning of Style. *Journal of Communication Inquiry, 33*(1) 58-70.

McGeehon, Z. (2018). Motivations in Cosplay. Southern Illinois University at Edwardsville, ProQuest Dissertations Publishing, 2018. 10843793. Retrieved from: https://search.proquest.com/open-view/2a13a299a150669c6c80c945133196c7/1?pq-origsite=gschol-ar&cbl=18750&diss=y

McGrane, C. (2018). Dungeons, Dragons and diversity: How the world's most influential RPG turned the tables on inclusion. Geek Wire. Retrieved from: https://www.geekwire.com/2018/dungeons-Drag-ons-diversity-worlds-influential-rpg-turned-tables-inclusion/

Perlman, M. (2019). The transformation of the word geek. Columbia Journalism Review. Retrieved from: https://www.cjr.org/language_corner/geek.php

Pettinger, P. (2014). Pierre Pettinger. In *Cosplay World*, Brian Ashcroft & Luke Plunkett (Eds).

Plunket, L. (October 22, 2014). Where the word "cosplay" actu-ally comes from. Kotaku. Retrieved from: https://kotaku.com/where-the-word-cosplay-actually-comes-from-1649177711

Post, S.G. (2005). Altruism, happiness, and health: It's good to be good. *International Journal of Behavioral Medicine, 12*(2), 66-77. https://doi.org/10.1207/s15327558ijbm1202_4

Webster's New world college dictionary. (2014). Boston: Houghton Mifflin Harcourt.

World Health Organization. (2007, November). Fact sheet: Mental health: strengthening mental health promotion. Retrieved from: https://mindyourmindproject.org/wp-content/uploads/2014/11/WHO-Statement-on-Mental-Health-Promotion.pdf

World Health Organization. (2013). Mental health action plan 2013-2020. Retrieved from: https://apps.who.int/iris/bitstream/handle/10665/89966/9789241506021_eng.pdf;jsessionid=C-3180C1F1E6BF7EF54F5FEEFE0FAAFF8?sequence=1

Zubernis, L. (2017). *Family Don't End With Blood*. Dallas, Texas: Smart Pop.

# Sexism in Geek Culture 16

Stephanie Orme, PhD

In the fall of 2014, a culture war that had been brewing within the video game community for decades came to a bubbling point. While games journalists and other public figures were calling more diverse representation in games, a vocal contingent of players began to publicly express their frustrations – and outright anger – with what they perceived as an attack on gaming culture. These players accused games reporters of favoring games with a "feminist agenda" at the expense of the games they had grown up with. The real spark came when the jilted ex-boyfriend of female game developer Zoe Quinn penned a scathing blog post accusing Quinn of sleeping with a games journalist in exchange for a positive review of her game *Depression Quest*. (It has been proven that said review does not exist (Illing, 2017)).

Rallying under the hashtag #Gamergate on social media, these individuals launched an online harassment campaign against so-called "Social Justice Warriors" – feminist game critics and others who advocate for more equitable representation of marginalized groups in games. Several prominent women in the gaming scene became primary targets of Gamergate, including Quinn, feminist media critic Anita Sarkeesian, and game developer Brianna Wu (Wingfield, 2014). The constant barrage of harassment and threats launched gaming culture into mainstream news coverage. By the summer of the following year, Gamergate had largely faded into the backdrop; yet, the anti-women sentiments that under-girded the movement far precede it, and continue to linger (Gray & Leonard, 2018).

While Gamergate gained mainstream notoriety due to the particularly vicious nature behind its harassment tactics, this anti-women ethos came as no surprise to (women) players who are part of geek culture. For them, gender-based harassment in the form of slurs, criticisms, and outright threats come hand-in-hand with being a woman in a historically male-dominated cultural territory. Yet, those who do not participate in "geeky spaces" (e.g. gaming, comics, sci-fi) often tend to not realize, or understand the depths of, the types of toxic behavior women in these spaces routinely endure. This chapter offers context on several key issues related to sexism in geek culture, and how the effects of these issues might be experienced by mental health practitioners' patients.

## Fake Geek Girls and the Politics of Geek "Authenticity"

Geek "authenticity" – what it means to *be a geek* – has been demarcated by the kinds of men who dominated the cultural spheres of gaming, comics, fantasy, and sci-fi for decades (Massanari, 2015). They have positioned themselves as the arbitrators of geek culture and, by extension, who gets to be part of its membership. As such, women who identify as geeks constantly find their geek identity called into question and challenged by male members of geek culture who, for a variety of reasons, feel the urge to gatekeep geek culture.

Women who publicly express their geek fandom may find themselves branded a "Fake Geek Girl," a timeworn trope used to describe women who merely pretend to enjoy aspects of geek culture for attention (Reagle, 2015) or any other reason. Editor in Chief for Uproxx Brett Michael-Dykes captured this anti-women mentality when he declared, "We all know girls like this. By now we're on to them. Yet they persist, like a fungus. I'm talking about attractive females who fancy themselves as nerds" (Dykes, 2011). Demarcating a woman as a "fake" geek delegitimizes her cultural capital within geek spaces by asserting she has no genuine passion or knowledge about geek subject matter, stripping her of any say within that community. Similarly, women who shop in physical retail outlets carrying geek products such as video games and comic books while in the company of a male friend or romantic partner are often assumed to be into geek culture *because* of their male companion (Orme, 2016). While not all women who follow their friends or significant others into a geek retail store are necessarily invested in the experience, many of them are – and their personal ties to geek culture are erased.

Women who wish to be viewed as "real" geeks find themselves having to prove themselves to the male gatekeepers of various geek communities. In gaming culture, for example, being a "real" gamer means playing certain types of games, or even specific titles. Casual and mobile gaming – which enjoy popularity among many female players – are not regarded as "real" games, and those who play them are not "real" gamers (Kubik, 2012). Many women in traditionally male-dominated geek spaces – comic book shops, sci-fi conventions, esports tournaments – routinely find themselves being literally quizzed on their knowledge of geeky lore by male members of those communities (Gardner, 2018). Because many geek spaces were historically male-dominated, men became the ones to dictate the standards for what constitutes an "authentic" geek. This places girls and women geeks in an unfortunate bind, as Scott (2019) so aptly notes:

> *"The "fake geek girl" presents a zero-sum game for female fans, not only because "fakeness" is predicated on the notion that fan affect is quantifiable and must be authenticated but also because within this paradigm, only male fans (or those who align themselves with an affirmational notion of "authentic" fan culture) are empowered to define and delimit what constitutes a "real" fan"* (p. 99).

One might ask, *What's the big deal about whether someone else thinks you're a "real" geek or not?* The cultural capital that comes with having "real" geek status can actually drastically affect the ways in which girls and women experience geek culture. Aside from feeling like they are on the margins of geek culture, with products and marketing being directed at a presumed male demographic (Scott, 2017), women are often deprived of having a voice in geek spaces. Their opinions in both face-to-face and online communities may be discredited by the gatekeepers who determine that they are not "real" geeks (Scott, 2019). At its worst, this may also lead to gender-based harassment that discourages women from participating in geek communities altogether.

## Harassment, Toxicity, and the Thot Police

Unfortunately, the internet has made it easier to bully and harass women geeks. There is ample evidence that women face unequivocally more harassment while playing online games than males (see Cote, 2015; Fox & Tang, 2016). For many women, logging into an online gaming environment comes with the expectation that she will experience some sort of gender-based discrimination, and even harassment, should her gender identity be revealed while playing (McLean & Griffiths, 2018). Examples of harassment range from the most "benign" insults ("quit the game and go make me a sandwich") to outright threats of violence. For years, the now-defunct blog *Fat, Slutty, or Ugly* documented instances of sexism and gender-targeted harassment experienced by women players, categorizing them under themes such as "lewd proposals," "Sandwich Making 101," and "death threats" (O'Leary, 2012). While "trash talk" is practically a staple of multiplayer gaming – and not something that women uniquely experience – sexist comments, rape jokes and threats, and other gender-based harassment exist in a whole other category, and have lasting impacts on women long after they turn off the game (Fox & Tang, 2016).

In fact, this type of behavior is so prevalent that many women hide their gender identity while playing online games with strangers, using gender-neutral usernames or forgoing the use of in-game voice chat features (Cote, 2015; McLean & Griffiths, 2018). Using voice chat affords players in team-based games competitive advantages, as they are able to communicate strategy quickly and more effectively. Thus, women (and other minority players) find themselves in a double-bind: risk the possibility of opening themselves up to gender-based toxicity or be forced to play with limited competitive capabilities (Loehr, 2018).

The rise of video game live-streaming – the broadcasting of oneself playing a video game – has created more opportunities for women's visibility in gaming culture. However, with that visibility comes the possibility of gender-based toxicity. The term "Twitch thots[3]" has become popular parlance for describing conventionally attractive women on the platform – the idea being that these women are merely relying on their physical attractiveness to "exploit" the presumed heterosexual male audience for views, donations, and paid subscribers rather than producing "quality" content (Dalbey, 2018). The term has spawned an entire ecosystem of memes ridiculing female broadcasters, perpetuating the misogynistic logic that a woman cannot be both attractive and a good content creator. High-profile female broadcaster Amouranth reported being harassed and doxxed[4] after users accused her of hiding her relationship status from the community so that male viewers might donate to her in hopes of developing a romantic relationship with her (Alexander, 2018).

Then there is the harassment levied at anyone perceived to be pushing "feminist agendas" in geek spaces. Post Gamergate, there exists a heightened resistance to attempts to critique and diversify the comics, sci-fi, and other geek industries. The comic book community has recently seen its own version of Gamergate – Comicsgate – unfold on Twitter. In July 2017, editor of *The Unbelievable Gwenpool* Heather Antos and several female Marvel staff members gathered for milkshakes to honor the passing of industry icon Flo Steinberg. After Antos tweeted a selfie of the group, dozens of individuals began accusing Antos and her colleagues of being "fake geek girls" and "the creepiest collection of stereotypical SJW[5]s anyone could possibly imagine" and flooded her private message inbox with sexual harassment (Francisco, 2018).

This added fuel to an already burning fire of resentment towards diversity from some comics retailers who blamed declining sales on Marvel's recent push for more diverse representation (Elbein, 2017). A handful of anti-feminist individuals began circulating a blacklist of comics creators including the likes of Kelly Sue DeConnick, Ta-Nehisi Coates, and Matt Fraction, among others who are women creators and creators of color. The posters encouraged anyone "concerned with the state of comics" to

---

[3] "Thots", which stands for "that ho over there.," is a term used to describe promiscuous women in general. It has been adopted by Twitch users to degrade women on the male-dominated platform.

[4] Doxxing refers to the process of searching for and publishing the personal information (e.g. address, contact information) online, typically with malicious intentions.

[5] SJWs (which stands for Social Justice Warrior) is a derogatory term used to describe anyone who advocates for diversity and inclusion.

boycott their work (Francisco, 2018). A similar campaign against diversity had transpired a couple of years prior within the science-fiction writing community. As with previous years, two right-wing groups known as the Sad Puppies and the Rabid Puppies, attempted to rig the voting for the 2016 Hugo Awards, the prestigious honoring of works in sci-fi literature and drama (Barnett, 2016). The effects of movements like Comicsgate and the Hugo Awards incident are also felt by fans, who may experience toxic behavior in communities where they express their enjoyment of certain creators and their works.

## Box Office Bullies and Resistance to Representation

Issues regarding representation in geek culture have continued to make headlines the past couple of years, following the recent surge of female protagonists in traditionally masculine subsets of geek culture. Perhaps the most notable of these cases is the *Star Wars* film sequels, *The Force Awakens* (2015) and *The Last Jedi* (2017), both of which feature more women and people of color than previous films in the franchise. *The Force Awakens* netted over $2 billion globally and become a worldwide cultural phenomenon, in large part due to its strong female protagonist Rey, which helped to usher in new fans. However, many (mostly male) fans of *Star Wars* were quick to label Rey a "Mary Sue," a term reserved for female characters who are perceived to be unrealistically and flawlessly adept at doing things, because she possesses naturally strong Jedi abilities without having had training like Luke Skywalker undertook in the original trilogy (Kain, 2017). Rey, in being a competent young woman, threatened the fabric of the *Star Wars* universe – and fans' masculinity.

The greatest backlash would come with the arrival of the second film in the sequel lineup, *The Last Jedi*. This film boasted *Star Wars*'s most diverse cast of characters yet and featured the franchise's first Asian-American actor or actress in a major role – Kelly Marie Tran as Resistance maintenance worker Rose Tico. After the film's release, Tran was subjected to months of harassing, racist, and sexist messages on her Instagram account, resulting in her deleting all of her photos and leaving the platform (Chuba, 2018). Some members of the *Star Wars* fandom felt betrayed when their fan theories about Rey being the descendent of a legendary Jedi (thus explaining her innate ability) were proven false (Barsanti, 2018). Others were enraged by the way that Vice-Admiral Holdo shut down "flyboy hot-shot" Poe Dameron's battle plans – the type of masculine bravado that had been a staple of older films (Ong, 2017).

Some enraged *Star Wars* fans took the internet to proclaim that the film had destroyed Luke Skywalker's legacy. One individual went so far as to post an edited, 46 minute long cut of *The Last Jedi* titled *The Last Jedi: The De-Feminized Fan Edit*, which strips all positive portrayals of female characters present in the original film, re-writing male characters as flawless heroes. Admiral Holdo is written out of the "film" entirely (meaning Poe gets to be the noble hero to carry out her self-sacrificial battle tactic), Rey is made less powerful while antagonist Kylo Ren is made emotionally more rigid, and Rose's sister Paige is deprived of her last heroic act before dying, among other changes (Barsanti, 2018). Another *Star Wars* fan created an online petition that garnered over 116,000 supporters begging for The Walt Disney Company (which owns Lucasfilm) to remove *The Last Jedi* from official *Star Wars* canon – in other words, pretend it never happened ("Have Disney Strike," n.d.). There has even been an online campaign to create a fan-remake of *The Last Jedi* that alleges to have received over $416 million in pledges as of May 2018 (http://remakethelastjedi.com). All of this backlash seems rather moot, as the final film in the trilogy, *The Rise of Skywalker*, is releasing in North American theaters in December 2019.

This has not stopped disgruntled fans concerned about "social justice warrior politics" from finding ways to express their displeasure with female-led franchises. The newest trend in anti-feminist online culture is review-bombing, the practice of flooding review-aggregating websites like Rotten Tomatoes with negative ratings to lower a film's overall score. Users have been exploiting the platform's "Want to See" feature, which was meant to indicate anticipation of upcoming releases. Marvel's first female-led superhero film *Captain Marvel* became the target of negative reviews prior to the film's release after right-wing trolls on Reddit and 4chan called upon users to "tank" the film's ratings (Kaplan, 2019). (*Captain Marvel* smashed several box office records and is currently the 24th highest grossing film globally (Box Office Mojo, n.d.)). The forthcoming *The Rise of Skywalker* received negative reviews on the website before the film's title had even be revealed. In response, Rotten Tomatoes has announced they are disabling the comment function from the review pages of films that have not yet been released (Alexander, 2019).

## Implications for Therapists, Clinicians, and Mental Health Professions

The video game and comic book industries, Hollywood, and other media producers all seem to be trying harder to create a more inclusive geek culture, but with it comes unprecedented levels of blowback, from "digital vandalism" like review bombing to direct harassment of marginalized creators and fans. The current tumultuous state of geek culture has very real ramifications for those who seek to be part of it.

Woo (2012) has argued that geek culture allows us to create a sense of community – something that we are increasingly desperate for in an increasing socially fragmented age. A lower sense of belonging has been linked to depression and declining mental health (Kitchen et al., 2012). Tocci (2009) explains that social outcasts tend to gravitate towards solitary interests, which tend to overlap with many segments of geek culture (e.g. gaming, reading, watching TV). Woo (2012) suggests that one way we cultivate geek community is by amassing consumer goods and cultural artifacts (e.g. collectible figures, merchandise) that give us a certain social capital within the community. However, this can become a challenge for fans from marginalized groups, like girls and women, who may not be the target demographic for product creators. The marketing of geek merchandise continues to cater to a male demographic, with limited options for girls and women (Scott, 2017). When geeky products are produced and marketed with only male fans in mind, others are restricted in how they can visibly participate in self-expression.

Aside from general feelings of alienation, many women geeks may also experience genuine fears about safety. In addition to online harassment and threats women geeks receive, there is a troubling history of sexual harassment of women at fan conventions, particularly among those who come in costume – known as cosplaying – as their favorite characters.

The internet is rife with horror stories from cosplaying women who have been stalked, photographed without permission, and sexually assaulted, resulting in petitions to convention organizers to help combat the problem (Waldman, 2014). The San Diego Comic-Con – one of geek culture's preeminent gatherings – has a notably vague code of conduct, leaving cosplayers to largely look after themselves and each other. Riding the #MeToo movement wave, anime convention attendees began circulating an online spreadsheet of abusers and harassers who frequent U.S. anime conventions (D'Anastasio, 2019). It is difficult to ascertain just how prevalent sexual assault is at geek events, as many cases go unreported, and convention security is limited to the convention center and not what happens off-site. To help fill this void, the Cosplayer Survivor Support Network, a support group for cosplay community members who are victims of harassment, abuse, and other trauma, was formed in 2016 (http://cosplayer-ssn.org).

Marginalized geeks are carving out their own spaces in geek culture, from women-owned comic shops to LGBTQ+ geek events. A few examples include:

- The Geek Initiative (http://geekinitiative.com): Hosts a crowd-sourced list of inclusive comic book stores in the U.S.

- Black Nerd Girls (http://blacknerdgirls.com): Entertainment news hub with a focus on Blackness and geeky hobbies.

- Geeks Out (http://geeksout.org): Hosts conventions and organizes queer spaces at events.

One can also find local communities and events by searching online or by asking at your local comic shops, game retailers, and geek hobby stores.

The ostracizing and harassment that many girls and women face as members of geek culture can be detrimental to their health and well-being. Yet, for all of the sexism that plagues it, geek culture can, at times, be a wonderful thing. Comic shops, video game tournaments, and fan conventions can all be hubs for connecting with like-minded individuals. Affinities for certain characters and stories can bring people from diverse backgrounds together, and give parents and their children something to bond over. Despite its growing pains, geek culture is worth saving, making it vital that mental health specialists are informed about it.

# References

Alexander, J. (2019, February 26). Rotten Tomatoes tackles review-bombing by eliminating pre-release comments. *The Verge*. Retrieved from https://www.theverge.com/2019/2/26/18241840/rotten-tomatoes-review-bomb-captain-marvel-star-wars-the-last-jedi.

Alexander, J. (2018, June 27). Streamer Amouranth is latest example of 'Twitch thot' harassment problem. *Polygon*. Retrieved from https://www.polygon.com/2018/6/27/17506414/amouranth-twitch-thot-streamer-cosplayer-alinity-backlash.

Barnett, D. (2016, August 21). Hugo awards see off rightwing protests to celebrate diverse authors. *The Guardian*. Retrieved from https://www.theguardian.com/books/2016/aug/21/hugo-awards-winners-nk-jemisin-sad-rabid-puppies.

Barsanti, S. (2018, January 15). Some creep made an overly sexist edit of *The Last Jedi* and even they think it's awful. *AVClub*. Retrieved from https://www.avclub.com/some-creep-made-an-overtly-sexist-edit-of-the-last-jedi-1822104868.

Box Office Mojo. (n.d.). Worldwide grosses. Retrieved from https://www.boxofficemojo.com/alltime/world.

Cote, A. (2015). "I can defend myself": Women's strategies for coping with harassment while gaming online. *Games and Culture, 12*, 136-155.

Chuba, K. (2018, June 5). 'Star Wars' actress Kelly Marie Tran leaves social media after months of harassment. *Variety*. Retrieved from https://variety.com/2018/biz/news/star-wars-kelly-marie-tran-leaves-social-media-harassment-1202830892.

D'Anastasio, C. (2019, January 18). As spreadsheet of accused abusers spreads, anime conventions get their MeToo movement. *Kotaku*. Retrieved from https://kotaku.com/as-spreadsheet-of-accused-abusers-spreads-anime-conven-1831879237.

Dalbey, A. (2018, December 21). Making fun of Twitch thots is still a thing, apparently. *The Daily Dot*. Retrieved from https://www.dailydot.com/parsec/xqc-felix-lengyel-twitch-thots.

Dykes, B. M. (2011, November 7). Meme watch: Idiot Nerd Girl is less nerd than idiot, but 100% annoying. *Uproxx*. Retrieved from https://uproxx.com/viral/meme-watch-idiot-nerd-girl-is-less-nerd-than-idiot-but-100-annoying/page/1.

Elbein, A. (2017, May 24). The real reasons for Marvel comics' woes. *The Atlantic*. Retrieved from https://www.theatlantic.com/entertainment/archive/2017/05/the-real-reasons-for-marvel-comics-woes/527127/.

Fox, J., & Tang, W. Y. (2016). Women's experiences with general and sexual harassment in online video games: Rumination, organizational responsiveness, withdrawal, and coping strategies. *New Media & Society*, *19*, 1290-1307.

Francisco, E. (2018, February 9). Comicsgate is Gamergate's next horrible evolution. *Inverse*. Retrieved from https://www.inverse.com/article/41132-comicsgate-explained-bigots-milkshake-marvel-dc-gamergate.

Gardner, K. (2018, September 23). Viral tweet about fandom gatekeeping proves we still have a male geek problem. *The Mary Sue*. Retrieved from https://www.themarysue.com/fandom-gatekeeping-male-geeks.

Gray, K. L., & Leonard, D. (2018). *Woke Gaming: Digital Challenges to Oppression and Aocial Injustice*. Seattle: University of Washington Press.

Illing, S. (2017, September 19). The woman at the center of #Gamergate gives zero fucks about her hates. *Vox*. Retrieved from https://www.vox.com/culture/2017/9/19/16301682/gamergate-alt-right-zoe-quinn-crash-override-interview.

Kain, E. (2017, December 21). No, Rey from 'Star Wars: The Last Jedi' is still not a Mary Sue. *Forbes*. Retrieved from https://www.forbes.com/sites/erikkain/2017/12/21/no-rey-from-star-wars-the-last-jedi-is-still-not-a-mary-sue/#9d1d7b945004.

Kaplan, A. (2019, February 20). Right-wing trolls attack Brie Larson and target *Captain Marvel* with negative reviews on Rotten Tomatoes. *Media Matters*. Retrieved from https://www.mediamatters.org/blog/2019/02/20/Right-wing-trolls-attack-Brie-Larson-and-target-Captain-Marvel-with-negative-reviews-on-Ro/222924.

Kitchen, P., Williams, A., & Chowhan, J. (2012). Sense of belonging and mental health in

Hamilton, Ontario: An intra-urban analysis. *Social Indicators Research*, *108*, 277-297. Retrieved from https://link.springer.com/article/10.1007/s11205-012-0066-0.

Kubik, E. (2012). Masters of technology: Defining and theorizing the hardcore/casual dichotomy in video game culture. In Gajjala, R., & Oh Y. J. (Eds.), *Cyberfeminism 2.0* (pp 135-152). New York: Peter Lang.

Loehr, S. (2018, February 5). Heroes of the Storm's voice chat would hurt minority communities. *Polygon*. Retrieved from https://www.polygon.com/2018/2/5/16964202/heroes-of-the-storm-voice-chat-blizzard.

Massanari, A. L. (2015). Participatory culture, community, and play: Learning from Reddit. New York: Peter Lang.

McLean, L., & Griffiths, M. D. (2018). Female gamers' experiences of online harassment and social support in online gaming: A qualitative study. *International Journal of Mental Health and Addiction*. doi.org/10.1007/s11469-018-9962-0

O'Leary, A. (2012, August 1). In virtual play, sex harassment is all too real. *The New York Times*. Retrieved from https://www.nytimes.com/2012/08/02/us/sexual-harassment-in-online-gaming-stirs-anger.html.

Ong, T. (2017, December 24). In The Last Jedi, being a space cowboy doesn't fly anymore. *The Verge*. Retrieved from https://www.theverge.com/2017/12/24/16766588/the-last-jedi-poe-dameron-star-wars.

Orme, S. (2016). Femininity and fandom: The dual-stigmatization of female comic book fans. *The Journal of Graphic Novels and Comics* 7(4), 403-416. doi: 10.1080/21504857.2016.1219958

Reagle, J. (2015). Geek policing: Fake geek girls and contested attention. *The International Journal of Communication*, *9*, 2862-2880.

Scott, S. (2019). *Fake geek girls: Fandom, gender, and the convergence culture industry*. New York: NYU Press.

Scott, S. (2017). #Wheresrey?: Toys, spoilers, and the gender politics of franchise paratexts. *Critical Studies in Media Communication*, *34*, 138-147.

Tocci, J. (2009). Geek cultures: Media and identity in the digital age. Ph.D. dissertation. University of Pennsylvania.

Waldman, K. (2014, June 3). Comic-con International has no interest in taking on sexual harassment. *Slate*. Retrieved from https://slate.com/human-interest/2014/06/sexual-harassment-at-comic-con-san-diego-convention-says-no-to-a-more-comprehensive-policy.html.

Walsh (n.d.) Have Disney strike Star Wars Episode VII from the official canon. *Change.org*. Retrieved from https://www.change.org/p/the-walt-disney-company-have-disney-strike-star-wars-episode-viii-from-the-official-canon.

Wingfield, N. (2014, October 15). Feminist critics of video games facing threats in 'Gamergate' campaign. *The New York Times*. Retrieved from https://www.nytimes.com/2014/10/16/ technology/gamer-gate-women- video-game-threats-anita-sarkeesian.html.

Woo, B. (2012). Nerds!: Cultural practices and community-making in a subcultural scene. Ph.D. dissertation. Simon Fraser University.

# Resource Groups for Clinicians

**Leyline's Geek Therapy Training** provides high-quality webinar trainings with the experts and leaders in the field. Clinicians and mental health experts are able to provide and share the knowledge that has been developed by working with their clients. These modalities have been resulting in clients having less anxiety (e.g., social), less depressive symptoms (e.g., after playing video games), improved self-esteem, richer interpersonal interactions, greater social and school engagement, and greater development of social skills and problem solving. They are being used to improve overall psychological well-being across all ages, as well as focusing on the specific needs of targeted populations, such as those with ADHD, ASD, PTSD, and mood and anxiety disorders. – www.geektherapytraining.com.

**Take This** is a mental health 501(c)3 non-profit organization providing comprehensive resources, support, and consultation tailored for the unique needs of the game community, and embraces its diverse cultures and needs. They provide mental health education and a variety of outreach programs to serve the game and game development communities. They work in a spirit of partnership with other organizations addressing these issues among game enthusiasts, streamers, and creators. – www.takethis.org.

**Geeks Like Us (GLU)** is a community-based media company designed to help geeks flourish. Created by geeky psychologists, GLU aims to celebrate the science and passion within geek culture through related articles (e.g. The Healing Laugh of Deadpool), podcasts (e.g., Brain Noodles),

YouTube Series (Psych at the Table), convention panels (SDCC, PAX) and streaming content (Thuppence, Clinical Roll). Above all else, GLU strives to help people grow and embrace what it means to be "unapologetically enthusiastic." — www.geekslikeus.com

**Game to Grow** is a 501(c)3 non-profit organization dedicated to the use of games of all kinds for therapeutic, educational, and community growth. Our therapeutic social skills groups help youth become more confident, creative, and socially capable through the intentional facilitation of customized, collaborative gaming experiences. We're most well-known for our use of tabletop role-playing games like Dungeons & Dragons. Many of the kids and teens in our groups struggle with social challenges related to autism, ADHD, anxiety, or depression, and the groups help them build social skills, reduce isolation, and develop friendships. We also provide training, consultation, and support to other therapeutic and gaming professionals, educators, parents, and advocates, so that even more individuals can benefit from the life-enriching power of games. - www.gametogrow.org

**The Bodhana Group** is a 501(c)(3) nonprofit organization that advocates the use of tabletop gaming as a directed therapeutic and clinical practice that can benefit personal growth, as well as enhance social and educational services to individuals and families. The Bodhana Group advocates the use of tabletop gaming as a directed therapeutic and clinical practice that can benefit personal growth as well as enhance social and educational services to individuals and families. We believe that the inherent benefit one gets from playing games can be focused and utilized to make one better. Better at math or reading. Better at socializing or emotional expression. Better at coping skills. Better at life. The Bodhana Group offers training, consultation and services for individuals, families and organizations. - https://www.thebodhanagroup.org/.

**RPG Research** is an international, 501(c)3 non-profit, 100% volunteer-run, human services charitable research and community services organization, studying the effects of collaborative music and all role-playing game formats and their potential to improve lives worldwide. Working with a wide range of regular and special needs populations from ages 2 through 102+. - http://www.rpgresearch.com.

**Gamenamic Leadership's Mission:** Using gaming to help people learn about themselves, group dynamics, and discovering how the world works. We facilitate games and workshops that promote leadership and team development. Facilitators guide players through the game experience, offer coaching throughout, and engage the participants in case-in-point learning. Following the game experience, a facilitated debrief prompts players to critically reflect on their own development, as well as how the mental models present in the game can contribute to leadership outside the game. - Gamenamic.org

It is **Roll Play Lead's** mission to support the social skill growth of teens who live with anxiety and other forms of mental illness through leadership development in the form of table-top role playing games (TTRPG), mainly Dungeons & Dragons.- rollplaylead.org/

**Women in Games** is an international non-profit designed to support women working, or interested in working, in the global digital games industry. WIGJ (formerly Women in Games Jobs) has a presence in 23 countries, representing Europe, North and South America, Asia, and Africa. On an international level, WIGJ has regional ambassadors dedicated to achieving WIGJ's mission of doubling the number of women working in games in 10 years. Every year, WIGJ hosts an annual European conference featuring industry guest speakers, panel discussions, and workshops. Local chapters in cities around the globe offer spaces for women game makers and allies to gather to promote inclusive hiring in game design through lectures, mentorship programs, and networking events. For more information, visit http://www.womeningames.org.

**AnyKey** is a non-profit advocacy group that works to cultivate an inclusive climate in the competitive gaming industry. Backed by research, their initiatives are to amplify the voices of individuals making strides towards inclusivity in esports, connecting marginalized members to resources for

262   RESOURCE GROUPS FOR CLINICIANS

support, and providing esports organizations with actionable items to make their spaces more inclusive. AnyKey hosts Women in Esports networking events and is a staple of Diversity Lounges at major geek events, where they invite discussion of important diversity and inclusion issues. AnyKey started the glhf Pledge ("Good luck, have fun!" Pledge), which players, live-streamers, and other members of esports culture can take to show their commitment to building an inviting esports community for all. For more information, and to take the glhf Pledge, visit http://www.anykey.org.

**Monte Cook Games** has always been about acceptance and inclusion. In their products, in the events they support, and in the gaming spaces they strive to create, they welcome people from all walks of life, all genders and orientations, all religions and cultures, and all ethnicities. Monte Cook Games support the civil liberties of all people, and manifest that support in our own small way: through the fun and imagination of games. They have created a "Consent In Gaming PDF" that is free to use and can be downloaded from their website: https://www.montecookgames.com/

# Recommended Book Reading List

| Recommended Book Reading | | |
|---|---|---|
| Title | Author | Publisher |
| Batman and Psychology: A Dark and Stormy Knight | Travis Langley | John Wiley & Sons |
| Blood, Sweat, and Pixels: The Triumphant, Turbulent Stories Behind How Video Games Are Made | Jason Schreier | Harper Paperbacks |
| Dungeons & Dragons Essentials Kit (D&D Boxed Set) | Wizards RPG Team | Wizards of the Coast |
| Dungeons & Dragons Monster Manual (Core Rulebook, D&D Roleplaying Game) | Wizards RPG Team | Wizards of the Coast |
| Dungeons & DragonS Player's Handbook | Wizards RPG Team | Wizards of the Coast |
| Extra Lives: Why Video Games Matter | Tom Bissell | Vintage |
| Fake Geek Girls | Suzanne Scott | NYU Press |
| First Person: New Media as Story, Performance, and Game | Noah Wardrip-Fruin and Pat Harrigan | The MIT Press |

| | | |
|---|---|---|
| Flow: The Psychology of Optimal Experience | Mihaly Csikszentmihalyi | Harper Perennial |
| Game Play: Therapeutic Use of Games with Children and Adolescents | Jessica Stone & Charles Schaefer | Wiley |
| Gaming at the Edge: Sexuality and Gender at the Margins of Gamer Culture | Adrienne Shaw | Univ Of Minnesota Press |
| Gaming Masculinity: Trolls, Fake Geeks, and the Gendered Battle for Online Culture | Megan Condis | University Of Iowa Press |
| Getting a Life: The Social Worlds of Geek Culture | Benjamin Woo | McGill-Queen's University Press |
| Getting Gamers: The Psychology of Video Games and Their Impact on the People who Play Them | Jamie Madigan | Rowman & Littlefield Publishers |
| Killing Monsters: Why Children Need Fantasy, Super Heroes, and Make-Believe Violence | Gerald Jones | Basic Books |

| | | |
|---|---|---|
| Moral Combat: Why the War on Violent Video Games Is Wrong | Patrick Markey & Christopher Ferguson | Ben Bella Books |
| Our Superheroes, Ourselves | Robin Rosenberg | Oxford University Press |
| Popular Culture Psychology Series | Travis Langley | Sterling |
| Ready Player Two: Women Gamers and Designed Identity | Shira Chess | Univ Of Minnesota Press |
| Reality Is Broken: Why Games Make Us Better and How They Can Change the World | Jane McGonigal | Penguin Books |
| Return of the Lazy Dungeon Master | Michael Shea | Independently published |
| Superhero Therapy | Janine Scarlet | Instant Help |
| The Psychology of Final Fantasy: Surpassing the Limit Break | Anthony M. Bean | Leyline Publishing |
| The Psychology of Zelda: Linking Our World to the Legend of Zelda Series | Anthony M. Bean | Ben Bella Books |

| The Ultimate RPG Gameplay Guide: Role-Play the Best Campaign Ever—No Matter the Game! | James D'Amato | Adams Media |
|---|---|---|
| The Video Game Debate | Rachel Kowert and Thorsten Quandt | Routledge |
| Video Games and Well-being: Press Start | Rachel Kowert | Palgrave Pivot |
| Woke Gaming: Digital Challenges to Oppression and Social Injustice | Kishonna Gray and David Leonard | University of Washington Press |
| Working With Video Gamers and Games in Therapy: A Clinician's Guide | Anthony M. Bean | Routledge |

# Index

Note: Page numbers in *italics* refer to figures;
numbers in **bold** indicate tables.

IF YOU LIKED THIS BOOK,
SEE WHAT ELSE WE ARE DOING AT:

# GEEKTHERAPYTRAINING.COM

BOOKS • COURSES • PROJECT DEVELOPMENT

Have an idea for a book? Let us know.

Get this badge by completing our Geek Culture
Certificate Program consisting of 12 courses.

geektherapytraining@gmail.com • leylinepublishing@gmail.com

 @GeekTherapyTraining

@TheGeekTraining  @GeekTherapyTraining